Contents

Readings

Balakian, Anna. *The Symbolist Movement* (New York: Random House, 1967).

Bowra, Cecil M. *The Heritage of Symbolism* (London: McMillan, 1967).

Charpentier, John. *Le Symbolisme* (Les Arts et le Livre, 1927).

Cornell, William K. *The Symbolist Movement* (New Haven: Yale University Press, 1951).

———. *The Post-Symbolist Period* (New Haven: Yale University Press, 1958).

Décaudin, Michel. *La Crise des Valeurs symbolistes* (Toulouse: Privat, 1960).

Jones, Mansell. *The Background of Modern French Poetry* (Cambridge University Press, 1951).

Lawler, James R. *The Language of French Symbolism* (Princeton: Princeton University Press, 1969).

Lehmann, A. G. *The Symbolist Aesthetic in France, 1885–1895* (Oxford: Blackwell, 1950).

Martino, Pierre. *Parnasse et Symbolisme* (Colin, 1925).

Michaud, Guy. *Message poétique du symbolisme* (Nizet, 1947). 3 vols.

———. *La Doctrine symboliste* (Nizet, 1947).

Peyre, Henri. *Qu'est-ce que le symbolisme?* (Presses Universitaires de France, 1974).

Raymond, Marcel. *De Baudelaire au Surréalisme* (Corti, 1933).

Schmidt, Albert. *La Littérature symboliste, 1870–1900* (Presses Universitaires de France, 1942).

Van Bever, Ad. et Léautaud, Paul. *Poètes d'aujourd'hui, morceaux choisis* (Mercure de France, 1910). 3 vols.

Visan, Tancrède de. *L'Attitude du lyrisme contemporain* (Mercure de France, 1911).

Introduction[1]

The Symbolist movement can be viewed today as a development and, in some respects, a fulfillment of the ideals set up by the earlier Romantic generations everywhere in Europe. It seems indeed a part of Romanticism, which, in the broad sense of the word, stands for the intuitive as opposed to the rational, the subjective as opposed to the objective, for individuality and liberty.[2] Thus philosophically and esthetically considered, Symbolism is a modern expression of one of the fundamental tempers of man, and, as such, can be properly placed in the line of all mystic, oracular, illuminist, or idealist traditions.[3] This is the broad view. It takes in some of the greatest writers of the nineteenth century in France and includes as well the chief creative geniuses of our own times. But if we take the narrow view, we see merely a swarm of poets loosely called Symbolists grouping and regrouping themselves during the last fifteen years of the nineteenth century into ephemeral schools and cliques. No poet of genius is within the field of our vision, nor, in spite of constant jockeying for position, any single great leader capable of rallying writers under a clearly defined banner marked Symbolism.

Understood in this very literal and limited sense, the Symbolist movement began in 1886 when Jean Moréas, smarting under the accusation that he and his associates were morbid and neurotic, denied the charge in the 18 September issue of the *Figaro* and went on to explain their lofty aims and ambitions. They were seeking, he affirmed, to create beauty through a search for the "pure concept" and the "eternal symbol." Although vague, verbose, and very abstract, Moréas's remarks pleased almost all the new poets. They approved his emphasis upon the positive quality and the grandeur of their aspirations and accepted the article as a manifesto. Symbolism became thereby officially baptized and Jean Moréas was constituted leader of a school so denominated.

The new poets soon proved themselves more enthusiastic and energetic than disciplined. Individual talents cried for expression, and vied with one another in the numerous little magazines that sprang up following Moréas's manifesto. Poetic circles were in a foment of activity, a general mêlée ensued. René Ghil became editor of a new periodical called *La Décadence* and challenged the leadership of Moréas. Moréas immediately took up the challenge and, with Gustave Kahn, founded another magazine, *Le Symboliste*. Other leaders and other magazines joined in the fray, with poets and supporters constantly shifting allegiance. Ghil, by 1890, had lost his following and was embarked alone on a course of poetic speculation leading away from Symbolism. The following year Moréas himself stepped down. In another letter to the *Figaro*, he announced that Symbolism, only a transitory phenomenon, was dead and that he was founding the Ecole Romane to succeed it. The movement went on without leaders or found new ones. Conflict, at least nominal, increased as new poets established their theory either outside the Symbolist cadre or in apparent opposition to it. In the name of nature, life, simplicity, or clarity, Symbolism came under attack. Chief among the adversaries were, besides the Ecole Romane, the Naturists, but there were many Lilliputian schools hoping to deal Symbolism a death blow. Magazines pronounced it already dead and covered it with ridicule. The general public, never vitally concerned, was more interested in the Dreyfus Case than in poetry. Poets themselves turned from their metaphysical speculation to affairs of the day; writers like Régnier or Samain moved away from Symbolism in proportion as their native genius declared itself. No champion of any stature would present himself to defend the cause that had been espoused with such pride and confidence. As the century drew to an end, there was little left to attack, the subject was scarcely discussed and, although for some time there would be attempts to rally old adherents and enlist "Neo-Symbolists," the period of the schools was over. As Michel Décaudin declares, "S'il y a encore des poètes symbolistes en 1900, il n'y a plus de symbolisme." [4]

The self-conscious and self-styled Symbolist poets represent, as I have already suggested, only an articulate and militant phase of a general development in French poetry stemming from the Romantic period and continuing to the present day. Moréas's manifesto did not begin the movement, nor did the ultimate abandonment of all hopes of founding an integrated and enduring Symbolist school alter the trend. Poets of the twentieth century have continued in theory and practice where nineteenth-century Symbolists left off. Among them we can count our greatest contemporary poets, far greater than any who wrote and argued

THE RHUMB LINE OF SYMBOLISM

French Poets from Sainte-Beuve to Valéry

THE
RHUMB LINE
OF
SYMBOLISM

FRENCH POETS
FROM SAINTE-BEUVE TO VALÉRY

Presentation and Selected Texts

LAURENT LeSAGE

THE PENNSYLVANIA STATE UNIVERSITY PRESS
UNIVERSITY PARK AND LONDON

I am grateful to the following publishers for permission to reprint some of their materials:
To the Philosophical Library, for passages from an article I wrote for the *Dictionary of French Literature*.
To Gallimard, Mercure de France, and Editions Messein for various poems that appear in this anthology.

I wish to acknowledge a grant from The Pennsylvania State University Office of Research and Graduate Studies, which aided in the preparation and publication of this book.

Library of Congress Cataloging in Publication Data

LeSage, Laurent, 1913–
    The rhumb line of symbolism.

    Includes bibliographies.
    1. French poetry—19th century—History and criticism. 2. Symbolism in literature. I. Title.
PQ439.L4   821'.8'08   77-8020
ISBN 0-271-00513-0

Printed in the United States of America

in the little magazines of the eighties and nineties. Poets of genius preceded and followed the movement strictly defined, whose chief significance is to have glossed and exploited the genius of the ones and to have thereby made possible the full flowering of the other. To trace the Symbolist heritage, I have chosen those poets whom I consider significant and representative. Doubtless other selections could have served and surely no claim is made for comprehensiveness. Some of the greatest poets— from Victor Hugo to Apollinaire or to Saint-John Perse—have been left out because their identity is only partially or incidentally defined by Symbolism. In the matter of emphasis, intrinsic merit has not served as sole criterion for the treatment given individual poets; if some of the major figures receive less than their due, it is because they have abundantly obtained it elsewhere. It has seemed more useful to present a minor figure difficult of access than to expatiate upon the familiar. Similar thinking prompted the choice of texts, although, when possible or useful, the most often anthologized pieces were used. Even these are not always easy to come by, and one of the justifications of this work is the broad sweep of pertinent texts, not to be found in translation or even in the original. Among the poets of the Romantic period, we now distinguish several who, somewhat off the main highway, seem to have followed a byway that would broaden into Symbolism. Hence our interest in Aloysius Bertrand, who recorded his hallucinations in prose poems; Gérard de Nerval, who strove to associate music and transcendental knowledge with poetry; Sainte-Beuve, whose poetry struck a rare intimate note; Charles Baudelaire, who integrated and gave the most complete expression to these early manifestations of the Symbolist spirit.

Baudelaire (1821–1867) is thus the first of the great Symbolist masters. In the words of Hugo, this poet had brought a "frisson nouveau" into French poetry, a "frisson" induced by intimate revelation and poetic suggestion of mystery, evil, unhealthy and melancholy beauty. The influence of the *Fleurs du Mal* operated through successive generations of latter nineteenth-century poets. The Parnassian craftsmen, following Gautier, were interested primarily in the technical aspect of Baudelaire's verse; Decadents and Symbolists, however, were attracted by its broad implications. A concept of beauty that included the ugly and the evil (the "frisson nouveau") strongly appealed to the Decadents. Symbolists saw in Baudelaire a poet on the track of a poetic magic that might conjure up, through a blending of rhythm, sound, and image, the veritable face of the universe. In his famous sonnet entitled "Correspondances" and in his article on Théophile Gautier ("L'Art romantique"), he had suggested that the poet was in moments of perfect evocation capable of perceiving the analogies in nature which bind the universe together, of establishing the symbols which stand for the absolute itself.

From these two aspects of Baudelaire, the artist and the seer, may be traced the two traditions that have threaded through poetic history down to the present day.[5] In the line of artists, there are the Mallarmés and the Valérys; in that of the seers, Rimbaud and the Surrealists.[6]

Verlaine (1844–1896), following his natural inclination, had moved slowly away from the Parnassian ideal toward a concept of poetry that anticipated Symbolism. Even in his earliest collection of verse, the *Poèmes saturniens* (1866), a strong current of Baudelairianism, running counter to its general Parnassian themes and techniques, indicated the direction which this young poet was going to follow. Not many years later, Verlaine formulated his anti-Parnassian notions about poetry in the piece which has become famous, "Art Poétique." Verse must be musical, a harmony of sounds inspiring revery. Rime, architecture, must be attenuated; rhetoric must be replaced by suggestion and nuance.

Toward 1885, the young poets discovered poor Lélian, as Verlaine had called himself. Captivated by the legend that had grown up around his name, they saluted him as a leader and tried to imitate his manner. His verses were eagerly sought after by all the Symbolist magazines. He had given in his *Poètes maudits* models for the young poets to follow: Tristan Corbière, the naive bohemian author of the *Amours Jaunes;* Mallarmé; Villiers de l'Isle-Adam, whom they called their Chateaubriand; Lautréamont, poet of Promethean revolt and the prodigious image.

Stéphane Mallarmé (1842–1898) is the third major force in the Symbolist movement. Like Verlaine he proceeded from Baudelaire, like Verlaine he was a guide and teacher to younger poets writing during the latter nineteenth century. Unlike Verlaine, his own poetic production was very limited. But his poetic ambitions exceeded those of Verlaine, and have interested successive generations at least as much as Verlaine's accomplishments. His poetry stands for the most sublime of all Symbolist dreams, one which has challenged the greatest poets and which is still the object of numerous and voluminous commentaries.

Obsessed by the notion of correspondences, which he had found in the *Fleurs du Mal*, Mallarmé saw everything in the universe bound by subtle analogies which the poet alone could detect. They might lead him beyond the world of appearances into that world of pure ideas whose existence had been affirmed by philosophers from Plato to Hegel. To serve him in his hermetic alchemy, Mallarmé deliberately made his verse obscure by omissions, peculiar syntax, and unconventional diction.

Mallarmé was made known to the poets of 1886 by Huysmans's description of him in the celebrated *A Rebours*. Soon he was surrounded by a fervent group who came every Tuesday to the apartment in the rue de Rome to listen to the master expound his doctrine. As Mallarmé spoke of the revelatory symbol, of Wagner and the possibility of synthesizing poetry with music, Moréas composed his manifesto and René Ghil mapped out his theory of "instrumentation verbale."

Rimbaud (1854–1891) completes the tetrad of the masters of Symbolism. Ten years younger than Mallarmé or Verlaine, Rimbaud nevertheless belonged to their generation. At fifteen he was already a poet. At twenty his career was over. But in three or four years he produced his amazing work and had improvised an esthetic that would inspire writers of future generations. The "Alchimie du verbe" proudly and defiantly states his accomplishments: "... avec des rythmes instinctifs, je me flattai d'inventer un verbe poétique accessible ... à tous les sens ... je notais l'inexprimable. ... Je m'habituai à l'hallucination simple. ... Je finis par trouver sacré le désordre de mon esprit."[7] Rimbaud's assertions define the poet's rôle as that of a seer, of a *voyant*. As such he acclaimed Baudelaire "le premier voyant, roi des poètes, *un vrai Dieu!*"[8] Rimbaud's sojourn in poetic circles was too brief—moreover, he was too young—to exert the personal influence upon poets that Mallarmé and Verlaine held. His work itself, only partially known during his lifetime, had to wait until recent times to receive its fullest acclaim. Except for a few copies, *Une Saison en Enfer* remained with the publisher until the work was discovered in 1901, and the discovery was not made known until 1914. The "lettre du voyant" was first published in 1912. But the poets of 1886 used the *Illuminations* to illustrate their new theories, and writers like René Ghil were quite patently in Rimbaud's debt.

If Baudelaire, Verlaine, Mallarmé, and Rimbaud were to triumph in the mid–eighties, it is because the youthful rebels against the poetic party then in office had finally gathered enough strength to require leadership for a full-scale revolt. The school of Parnasse had ruled officially since 1866. But by the end of the seventies, a decade marked by poetic lethargy, opposition to the values upon which Parnassianism rested or with which it was associated became general enough to indicate a new poetic movement was underway. Positivistic philosophy, bourgeois society, the cult of form in art were under attack by an increasingly large proportion of the younger generation. The Hydropaths, the Hirsutes, and the others sought to outrage the bourgeois by their unconventional ideas and manners. Contemptuous society called the bearded and Bohemian revolutionaries the Decadents, and they accepted the label with bravado.

Although neither bearded nor Bohemian, the poet who represents the highest achievement of Decadentism is Jules Laforgue. To convey anguish and irony, cosmic visions and timid complaints, Laforgue found new and subtly effective measures. Fellow Decadents copied his neologisms, the liberties that he took with rhythm and rime. He is said to have invented free verse.

When Jean Moréas, in retort to the contemptuous attack upon himself and his colleagues, proposed the name of *Symbolist* to replace that of *Decadent*, the latter term soon fell into disuse. For a time there was conflict between poets calling themselves Symbolists and others calling themselves Decadents, but before long their differences were lost in the general Symbolist mêlée. The Decadent period had been one of general revolt and fierce defiance; the new one was in the main more constructive and more exclusively concerned with literature. The differences which soon cropped up among the Symbolists were on purely literary matters.

René Ghil founded a school called "symbolique et harmoniste" to oppose Moréas. Exploiting the implications of Rimbaud's vowel sonnet, Ghil developed his theory of "instrumentation verbale" to reduce the poem to pure music and suggestivity. Several magazines of the times supported Ghil and numerous poets studied with him.

The question of free verse for some critics summarizes the entire Symbolist movement. Gustave Kahn declared that it was his invention. He described, defined, and defended it in the *Revue Indépendante* in 1888, but his claim for paternity was hotly contested. The entire issue of free verse incited passionate and widespread controversy for years to come. It was the most radical alteration French verse had ever in its entire history undergone. The public was shocked and the poets dazzled by their own daring. But it was the logical step in the direction away from the visual toward the auditory in poetry. Less ambitious than Kahn, Vielé-Griffin nevertheless contributed much discussion to the theory of free verse. His own poetry is something between the regular stanza and free verse. The other outstanding *vers-libriste*, Stuart Merrill, likewise avoided excessive metrical eccentricities. In 1897, another innovation in poetic forms made a stir: Paul Fort had devised for his ballads a very personal sort or rhythmic prose that accommodated itself easily to the poet's moods.

When the critic Brunetière defined Symbolism as simply the "réinté-
gration de l'idée dans la poésie" he was oversimplifying, but less so than
those who found Symbolism merely a matter of free verse or music. His
statement points out a very fundamental attitude of the poets who fol-
lowed Mallarmé and accepted the metaphysic of Baudelaire's "Sonnet des
Correspondances." They all sensed the presence of a higher reality behind
the world of appearances which they called the world of ideas. Accord-
ingly, all phenomena assumed symbolic value, indications of that higher
reality. Phenomena are linked to the ideas behind them and to one another
by the mysterious bonds of analogies which are detected only in the
poetic experience. Given this fundamental philosophic assumption and
ambition, the matters of poetry=music, of free verse, of suggestion and
obscurity take their place as secondary manifestations of the Symbolist
thought.

Lying at the heart, therefore, of the Symbolist doctrine is the symbolic
image. Each poet sought to translate his aspirations, his thoughts and
emotions by its means. Mallarmé had taught that the humblest objects
could serve, and many poets attempted to use familiar objects of daily
existence. But the pictures tended to conventionalize: fountains and pools
of water, moonlight, dawn, twilight, fogs, old parks, and dead cities.
Antiquity and the Middle Ages were ransacked to build up a common
fund of imagery. Greco-Latin lore offered sirens, chimeras, nymphs,
satyrs; the recently discovered Middle Ages provided princesses and
saints, figures from Celtic and Germanic legends. Henri de Régnier used
legendary beasts, all sorts of medieval material, and gardens so dear to
Marcel Proust. Albert Samain was fond of antique images and great
sustained metaphors. Some studded their verse with novel images, some
with quaint and some with modern metropolitan.

Symbolist poets were eager to carry their theories into the theater.
Wagner's prodigious dream of combining the arts in theatrical presenta-
tion had fascinated Mallarmé and continued to inspire his successors. Not
that they, any more than Mallarmé, hoped to emulate the German master,
but in their modest way they hoped to challenge the monopoly of the
Naturalistic play and the *pièce à thèse*. Numerous poets, following Mal-
larmé's example in *Hérodiade*, composed poems in dramatic form. These
could be adapted for the stage. Other poems and prose in dialogue could
be recited effectively against scenery and accompanied by music, illus-
trated by mime or the dance. Lights and even perfumes might prove
effective auxiliaries. Audiences, the Symbolists hoped, would become
accustomed to this sort of dramatic entertainment just as they went to

concerts made up of fragments of operas and symphonies. Between 1890 and 1900, several theaters made such experiments, notably the Théâtre d'Art of Paul Fort and the Théâtre de l'Œuvre of Lugné-Poe. However interesting these attempts may seem, the only real success that the Symbolist theater could claim was the work of Maurice Maeterlinck.

If by 1900 Symbolism was dead officially, it has nevertheless lived on in the most significant poets of the twentieth century. Apollinaire, in treating his whimsical and wistful themes, made full use of the metrical freedom that the Symbolists had won. Charles Péguy embroidered his medieval themes on Symbolist-inspired patterns. Paul Claudel throughout a long lifetime defended Symbolist theses and illustrated them in the most sumptuous theater of our century. Jean Giraudoux, who was hailed as having realized Symbolism in the novel, went on to create a theater that accomplished the Symbolist ambition to discredit Realism. The early plays and prose pieces of André Gide were written under Symbolist masters, and his style was marked forever by the Symbolist associations of his youth. His ethic, too, one might say. Proust's esthetic and metaphysic derive quite clearly from the great nineteenth-century poets. Paul Valéry is Mallarmé's successor. Dadaism and Surrealism, the chief poetic movements of the between-wars period, pushed Symbolist theories to their ultimate conclusion. In many respects, one may say that French poetry of the twentieth century comes out of Symbolism, and that from Baudelaire to the poets of the present age we can trace an almost unbroken line.

Nor has Symbolism's influence been restricted to France. Poets from all over the world have received inspiration from Symbolists, and carried into their own countries the ideas and techniques they found in France. Throughout Europe, the Americas, and even in Asia, Symbolism has stimulated great poetic revivals and oriented native geniuses. France, once described by Emerson as that country "where poets were never born," has thereby acquired a prestige and importance that can scarcely be challenged.

Notes

1. To introduce my subject, I have repeated here, in the main, an article which I wrote for the *Dictionary of French Literature*, edited by Sidney D. Braun (New York: Philosophical Library, 1958).

2. It is always convenient, in such matters, to begin with Rousseau. In the *Rêveries du Promeneur Solitaire* and in the *Profession de foi du vicaire Savoyard*, we find implicit already the Romantic attitude toward nature, the artist, and his work. Down through Surrealism, poets will continue to affirm the authority of the subjective ego, passivity as a condition of inspiration, etc. They will furthermore note that in revery, where the creative imagination plays freely, the subject seems to move into a blissful state of timelessness and of direct contact with the absolute.

3. For ample treatment of this affiliation, see Georges Cattaui, *Orphisme et Prophétie chez les poètes français, 1850–1950* (Plon, 1965); Alain Mercier, *Les Sources esotériques et occultes de la poésie symboliste* (Nizet, 1969); Jacques Roos, *Aspects littéraires du mysticisme philosophique* (Strasbourg: P. H. Heitz, 1951); Auguste Viatte, *Les Sources occultes du Romantisme* (Champion, 1928).

4. Décaudin, *La Crise des Valeurs symbolistes*, p. 101. Literary historians like Décaudin and William Cornell have studied the fluctuations of Symbolism year by year, the personal quarrels, the ideological and political pressures, the shifting emphasis in doctrine and point of view. See Readings, p. vi.

5. The emphasis on inspiration starting with Rousseau's *Rêveries* and Madame de Staël's *Le Sentiment de l'Infini* surely paves the way for the concept of the poet as seer. However, among the chief Romantic authors, inspiration may mean little more than exaltation of sentiment over reason, spontaneity over craftsmanship, particularity of the artist's rôle in society (Lamartine's "son cœur dicte, la plume obéit"; Hugo's "écho sonore," etc.). Some of the lesser Romantics, such as those previously mentioned, did hold a more transcendental concept of the poet.

6. The differences between Baudelaire and his successors have been emphasized by Marcel Ruff in *L'Esprit du Mal et l'Esthétique Baudelairienne*, Colin, 1955. Other critics have reminded us that the inclusion of evil and the ugly in the concept of beauty as well as the doctrine of correspondences was not peculiar to Baudelaire. Baudelaire's impact on subsequent poets has been nonetheless strong, and the genealogical scheme made famous by Marcel Raymond (*De Baudelaire au Surréalisme*, Corti, 1933) does not seem to be invalidated by such strictures.

7. Arthur Rimbaud, "Une Saison en Enfer," in *Œuvres complètes de Arthur Rimbaud* (Gallimard, 1946), p. 220.

8. "La lettre du voyant," ibid., p. 257.

Poetry of Sainte-Beuve

Vie, Poésies et Pensées de Joseph Delorme (Delangle, 1829).
Les Consolations (Urbain Carrel, 1830).
Pensées d'août (Renduel, 1837).
Poésies complètes (Charpentier, 1840).
Vie, Poésies et Pensées de Joseph Delorme (Nouvelles Editions Latines, 1956).
Critical edition by Gérald Antoine.

Readings

Barlow, Norman H. *Sainte-Beuve to Baudelaire: A Poetic Legacy* (Durham, N.C.: Duke University Press, 1964).
Choisy, Louis-Frédéric. *Sainte-Beuve, l'homme et le poète* (Plon-Nourrit, 1921).
Clancier, Georges-Emmanuel. *De Chénier à Baudelaire* (Seghers, 1963), pp. 136–48.
Lalou, René. *Vers une alchimie lyrique* (Les Arts et le Livre, 1927), pp. 18–40; 105–43.
Lehmann, A. G. *Sainte-Beuve* (Oxford: Clarendon Press, 1962), pp. 58–73.

Charles Sainte-Beuve

1804–1869

Bereft of his father before he was born, Sainte-Beuve was brought up by his mother and his aunt in Boulogne-sur-Mer. There, in a widowed household, Sainte-Beuve spent a lonely, melancholy childhood given over chiefly to study and religious practice. When he was fourteen, he went to Paris for his schooling.

Sainte-Beuve's interest in poetry dates from 1820. Lamartine's *Méditations* were a revelation for this schoolboy of sixteen. He was fond too of Chateaubriand, whose fame was reaching its zenith about now. He himself began to write verse. At the same time, Sainte-Beuve became interested in science and, under the influence of his new studies, his Christian convictions began to pale. By the time he was ready for medical school in 1823, his agnosticism became complicated by a taste for libertinage, both tendencies being in contradiction to the religiosity and moralism of his poetic inspiration. Here is the source for those conflicts which Sainte-Beuve describes in *Les Poésies de Joseph Delorme*. The havoc wreaked in his views extended to politics, for after being an ardent legitimist like his mother, he became intensely democratic.

Still in medical school but bitten seriously by the literary bug, Sainte-Beuve began to contribute to the *Globe*, a magazine founded by one of his former professors. Eventually he left school and gave himself up entirely to literature. His work on the *Globe* had put him in contact with writers; their company excited and inspired him, particularly that of the young Romantics. In the movement that would triumph in 1830 Sainte-Beuve participated ardently. Lamartine describes him at the time: "C'était en 1829. J'aimais alors beaucoup un jeune homme pâle, blond, frêle, sensible jusqu'à la maladie, poète jusqu'aux larmes ... il s'appelait Sainte-Beuve. Il vivait à Paris avec une mère âgée, sereine, absorbée en lui, dans

une petite maison sur un jardin retiré, dans le quartier du Luxembourg."[1]
This is the year of *Vie, Poésies et Pensées de Joseph Delorme*, a collection of
poems preceded by a fictitious biography and followed by a miscellany
of thoughts on literary matters. In the verses ascribed to this unhappy
victim of the *mal du siècle*, Sainte-Beuve strikes chords in a minor key
rarely heard in the works of his greater contemporaries. This is his strongest
claim to fame as a poet: he introduced the humble and the familiar into
French poetry, extolling tranquil pleasures, life with a tender companion,
children, a cottage with green shutters. Lamartine describes him as "ayant
une grande analogie avec Novalis en Allemagne, avec les poètes intimes
qu'on nomme les Lakistes en Angleterre."[2] Sainte-Beuve's modest claim
in the territory of poetry is set forth in "Promenade," where he alludes
with gentle irony to the grander claims staked out by his peers: "Laissons
Chateaubriand, loin des traces profanes, / A vingt ans s'élancer en d'im-
menses savanes ..." "Laissons à Lamartine, à Nodier, nobles frères, / Leur
Jura bien-aimé ..." "Qu'aussi Victor Hugo, sous un donjon qui croule,
/ Et le Rhin à ses pieds ..." In *Les Consolations*, Sainte-Beuve's second
volume of verse, he works on in the vein struck in the first. His themes
are those of ordinary life—a walk, a conversation, a domestic incident.
The emotion of friendship (for the Hugos) and of newly recovered
Christian piety make it for some critics his best work; for others like
Ferdinand Brunetière, humdrum material always remains humdrum.[3]
Perhaps Brunetière is right in thinking that Sainte-Beuve lacked the
sincerity and moral elevation of Wordsworth and the other Lake poets
that he was imitating. He created, nevertheless, something novel in France,
and his depiction of the simple life is not altogether without charm. We
are tempted to think that the quaint winsomeness that his poetry possesses
for us may be in a measure due to the patina that the years have added;
yet nineteenth-century readers relished it as well and were just as amused
as we are when Sainte-Beuve pushes his Muse too far. "Sur sa table un
lait pur, dans son lit un œil noir" was a line widely made sport of in Sainte-
Beuve's own day. In the Antoine edition of *Joseph Delorme*, there is a
caricatural drawing of Sainte-Beuve before a bowl of milk and a bed
which contains a single black eye! Sainte-Beuve's final effort to establish
in poetry "un certain genre moyen" is the volume entitled *Pensées d'août*,
which appeared in 1837. It is a miscellany of themes and styles, tending
perhaps more than his previous works toward the didactic.

Although Sainte-Beuve's place in French literary history is assured by
his cultivation of the homely genre, his seminal force is not precisely

here. That is to say, no one following him chose to work in this genre as such, but many subsequent French poets found inspiration in certain incidental features of his poetry. In later life Sainte-Beuve uttered these words which were more prophetic than he knew: "Aujourd'hui on me croit seulement un critique; mais je n'ai pas quitté la poésie sans y avoir laissé tout mon aiguillon."[4] This "stinger" has been given various interpretations, pointing in the main to a certain psychology that we think of as modern. Sainte-Beuve translated the *mal du siècle* into the idiom of his own experience and temperament: the result was, as René Lalou calls it, "une poésie intime jusqu'à l'excentricité, originale jusqu'à la création des valeurs paradoxalement neuves."[5] Already in Sainte-Beuve we perceive the accents of Baudelaire, who, in his reference to *Joseph Delorme* as "*Les Fleurs du Mal* de la veille," was not merely currying favor with the important critic. Doubtless he could recognize in Joseph Delorme a kindred spirit, another victim of those inner conflicts which he summarized by the paradox of his own title: "Flowers of Evil." Both *Joseph Delorme* and *Les Fleurs du Mal* set up the opposing poles of the profane and the sublime, between which each poet feels his soul vacillate. The resulting moral and metaphysical suffering made acute by full intellectual awareness of his problem creates the state of mind which Baudelaire recognized as common to himself and his predecessor. Albert Thibaudet defines the affinities between Baudelaire and Sainte-Beuve as: critical intelligence (analysis of the heart instead of the typical Romantic effusions of the heart); inner Christianity (the theological implication of this analysis, the preoccupation with original sin); and a keen awareness of Paris.[6] This last named point is more important than it sounds because it ties together the theme of the homely and familiar with the spleen theme. The poet projects the Romantic psyche into a depiction of the modern metropolis, making of it a swarming culture of misery and vice. But Sainte-Beuve's realism moved away too soon from city scenes into the purely domestic, leaving the field to Baudelaire. The effect, however, of his "stinger" may be observed not only in the "Tableaux parisiens" of *Les Fleurs du Mal* but also in the "Petits Poèmes en prose," some of which first appeared under the title "Spleen de Paris."

Among the points in common, Thibaudet does not include that of the concept of universal analogies or correspondences. Yet Joseph Delorme heard the harmonies of the "analogie universelle" and saw in material nature the signs of a divine unity. In "Les Rayons Jaunes," the series of associations awakened by the color of the sun's rays is an early exploitation in verse (before Gautier's "Symphonie en blanc majeur" and Banville's "Symphonie de la neige") of the theory of correspondences. Although rudimentary and inexplicit in the poem, it is stated precisely elsewhere in *Joseph Delorme*.[7]

Sainte-Beuve's importance as an initiator is not limited to matters of theme and mood: he left his mark too on poetic techniques. We know about his recovery of the Pléïade poets of the sixteenth century ignored or forgotten by the classical generations that followed them. A great part of his recovery was in metrics and in poetic diction. He promoted sixteenth-century verse forms, pleaded for renewed emphasis on rime, and advocated poetic procedures such as alliteration and assonance proscribed by the arbiters of classical taste.[8] Baudelaire, who would be first admired chiefly as a technician of poetry, was an attentive pupil. An additional feature of Sainte-Beuve's technical innovation is his predilection for the specific and realistic epithet. Here again Sainte-Beuve reaches back to pre-Classical literature to create models for poets to come. In spite of the general impression that he may give us today of being terribly conventional and rhetorical, he does say something new whereas Lamartine and other Romantic poets remained true to the tradition of the colorless generality.

It is to be feared, however, that in spite of its interesting features, the poetry of Sainte-Beuve may be destined to remain in the histories of literature. The homely genre as he practiced it has, as we have asserted, a quaint charm. Yet at bottom if it seemed ridiculous to his generation, it surely seems more so today. What seems even more alien to modern sensibility is Saint-Beuve's *mal du siècle*, although it was once thought to be very moving.

Notes

1. Alphonse Lamartine, *Harmonies poétiques et religieuses* (Hachette, 1879), vol. 14, *Œuvres*, pp. 226–27.

2. Ibid., p. 226.

3. Ferdinand Brunetière, "L'œuvre poétique de Sainte-Beuve," in *Evolution de la poésie lyrique en France au XIXe siècle* (Hachette, 1909).

4. Cited by René Lalou in *Vers une alchimie lyrique*, p. 39.

5. Ibid. See also J. Charpentier, *De Joseph Delorme à Paul Claudel*, pp. 51–52 (Les Œuvres Représentatives, 1930).

6. Albert Thibaudet, *Histoire de la littérature française* (Stock, 1936), pp. 322–23.

7. See *Joseph Delorme*, Texte XVIII (p. 150 of the Antoine edition). Is yellow here "yellow for mourning" of Swedenborgianism? See Anna Balakian, *The Symbolist Movement*, p. 25.

8. "A la Rime." This poem, resuscitating a strophe not used in French poetry since the Pléiade and exhibiting lexigraphical reminiscences of Ronsard and his group, calls for a return to the sixteenth-century emphasis upon rime. Throughout the nineteenth century, it served as a point of reference, a nail from which to hang reaffirmations of the importance of rime or repudiations of rime. See Antoine edition, p. 164, where its importance to Baudelaire is cited.

LES RAYONS JAUNES [1]

Les dimanches d'été, le soir, vers les six heures,
Quand le peuple empressé déserte ses demeures
      Et va s'ébattre aux champs,
Ma persienne fermée, assis à ma fenêtre,
Je regarde d'en-haut passer et disparaître
      Joyeux bourgeois, marchands,

Ouvriers en habits de fête, au cœur plein d'aise;
Un livre est entr'ouvert, près de moi, sur ma chaise;
      Je lis ou fais semblant;
Et les jaunes rayons que le couchant ramène,
Plus jaunes ce soir-là que pendant la semaine,
      Teignent mon rideau blanc.

J'aime à les voir percer vitres et jalousie;
Chaque oblique sillon trace à ma fantaisie
      Un flot d'atomes d'or;
Puis, m'arrivant dans l'âme à travers la prunelle,
Ils redorent aussi mille pensers en elle,
      Mille atomes encor.

Ce sont des jours confus dont reparaît la trame,
Des souvenirs d'enfance, aussi doux à notre âme
      Qu'un rêve d'avenir;
C'était à pareille heure (oh! je me le rappelle)
Qu'après vêpres, enfants, au chœur de la chapelle,
      On nous faisait venir.

La lampe brûlait jaune, et jaune[2] aussi les cierges;
Et la lueur glissant aux fronts voilés des vierges
      Jaunissait leur blancheur;
Et le prêtre vêtu de son étole blanche,
Courbait un front jauni, comme un épi qui penche
      Sous la faux du faucheur.

Oh! qui dans une église, à genoux sur la pierre,
N'a bien souvent, le soir, déposé sa prière,
      Comme un grain pur de sel?
Qui n'a du crucifix baisé le jaune ivoire?

Qui n'a de l'homme-Dieu lu la sublime histoire
    Dans un jaune missel?

Mais où la retrouver, quand elle s'est perdue,
Cette humble foi du cœur, qu'un ange a suspendue
    En palme à nos berceaux;
Qu'une mère a nourrie en nous d'un zèle immense;
Dont chaque jour un prêtre arrosait la semence
    Aux bords des saints ruisseaux?

Peut-elle refleurir lorsqu'a soufflé l'orage,
Et qu'en nos cœurs l'orgueil, debout, a dans sa rage
    Mis le pied sur l'autel?
On est bien faible alors, quand le malheur arrive,
Et la mort ... faut-il donc que l'idée en survive
    Au vœu d'être immortel!

J'ai vu mourir, hélas, ma bonne vieille tante,
L'an dernier; sur son lit, sans voix et haletante,
    Elle resta trois jours,
Et trépassa. J'étais près d'elle dans l'alcôve;
J'étais près d'elle encor, quand sur sa tête chauve
    Le linceul fit trois tours.

Le cercueil arriva, qu'on mesura de l'aune;
J'étais là ... puis, autour, des cierges brûlaient jaune,
    Des prêtres priaient bas;
Mais en vain je voulais dire l'hymne dernière;
Mon œil était sans larme et ma voix sans prière,
    Car je ne croyais pas.

Elle m'aimait pourtant; ... et ma mère aussi m'aime,
Et ma mère à son tour mourra; bientôt moi-même
    Dans le jaune linceul
Je l'ensevelirai; je clouerai sous la lame
Ce corps flétri, mais cher, ce reste de mon âme;
    Alors je serai seul;

Seul, sans mère, sans sœur, sans frère, et sans épouse;
Car qui voudrait m'aimer, et quelle main jalouse
    S'unirait à ma main? ...[3]
Mais déjà le soleil recule devant l'ombre,

Et les rayons qu'il lance à mon rideau plus sombre
S'éteignent en chemin ...

Non, jamais à mon nom ma jeune fiancée
Ne rougira d'amour, rêvant dans sa pensée
          Au jeune époux absent;
Jamais deux enfants purs, deux anges de promesse
Ne tiendront suspendu sur moi, durant la messe,
          Le poêle jaunissant.

Non, jamais, quand la mort m'étendra sur ma couche,
Mon front ne sentira le baiser d'une bouche,
          Ni mon œil obscurci
N'entreverra l'adieu d'une lèvre mi-close!
Jamais sur mon tombeau ne jaunira la rose,
          Ni le jaune souci!

—Ainsi va ma pensée, et la nuit est venue;
Je descends; et bientôt dans la foule inconnue
          J'ai noyé mon chagrin:
Plus d'un bras me coudoie; on entre à la guinguette,
On sort du cabaret; l'invalide en goguette
          Chevrotte un gai refrain.

Ce ne sont que chansons, clameurs, rixes d'ivrogne;
Ou qu'amours en plein air, et baisers sans vergogne,
          Et publiques faveurs;
Je rentre; sur ma route on se presse, on se rue;
Toute la nuit j'entends se traîner dans ma rue
          Et hurler les buveurs.

---

1. This is the most celebrated of Sainte-Beuve's poems, mocked by many but admired by many more. Lamartine, Banville, Gautier, Musset, Verlaine, and of course Baudelaire seem to have been fond of it. In a letter to Sainte-Beuve (25 January 1862), Baudelaire declares himself to be the "amoureux incorrigible" of "Les Rayons Jaunes." Besides the synesthesia developed by the imagery, there is the depiction of Paris that admittedly attracted Baudelaire. Indeed the poet looking down from his window at the populace thronging the streets, the city given over to debauchery when night falls are strongly suggestive of Baudelaire's "Recueillement." Other poems besides "Les Rayons Jaunes" in which Baudelaire specifically recognizes the melancholy Parisian tone which he himself would adopt are four in the *Pensées d'août* collection: "Dans ce cabriolet de place

j'examine," "La voilà, pauvre mère, à Paris arrivée," "En revenant du convoi de Ga-
brielle," and "Le Joueur d'orgue."

2. Just as the repetition of the jaundiced color, the repetition of the closed *o* sound
sustains the melancholy character of the poem. Sound and image together help create
what L. F. Choisy calls its ambiguous charm—"quelque chose de doux et de malsain,
à la fois paisible et vermoulu, tenant de la sacristie et de la salle d'opération." See Choisy,
Sainte-Beuve, l'homme et le poète, p. 16.

3. A true and moving note in the middle of an exercise of virtuosity, according to
Gérald Antoine (see *Vie, Poésies et Pensées*, Antoine edition, p. 185).

LA VEILLEE[4]

A mon ami V. H.
Minuit, 21 octobre

Mon ami, vous voilà père d'un nouveau-né;
C'est un garçon encor; le ciel vous l'a donné
Beau, frais, souriant d'aise à cette vie amère;
A peine il a coûté quelque plainte à sa mère.
Il est nuit; je vous vois; ... à doux bruit, le sommeil
Sur un sein blanc qui dort a pris l'enfant vermeil,
Et vous, père, veillant contre la cheminée,
Recueilli dans vous-même, et la tête inclinée,
Vous vous tournez souvent pour revoir, ô douceur!
Le nouveau-né, la mère, et le frère et la sœur,
Comme un pasteur joyeux de ses toisons nouvelles,
Ou comme un maître, au soir, qui compte ses javelles.
A cette heure si grave, en ce calme profond,
Qui sait, hors vous, l'abyme où votre cœur se fond,
Ami? qui sait vos pleurs, vos muettes caresses;
Les trésors du génie épanchés en tendresses;
L'aigle plus gémissant que la colombe au nid;
Les torrents ruisselants du rocher de granit,
Et, comme sous les feux d'un été de Norvège,
Au penchant des glaciers mille fontes de neige?

Vivez, soyez heureux, et chantez-nous un jour
Ces secrets plus qu'humains d'un ineffable amour!

—Moi, pendant ce temps-là, je veille aussi, je veille,
Non près des rideaux bleus de l'enfance vermeille,
Près du lit nuptial arrosé de parfum,
Mais près d'un froid grabat, sur le corps d'un défunt.
C'est un voisin, vieillard goutteux, mort de la pierre;
Ses nièces m'ont requis, je veille à leur prière.
Seul, je m'y suis assis dès neuf heures du soir.
A la tête du lit une croix en bois noir,
Avec un Christ en os, pose entre deux chandelles
Sur une chaise; auprès, le buis cher aux fidèles
Trempe dans une assiette; et je vois sous les draps
Le mort en long, pieds joints, et croisant les deux bras.
Oh! si, du moins, ce mort m'avait durant sa vie
Eté longtemps connu! S'il me prenait envie
De baiser ce front jaune une dernière fois!
En regardant toujours ces plis raides et droits,
Si je voyais enfin remuer quelque chose,
Bouger comme le pied d'un vivant qui repose,
Et la flamme bleuir! si j'entendais crier
Le bois de lit! ... ou bien si je pouvais prier!
Mais rien: nul effroi saint; pas de souvenir tendre;
Je regarde sans voir, j'écoute sans entendre,
Chaque heure sonne lente; et lorsque, par trop las
De ce calme abattant et de ces rêves plats,
Pour respirer un peu je vais à la fenêtre
(Car au ciel de minuit le croissant vient de naître),
Voilà soudain, qu'au toit lointain d'une maison,
Non pas vers l'orient, s'embrase l'horizon,
Et j'entends résonner, pour toute mélodie,
Des aboiements de chiens hurlant dans l'incendie.

---

4. This poem was mentioned in a letter from Baudelaire to Sainte-Beuve, 15 January 1866. Designed as a contrast of mood and situation—the felicity of Hugo watching at the bedside of his wife and newborn son and the melancholy vigil of Joseph Delorme over a neighbor's corpse—the poem creates an atmosphere of bitter depression, of spleen, which is doubtless the appeal for Baudelaire. Modern readers are less likely to sympathize

with Joseph Delorme's troubles. Although contemporaries like Alfred de Vigny and Hugo found his complaints as pathetic as did Sainte-Beuve himself, a recent English critic writes: "Here one touches on the really glaring defect of the *Poésies*. . . . The self-pity on every page is intolerable: never a grain of irony in these elegies . . . , nothing to palliate Joseph's endless whine. *La Veillée* . . . an endless whine, maudlin and crude. No doubt it is part of the character, the *persona*; but that does not make it more acceptable. Nerval, Baudelaire, Corbière, Laforgue, Verlaine, all in fact indulge in the same self-pity as their ancestor, but in one way or another ironize or distance the theme of Pierrot, the *poète disgracieux*." See A. G. Lehmann, *Sainte-Beuve*, p. 69. The French critic Barat finds *Joseph Delorme* just as irritating. He defines the cause in somewhat different fashion, however, calling it Joseph Delorme's "ennui communicatif." As for "La Veillée," he says, "Il s'ennuie encore en veillant son voisin...; il passe sa veillée à faire des 'rêves plats,' et le feu prend à la maison sans le tirer de sa torpeur." E. Barat, *Le Style poétique et la Révolution romantique* (Hachette, 1904), p. 232. Barat is not very much taken by Sainte-Beuve's poetry anyway, tending to find it generally bad and unoriginal. Incidentally, his claim that *Delorme* was a failure is to be weighed against Lehmann's description of its popular success.

Gaspard de la Nuit. Fantaisies à la manière de Rembrandt et de Callot

Gaspard de la Nuit (Victor Pavie, 1842).

Gaspard de la Nuit (Pincebourde, 1868). New edition with addition of prose pieces and verse found in periodicals and collections. Introduction by Charles Asselineau.

Gaspard de la Nuit (Payot, 1926). Text conforms to the 1836 manuscript found by M. B. Guégan, which differs slightly from that of the Pavie edition.

Gaspard de la Nuit (Monte Carlo: Cap, 1956–1957). Illustrations by Rembrandt, Callot, etc., and notes and drawings of the author designed for the edition Renduel was to have done.

Gaspard de la Nuit (Colombe, 1962). Preface, introduction, and notes by Jean Palou.

A Selection from Gaspard of the Night (Minard, 1964). Introduction and translation by Paul Zweig.

Readings

Bernard, Suzanne. *Le Poème en prose de Baudelaire jusqu'à nos jours* (Nizet, 1959), pp. 49–73.

Lalou, René. *Vers une alchimie lyrique* (Les Arts et le Livre, 1927), pp. 40–48; 144–55.

Milner, Max. *Le Diable dans la littérature française* (Corti, 1960), vol. 1, pp. 594–97; vol. 2, pp. 198–205.

Rude, Fernand. *Aloysius Bertrand* (Seghers, 1971). Poètes d'aujourd'hui.

Sprietsma, Cargill. *Louis Bertrand dit Aloysius Bertrand* (Champion, 1926).

Tessier, Yves. "Aloysius Bertrand." In Francis Dumont, *Les Petits Romantiques* (Cahiers du Sud, 1949), pp. 65–73.

Louis Bertrand

1807–1841

Toward the end of 1828, there appeared in the Romantic "cénacles" of Paris a tall and thin young man with a wild look in his eye, a figure that might have come right out of one of those tales of Hoffmann that would be published in French the following year. The person was Louis Bertrand, freshly arrived from his hometown of Dijon and not yet known by the Romantic name he gave himself, Aloysius. Sainte-Beuve, in recalling a November evening at Victor Hugo's, tells how the newcomer read some of his own work and made a deep impression upon all present. Actually his audience was already disposed in his favor, for his name had preceded him to Paris. The group of young men who made up the Société d'Etudes de Dijon put out a literary journal, *Le Provincial*, which, according to Sainte-Beuve and Hugo, compared favorably with *Le Globe*. As its first editor and frequent contributor, Bertrand enjoyed a certain reputation. But in spite of the welcome accorded him at Hugo's in the rue Notre-Dame-des-Champs or at the Arsenal where Nodier received on Sundays, in spite of the solicitations of Sainte-Beuve, Louis Bertrand seldom put in an appearance. He was either too much embarrassed by his shabby clothes or too ill, this poor poet who deserves as much as any to have figured in Verlaine's gallery of "poètes maudits."

At the age of twenty, he had come to Paris with the manuscript of a volume of ballads and a play in his luggage. The play was refused and the publication of the ballads deferred. Before long Bertrand was penniless and gravely ill. The following year he went back to Dijon. He involved himself in provincial politics, played a somewhat inglorious part in the July revolution there, and finally returned to Paris for another try at fame and fortune. But neither came his way. In bad health and without money, he faced a really hopeless future. Toward the end of 1833, his mother and sister came to live with him, thus adding to his burden of poverty. Yet Bertrand persisted in his writing, preferring to starve as a poet rather than take a job and compromise his vocation. Bertrand seems the likeness in life of all the Chattertons and Werthers of *mal du siècle* fiction. He even loved like a Romantic hero, since it was perhaps not common sense but morbid preference for unfulfillment that prompted a letter to his sweetheart Célestine telling her that they could never know happiness together.

Célestine abandoned him, publishers and producers refused his work. The years went by, Bertrand filling his days with writing and studying art. He became enamored of painting and drawing, and even did some sketches in the manner of Hugo with which he intended to illustrate *Gaspard de la Nuit*. But negotiations with the publisher Eugène Renduel did not get anywhere. Finally Bertrand entered the hospital.

The last years of this young poet's unhappy life were brightened by the kindness of the sculptor Jean-Pierre David, known as "David d'Angers," who worked assiduously to get *Gaspard de la Nuit* in print. When David learned that Renduel had given up all notion of bringing it out, he enlisted the support of the Pavie brothers who agreed to take over the publication. However, Bertrand did not live long enough to see his dream accomplished. On the morning of 29 April 1841, when David, who had been visiting him regularly, arrived at the hospital, he was told that Bertrand had just expired. The following year, *Gaspard de la Nuit* finally appeared, thanks to David's efforts and the cooperation of Sainte-Beuve and Victor Pavie. In the prospectus we may read a report of their conversation:

> Je le publierai, dit-il (David) et puisse la mort lui réussir mieux que la vie.
> Et moi, dit Sainte-Beuve, je lui mettrai au front une notice originale.
> Et moi, dis-je (Pavie), je l'imprimerai.[1]

The public, however, took little heed. *Gaspard de la Nuit* was not—and has never been—a popular success. It is significant that there is still today no full translation of it into English.

On the other hand, *Gaspard* has had always a strong appeal for a few, a few that include several of the greatest writers of France. Sainte-Beuve esteemed the work, Baudelaire said that at least twenty times he had leafed through it and, in his own *Spleen de Paris*, had tried to do something similar—that is to say, "appliquer à la description de la vie moderne, ...

le procédé qu'il avait appliqué à la peinture de la vie ancienne, si étrange-ment pittoresque."[2] Mallarmé wrote to his daughter, "Prend Bertrand, on y trouve de tout." Among more recent writers, Max Jacob had certain reservations, suspecting that as an artist, Bertrand had lingered too lovingly over details.[3] Yet André Breton hailed him as a Surrealist,[4] and two postwar critics placed him above Baudelaire.[5] This praise is excessive; notwithstanding, Bertrand deserves to be read for the real charm of his pieces as well as for their historical interest. Although in a sense the prose poem has always existed, the modern variety which is a conscious art form begins with *Gaspard de la Nuit*. Louis Bertrand is the inventor of a new literary genre.

It has been suggested that Bertrand invented the prose poem because he dared not rival his great contemporaries in verse. This explanation is perhaps true, but without elaboration it may be misleading. In the first place, Bertrand wrote considerable verse too, and what he chose for his maiden recitation in Paris was not a poem in prose (as Sainte-Beuve erroneously recalled thirteen years later) but a poem in verse.[6] Moreover, if he cultivated the prose poem, it was probably more because of tem-perament and circumstance than because it was the only sort in which he could excel. The noble genre as practiced by the Romantics was chiefly a vehicle for lyrical effusions, to which Bertrand was not particularly given. On the other hand, he felt an attraction to the themes of the foreign ballads which he read in prose translation. There he could find the spooks and spirits of the Middle Ages that this dreamy youth evoked in his walks around old Dijon. He called his own prose pieces ballads or *bambochades*.[7] Any conscious decision in favor of the prose poem must have come after a gradual realization of what he had achieved by inclination and circum-stance. When Bertrand said that with *Gaspard de la Nuit* he had tried to create "un nouveau genre de prose," his book was already finished and he would have only four more years to live.[8]

Whatever may have been the part of foreign models in Bertrand's decision to write his poems in prose, their role in determining his subject matter is manifestly very great. The *maerchen* of the German Romantics come strongly to mind as we read along in the author's introduction to *Gaspard de la Nuit*. In a garden he encounters a stranger with a weasel-like face and an unkempt beard who strikes up a conversation with him on art. For a long time, this odd fellow explains, he had sought to answer the riddle of art. Ultimately he found what seemed to be the secret pre-cisely formulated in the two words *Gott* and *Liebe* which he noticed on a scroll ornamenting the title of an old book of magic. Henceforth reality turned into fairyland for him—beneath his window he could perceive a mysterious terrace where an old man, on his knees, was praying and a girl (or a wraith) was playing on a harp. He set out to explore nature and ruins—a gargoyle laughed from a nook on the cathedral. God and Love equated in his mind with sentiment. But sentiment is only half of the answer to the question art poses. The other half is idea. Perhaps this is the devil's half and perhaps the poor devil of the garden is the Devil himself. At any rate, since the Cologne Cathedral was built by the lord of darkness in homage to the lord of light, Bertrand solicits the support of the Devil to compose his poems as an offering to God.

All this medievalism and magic, controlled by a certain amount of *romantische ironie*, are surely reminiscent of the German. Yet Bertrand's borrowing may not be direct. The medieval setting had already been used by Victor Hugo. As a matter of fact, Bertrand expressly acknowledges his debt to Hugo: "Vous m'avez communiqué une passion d'architecture gothique..."[9] It is also Hugo who could have given Bertrand a taste for the grotesque so apparent throughout the poems. Perhaps it was even Hugo who first led Bertrand to Jacques Callot and the Flemish genre painters with whom Bertrand would vie in poetry. In expounding his theory of the grotesque, Hugo mentions Rubens and Callot, the burlesque Michelangelo—as Hugo calls him.[10] And there were, of course, other influences besides Hugo. Scarbo reminds us very strongly of Charles Nodier's *Smarra*—Scarbo, the gnome who gets drunk on the oil from the poet's lamp, who bites him in the neck and, to cauterize the wound, sticks in his iron finger reddened by the fire.[11] Bertrand need not to have gone directly to the German to find gnomes, dwarfs, and sprites, for they were already popular in Paris; they had been introduced largely through the translations, adaptations, and imitations that filled the magazines and collections of the day. Soon after Bertrand's arrival in the capital, the French public was to know E. T. A. Hoffmann firsthand through an essay presentation by Walter Scott himself and a subsequent translation of the German writer's works. But his name and reputation had been known in Paris for some years. Toward 1830, he enjoyed a great deal of notoriety in the Romantic press where the relative merits of Hoffmann and Scott were argued out. For Paris, already in love with the fantastic, Hoffmann was a hero, and Bertrand borrowed for the subtitle of his own book the title of Hoffmann's first: *Fantasiestücke in*

Callot's Manier. In 1844, when Bertrand's *Fantaisies* finally appeared, the mark of 1830 was apparent upon it, and Sainte-Beuve somewhat condescendingly alludes in his preface to the old-fashioned "diableries" that it contains. Directly or indirectly, Louis Bertrand is an extremely derivative writer; his poems reflect the modes of his day and his reverence for the writers who set them.

The originality of Bertrand is therefore chiefly in his approach to material that was in the common domain. If we compare his ballads with those that appeared in the Romantic keepsakes, with those of Alphonse Rabbe, or with the "translations" of Charles Nodier, we find a far more personal manner. If we compare them with any previous so-called "prose poem," instead of merely rhythmic prose, we find real poems. The great innovation of Bertrand is indeed to have preferred to the spontaneous writing then in style a composition carefully worked out. The prose ballad, as Bertrand conceives of it, has a form almost as fixed as that of one in verse. Characteristically it is made up of six "stanzas," the first being a prologue and the last an epilogue. The stanzas between are symmetrically arranged, with identical beginnings to lines, parallels, and other devices of repetition. Such an organization resembles musical composition and is far different from one based (like most prose pieces and some verse forms) upon chronology or anecdote. Within the stanza, Bertrand shows the same concern to create a unit. He articulates the parts of the sentence to obtain the rhythmic effect he desires, often complementing the thought or enhancing the mood by syntactical manipulation. In this connection, his use of the dash is particularly noteworthy.

Doubtless the form of his ballads is too rigid and his expression too carefully wrought. His poems risk seeming mechanical and arbitrary. A greater artist might have broken the monotony by some bold, spontaneous thrusts and been less mindful of possible incorrections or negligences. But these criticisms, at most, imply the errors of a craftsman rather than an indictment against craft as such: Bertrand's concern for precise technique and form is, in principle, highly commendable. We may approve also his avoidance both of the lyrical expansiveness that marked the poetry of the time and of the moralizing that characterized the prose. His tendency was all toward concentration, distillation, as a comparison of successive versions of a work clearly shows. By the plasticity that he achieves in the final version, he anticipates the Parnassian ideal; the preference he shows for evocation over description and exposition anticipates an attitude of

Symbolism. If Louis Bertrand is a man of his times by certain themes such as the quaintly fantastic, his technique qualifies him as a precursor of modern poets, one of the first "alchemists of the verb."

Notes

1. Sprietsma, *Louis Bertrand*, p. 243.
2. See the letter that precedes *Le Spleen de Paris, petits poèmes en prose.*
3. Mallarmé and Jacob are cited by Pierre Moreau in *Le Romantisme* (Del Duca, 1957), pp. 304–5.
4. André Breton, *Premier Manifeste du Surréalisme* (1924).
5. Jean Marcel and Arpad Mezei, *Genèse de la pensée moderne dans la littérature française* (Corrêa, 1950), p. 48.
6. Sprietsma, *Louis Bertrand*, p. 130.
7. *Ballad* may come from Scott and *bambochade* from Ludwig Tieck (*Bambocciaden*). Or directly from the seventeenth-century Dutch painter Pieter van Laer, who was called Bamboccio. He did popular and burlesque country scenes, which David Teniers the younger later used.
8. Sprietsma, *Louis Bertrand*, p. 202.
9. See J. Marsan, "Notes sur Aloysius Bertrand," *Mercure de France* (March 1925), p. 320.
10. Victor Hugo, Preface to *Cromwell*.
11. *La Chambre gothique.*

HARLEM[1]

Quand d'Amsterdam le coq d'or chantera,
La Poule d'or de Harlem pondera.
                    Nostradamus (*Les Centuries*).

HARLEM, cette admirable bambochade qui
résume l'école flamande, Harlem peint par
Jean Breughel,[2] Peeter Neef, David Téniers
et Paul Rembrandt;

Et le canal où l'eau bleue tremble, et
l'église où le vitrage d'or flamboie, et le
stoël où sèche le linge au soleil, et les toits,
verts de houblon;

Et les cigognes qui battent des ailes
autour de l'horloge de la ville, tendant le
col du haut des airs et recevant dans leur
bec les gouttes de pluie;

Et l'insouciant bourgmestre qui caresse
de la main son menton double, et l'amoureux
fleuriste qui maigrit, l'œil attaché à une
tulipe;

Et la bohémienne qui se pâme sur sa
mandoline, et le vieillard qui joue du
rommelpot,[3] et l'enfant qui enfle une vessie;

Et les buveurs qui fument dans l'estaminet borgne, et la
servante de l'hôtellerie qui accroche à la fenêtre
un faisan mort.[4]

---

1. The Flemish genre painters of the seventeenth century charmed Romantic poets for
the light of quaint fantasy they cast over the commonplace. Hugo saw in their works
illustration of his theory of antithesis and praised Rubens for including the grotesque in
his paintings. No one, however, it might seem, found in them greater inspiration than
Louis Bertrand, who transferred their odd little scenes from canvas quite graphically to
the printed page. In "Harlem," which opens his collection of word paintings, he pays
them formal homage.

Yet there are indications that the Flemish school was less important to Bertrand than one generally supposes. In the first place, we remember that he did not owe it his original inspiration but only a certain form through which he realized it. But the question is whether those Flemish scenes that he never knew firsthand were copied by him only because they were in vogue and, as Jean Palou suggests (*Gaspard de la Nuit*, Colombe, 1962, Introduction, p. 15), whether they always remained foreign to him. I suspect that Palou is on the wrong track here. Anyone would agree that Bertrand is first a son of Dijon, but that in itself does not preclude Flanders as a spiritual homeland since it was through Flemish art that he saw his own town. In the vignettes of genre painting which constitute *Gaspard de la Nuit*, the differences between Harlem and Dijon disappear. But there is another aspect of the problem, one suggested by the allusions in this poem evoking the Dutch city. For one who was as enamored of Flemish painting as Bertrand is supposed to have been, he seems to have made some odd mistakes. Why he calls Rembrandt, Paul, I do not know, unless he confuses him with Rubens. If so, he does it in his introduction as well as in this poem; which makes this explanation not very likely. Yet Rubens would have served his purpose just as well as Rembrandt and surely been more at home with the other painters mentioned than the Dutchman.

Another little puzzle involves the Dutch word *stoël* that Bertrand uses in the second stanza. A note in the 1842 edition and in several subsequent ones explains this to mean "stone balcony." *Stoël* means chair. Probably there was confusion with the word *stoep*, which is cognate with the English word *stoop*. If so, no edition, to my knowledge, has corrected the mistake. Faults of erudition are less grave with artists than with editors and scholars, and if Bertrand's knowledge in language and art history were defective, this would not necessarily mean that the Flemish painters were any less important to him. The problem is not a serious one, but it is an interesting one. We know Bertrand studied painting assiduously during the last years of his life and visited collections in Paris. Perhaps he became really knowledgeable only after his poems were composed. Incidentally, he recorded his studies and visits in notebooks which exist today in private collections. Perhaps research will sometime turn up specific prototypes for some of his poems. Until then, we can say that they are suggestive of a great many paintings by Jacques Callot and the genre painters to whom he refers in this poem.

2. The painters mentioned here, with the exception of Rembrandt, are late sixteenth-early seventeenth-century Flemish. Jan Breughel the elder (1568–1625) is one of the masters of genre painting, portraying a wide variety of ordinary people in everyday scenes. Rubens worked with him. In the preface signed "Gaspard de la Nuit," Bertrand speaks of Brueghel de Velours, which is a name given to the elder Breughel, and of Brueghel d'Enfer. Pieter Neefs the elder (1578–1656/61) and the younger (1620–1675). David Téniers the elder (1582–1649) and the younger (1610–1690). Téniers the younger married Anna, the daughter of Breughel the elder and the ward of Peter Paul Rubens.

3. A note in the 1842 edition defines this as a musical instrument. Today it is the word for a child's noisemaker (a tin can and a stick).

4. Suzanne Bernard quotes this line to show how Bertrand avoids the suave harmonies of eighteenth-century poetic prose. Just the contrary of the oratorical rhythm which swells and builds up, Bertrand's rhythm is often broken and marked at the end of the line by a sudden drop. See *Le Poème en prose*, p. 66.

LE FOU[5]

Un carolus, ou bien encor,
Si l'aimez mieux, un agneau d'or.[6]
(Manuscrits de la Bibliothèque du roi)

La lune peignait ses cheveux avec un
démêloir d'ébène qui argentait d'une pluie
de vers luisants les collines, les prés et
les bois.

Scarbo, gnome dont les trésors foisonnent,
vannait sur mon toit, au cri de la girouette,
ducats et florins qui sautaient en cadence, les
pièces fausses jonchant la rue.

Comme ricana le fou qui vague, chaque nuit,
par la cité déserte, un œil à la lune et l'autre
—crevé!

"Foin de la lune! grommela-t-il, ramassant
les jetons du diable, j'achèterai le pilori
pour m'y chauffer au soleil."

+++

Mais c'était toujours la lune, la lune qui
se couchait,—et Scarbo monnoyait sourdement
dans ma cave ducats et florins à coups de
balancier.

Tandis que, les deux cornes en avant, un
limaçon qu'avait égaré la nuit, cherchait sa
route sur mes vitraux lumineux.

5. *La Nuit et ses Prestiges* from which both this poem and "Ondine" are taken is considered the finest section of Bertrand's work. Bertrand is a poet of night, of shadows and glimmering lights. It is at night that witches fly off to their sabbath, that the persecuted Jews meet in their dimly lit synagogues, that beggars lie asleep on the river boats, that

dogs bay at the moon and the whole city slips back into the fourteenth century. "Qui sait mieux que lui utiliser tout l'arsenal de l'occultisme, en célébrer les ténébreux prestiges?" Alan Mercier, *Les Sources esotériques et occultes de la poésie symboliste*, p. 25.

   6. The moon is likened to a gold coin.

ONDINE

.... Je croyais entendre
Une vague harmonie enchanter mon sommeil,
Et, près de moi, s'épandre un murmure pareil
Aux chants entrecoupés d'une voix triste et tendre.
                     (Ch. Brugnot—*Les Deux Génies*)[7]

"Ecoute! Ecoute! C'est moi, c'est Ondine[8]
qui frôle de ces gouttes d'eau les losanges
sonores de ta fenêtre illuminée par les mornes
rayons de la lune; et voici, en robe de moire,
la dame châtelaine qui contemple à son balcon
la belle nuit étoilée et le beau lac endormi.

"Chaque flot est un ondin qui nage dans le
courant, chaque courant est un sentier qui
serpente vers mon palais, et mon palais est
bâti fluide, au fond du lac, dans le triangle
du feu, de la terre et de l'air.[9]

"Ecoute! Ecoute! Mon père bat l'eau
coassante d'une branche d'aulne verte, et mes
sœurs caressent de leurs bras d'écume les
fraîches îles d'herbes, de nénuphars et de
glaïeuls, ou se moquent du saule caduc et barbu
qui pêche à la ligne."

Sa chanson murmurée, elle me supplia de
recevoir son anneau à mon doigt, pour être
l'époux d'une Ondine, et de visiter avec elle
son palais, pour être le roi des lacs.

Et comme je lui répondais que j'aimais une
mortelle, boudeuse et dépitée, elle pleura
quelques larmes, poussa un éclat de rire, et
s'évanouit en giboulées qui ruisselèrent
blanches le long de mes vitraux bleus.[10]

7. Brugnot was a friend of Bertrand's from Dijon. He was an active member of the Société d'Etudes and collaborator on *Le Provincial*.

8. Celebrated by Jean Giraudoux after Bertrand, La Motte Fouqué, and many other writers stretching far back into the Middle Ages, the water nymph is perhaps the most engaging of all the elemental spirits. Her attempts to marry a mortal and thereby gain a soul have been far more inspiring than the magic transformations of the salamander or the impish industry of the cobalt. Bertrand depicts her as the very incarnation of water in movement, water that splashes in clear pools, ripples along brooks, glistens as it spatters and runs on windowpanes. Images of fluidity and luminosity reinforce the water theme, while the marked cadences of the stanzas add to the general loveliness of this whimsical evocation.

The rhythm of this poem is assured by devices characteristic of Bertrand's technique. Here and there one may note perfect metrical patterns as in the two alexandrines:

Chaque flot est un ondin qui nage dans le courant,
....
Boudeuse et dépitée, elle pleura quelques larmes.

Sometimes there are approximations of rime schemes, as in the fourth strophe with the pattern a b a b: ... de recevoir ... / ... pour être ... / ... de visiter ... / ... pour être.... Usually, however, it is repetition that gives the rhythm. One notes the refrain "Ecoute! Ecoute! ..." of the first and third strophes and the prominent and identical positions of the relative clauses: "C'est Ondine qui frôle ...," "... la dame châtelaine qui contemple ...," "... un ondin qui nage ...," "un sentier qui serpente ..." Like the dash, the conjunction *et* serves Bertrand as a device of repetition. In this poem it occurs with almost metronomic regularity.

9. Jean Palou is reminded here of the three initiation trials in the Masonic ritual. See *Gaspard* (Colombe, 1962), Introduction, p. 20.

10. Palou sees these colors as having symbolic value. Ibid. For a discussion of colors in Bertrand see René Riese Hubert, "The Cult of the Visible in *Gaspard de la Nuit*," *Modern Language Quarterly* 25 (1964): 76–85.

Les Chimères

The first appearance in volume of the twelve sonnets comprising the "Chimères" is at the end of *Les Filles du Feu* (Giraud, 1854). Some had appeared previously in *Petits Châteaux de Bohème* (Didier, 1853). Eleven of the "Odelettes" appeared also in this book. Nerval's bibliography is extremely complicated because of his habit of constantly redoing or regrouping his works. For successive publication, see Aristide Marie, *Bibliographie des Œuvres de Gérard de Nerval* (Champion, 1926). Probably the most accessible texts for all Nerval's poetry are in the collected works, such as:

Œuvres complètes de Gérard de Nerval (Champion, 1926–1931). 6 vols. completed. Edited by Aristide Marie and others.

Œuvres complètes de Gérard de Nerval (Divan, 1927–1929). 10 vols. Edited by Henri Clouard.

Œuvres complètes de Gérard de Nerval (Gallimard, 1952–1956). 2 vols. Edited by Albert Béguin and Jean Richer for the Bibliothèque de la Pléiade.

Readings

Cellier, Léon. *Gérard de Nerval, l'homme et l'œuvre* (Hatier-Boivin, 1956).

Dédéyan, Charles. *Gérard de Nerval et l'Allemagne* (Société d'Édition d'Enseignement Supérieur, 1957).

Geninasca, Jacques. *Les Chimères de Nerval* (Larousse, 1973).

Jones, Robert Emmet. *Gérard de Nerval* (Boston: Twayne, 1974).

Marie, Aristide. *Gérard de Nerval, le poète et l'homme* (Hachette, 1914 and 1955).

Moulin, Jeanine. *Les Chimères*, exégèses (Droz, 1949).

Rhodes, S. A. *Gérard de Nerval, poet, traveler, dreamer* (New York: Philosophical Library, 1951).

Richer, Jean. *Nerval: expérience et création* (Hachette, 1963).

Gérard de Nerval (pseud. of Gérard Labrunie)

1808–1855

For about seventy years after his death, Gérard de Nerval, in spite of his historical significance and original merit, was thought of merely as one of the minor Romantics. His friends are partly responsible, having created the image of a "fol délicieux,"[1] a harmless but quite mad poet who carried in his pocket an apron string that he thought was the garter of Marguerite de Navarre or led a lobster on a leash through the Palais-Royal. Not until the 1920s did his absence in textbooks of French literature cause indignation. In Lanson's *Histoire de la littérature française* (1894) Nerval had rated only a brief entry and that for his translation of *Faust*. To Aristide Marie, an attorney from Fontainebleau, should go the credit of "discovering" Nerval. Marie had written already in 1914 a biography which passed unnoticed, but from 1926 on, the year he undertook to publish a complete edition of Nerval, interest began to increase. During the last twenty years, it has accelerated enormously to the point that one may suspect that, if preceding generations did him injustice, we may have gone far beyond repairing that injustice.[2] Be that as it may, it is scarcely our purpose here to begin to "de-emphasize" Nerval. His direct knowledge of German poets plus the similarities to them that he exhibits in his own work makes him a very important link in the current of poetry that passes from German Romanticism to French Symbolism.

Gérard de Nerval was born in Paris in 1808 but was taken immediately afterwards to a village in the Valois region to be cared for by his maternal grandparents. His father was a doctor with Napoleon's armies, and his mother accompanied Dr. Labrunie in his tours of foreign duty. Gérard never knew his mother, for she died in Silesia in 1810, and he saw very little of his father. His childhood was entirely spent with relatives in that part of France which he would paint in *Sylvie* and which he would always hold dear. When he was twelve, his father sent him to school in Paris at the Collège Charlemagne. Gérard distinguished himself as a student and developed a particular interest in classical literature and the German Romantics. Novalis, Richter, Heine, and Hoffmann may all have been important to him, but it is Goethe who attracted him most. His translation of *Faust* dates from his eighteenth year. As he was working on it, his own first verse, *Les Elégies nationales*, was published.

The very precocious scholar and poet became one of the young Romantics who moved in Victor Hugo's orbit. He was present at the famous performance of *Hernani* and counted among his friends Théophile Gautier of the unforgettable waistcoat, Arsène Houssaye, the truculent Petrus Borel. Gautier leaves us a pen portrait of Nerval to complement the profile on Jean Duseigneur's medal: in *Souvenirs Romantiques*, Gautier describes Nerval's "visage d'un blanc rosé animé d'yeux gris et doux, de jolis cheveux blonds pareils à une fumée d'or."[3] In the excitement of his surroundings and his own successes, Nerval dreamed of fame and glory. In 1834, he went to Italy, his first of many trips abroad. Doubtless he saw himself already as a sort of foreign correspondent for the young literature of France, returning from each trip with revelations of new techniques and themes. The year 1835 seems to have been a high point in the gay and gilded youth of the poet. He had already produced much. In addition to the political poems aforementioned, he had written the *Odelettes* and *La Main de la Gloire*, a fantastic story in the manner of Hoffmann. He had also started to write for the theater and had founded a literary review. There is not enough, however, in these youthful efforts to guarantee a great and original genius. Perhaps the reason is that, so far, Nerval was too much taken up by living. In 1835, he and some of his friends moved into an old house in the rue du Doyenné, where every night they held open house for a throng of revelers. Gérard was young, expensively dressed, and blessed with a little inheritance. "Nous étions jeunes, toujours gais, souvent riches."[4]

Alas, no serious maturity followed this lighthearted youth. Gérard de Nerval seems to have been constitutionally incapable of settling down to anything. This may explain his numerous trips abroad, his incurable wanderlust. For the next seven years, he was away from France for sojourns of various lengths: Italy, Belgium, Germany, the Near East. This may also be the explanation for his frustrations in love: Jenny Colon, Marie Pleyel, and others are pursued, then abandoned. We know that is the reason why, as a writer, Nerval did not produce more and why so much of what he did produce is scrappy and unorganized. He frittered away much of his life on grand projects never realized and schemes to win fortune and fame that did not pan out. If he was obliged to fall back on journalism and hack work to earn his living, it was because here again, he could not stay with any one job. Someone else might have done very well on the money Nerval got from his inheritance, his numerous grants from the government, and his many literary assignments. Actually Gérard de Nerval was given more in life than most.

In 1841, he had his first fit of insanity. His violent passion for the actress Jenny Colon may have precipitated it; perhaps his professional failures played a part. Not one of his melodramas, comedies, libretti had met with the success he had counted on. The failure of his magazine saddled him with debts. When he was once more himself, he set out for the Near East. *Le Voyage en Orient* is a record of this trip; so precise and realistic in its factual portions that one can suspect that the author wished thereby to establish proof that he had completely recovered and that the attack had in no way impaired his faculties. It would be true of each succeeding attack that a period of normal lucidity followed. This is when he wrote, but the material of his writing was taken in great part from his periods of derangement. Already in the *Voyage* one may see, with its combination of travel sketches and sentimental revery, the process of "l'épanchement du rêve dans la vie" which is characteristic of Nerval's greatest pieces. One may see also a strong preoccupation with the esoteric. This preoccupation, increased perhaps by two more attacks of insanity, is the basis of *Les Illuminés* (1852), which present a collection of "seers."

In August of 1853, the same month that *Sylvie* appeared, Gérard de Nerval was hospitalized again. He did not leave the famous clinic of Doctor Blanche until the following May. *Aurélia* is the work of those months of internment. It is the story of the progressive metamorphoses of his lost love Jenny Colon through other feminine figures and divinities to combine ultimately into the image of the Virgin Mother. As soon as he was free, Nerval set out for Germany. Upon his return two months later, he set about trying to reestablish himself professionally. His reason was too unstable, however, and from now until the end, Gérard de Nerval would live increasingly in his dreams. Nevertheless, his writing continued to appear. It would seem that during the last years of his life, he was in a great hurry to finish what he had to say and to get everything—old, new, good, bad—quickly into print. He put together collections of prose and poetry from various periods and even included texts from another hand to fill out a volume. Thus in 1853 appeared *Contes et Facéties* and *Petits Châteaux de Bohème*, in 1854, the *Filles du feu* followed by "Chimères" in the same volume. Seven of the twelve sonnets composing the "Chimères" had already appeared in the *Petits Châteaux*.

One January night of 1855, Nerval was found hanged in the rue de la Vieille Lanterne, a little street leading off from Châtelet. The manuscript of *Aurélia* was in his pocket. All these latter works are constructed out of mad dreams, lore, and fond nostalgia—bits and pieces of the poet's life turned into the loveliest of visions. It is chiefly this exploitation of the oneiric imagination that links Nerval with the German Romantics on the one hand and the French Symbolists on the other.

Charles Dédéyan has thoroughly demonstrated that all Nerval's writings are permeated by elements from beyond the Rhine.[5] The contacts with Germany were made early. It was his father who gave Nerval his first lessons in the German language, thereby lending him a certain advantage in his courses at Charlemagne and in the Romantic circles where German literature was very much in vogue. Madame de Staël must have served him as guide in his investigations of the Germans; in some of his writings there are remarks that are too reminiscent of *De l'Allemagne* to permit any doubt. He read widely and made translations that appeared in magazines and in volumes. After *Faust*, he undertook ballads (including Bürger's "Leonore") and a quantity of other pieces. Hardly more than twenty years old, Gérard de Nerval was considered the chief German specialist in the milieux of the *Jeune France*.

It is not certain exactly when Nerval made his first trip to Germany, but it was not until he was approaching thirty. In the meantime, he had improved his German and broadened his knowledge of German literature. When at long last he found himself in the country, his enthusiasm was tremendous: Germany was the incarnation of his dreams. It remained so during the rest of his life, and even the familiarity that he acquired through subsequent trips never disturbed the picture that he held of a land of *Sehnsucht* and *Gemütlichkeit*. He was pleased even to fancy himself of German extraction, tracing his family back to Teuton knights.

The image that he held was, of course, obtained from German writers. Through them Nerval saw their country and, by extension, all the world.

In the poetic representation he would make of the world in his own writing, their contribution was very great. The parallels in theme and treatment suggest heavy borrowings: from Goethe, the Faustian striving and concept of elective affinities; from Hoffmann, the fantastic; from Heine, romantic irony and the idealization of love; from Novalis (whom he never mentions) esoteric motifs. These are just a few of the parallels that Professor Dédéyan discusses. Altogether they constitute a philosophy and an esthetic that anticipate Symbolism. Through Nerval, the concept of the poet as a seer became established in France—and the concept of poetry as a quest for esoteric knowledge. Nerval was a *voyant* before Rimbaud; he perceived the *correspondances* of nature before Baudelaire. In his work, the dream was annexed to the domain of poetry, and the irrational was explored for its revelation of truth and beauty. The ideal of totality in human faculties and knowledge, totality in concept of the cosmos, the fusion of art and life emerge with this poet, setting him apart from his chief contemporaries in France but linking him with German Romanticism and the French poetry to evolve later in the century. In technique as well, Nerval anticipates Symbolism by moving from the pictorial emphasis of his contemporaries to the musicality favored by the school of the eighties.

In prefacing a new edition of *Aurélia*[6] Jean Giraudoux remarks that the works of Gérard de Nerval are less important than his life, that he is one of those authors whose personal drama stands as a sort of exemplum but whose works are generally mediocre. Giraudoux is right, of course, for aside from *Sylvie*, *Aurélia*, and *Les Chimères*, Nerval's work is primarily of interest in documenting his life. Yet if these exceptions constitute quantitatively so little that they cannot obtain for their author a place among the major literary geniuses of France, their quality is such as to put him high among these we call minor. Marcel Proust considered *Sylvie* one of the masterpieces of French literature,[7] and present-day writers and critics all agree on the importance of *Les Chimères*.

The charm of these poems is unlike what we find in most other French Romantic verse. They are neither descriptive nor confessional. Autobiography has been transfigured through sibylline parable and imagery completely liberated from sensation or earthbound perception. It goes without saying that there is no story and no message. What there is reads like pure incantation, some awesome ritual of prophecy or exorcism. The extraordinary character of *Les Chimères* can be explained by the hallucinations that Nerval actually suffered and by his cultivation of the esoteric sciences. They are products, as it were, of madness and magic. From 1843 to 1854, the years during which he was composing the *Chimères*, Nerval lived often in a world of his own; the cabalistic lore to which he had all his life been addicted nourished his folly: for Nerval, reality had become merely sign or omen and life was something to be deciphered. In the latter 1940s, two critics demonstrated that the poems of the *Chimères* can be read as experiments in alchemy. Georges LeBreton introduced the subject in two articles in the magazine *Fontaine*,[8] and Jean Richer treated it at length in a volume study.[9] Without denying Nerval's debt to alchemy, Jeanine Moulin[10] and Marie-Jeanne Durry[11] protest against a systematic application of the thesis advanced by LeBreton and Richer. The problem is interesting but does not actually concern the poems as poems. It is as marvelously ambiguous symbols, not as esoteric formulas, that the images that Nerval creates seem to us magic, and it is as a poet, not as a practitioner of the occult, that Nerval can be called a seer.

More conventional, although gems of Romantic lyric verse, are the *Odelettes*. Nerval had Ronsard in mind when he called them little odes; Edouard Maynial[12] points out, however, that their similarity to works of the sixteenth-century poet does not go beyond a vague resemblance in form and rhythm. In theme and tone they are typical of the 1830s when they were written. The gulf between them and the *Chimères* may be indicated by Nerval's pitiful assertion: "La Muse est entrée dans mon cœur comme une déesse aux paroles dorées; elle s'en est échappée comme une pythie en jetant des cris de douleur."[13] Yet different as they are, the *Odelettes* sound already, in a minor key, the tragic notes that will be heard in the *Chimères*.

Notes

1. The expression is from Maurice Barrès, uttered in his reception speech at the Académie Française, 17 January 1907.

2. Jacques Geninasca, *Les Chimères de Nerval*, and Jacques Dhaerens, *Le Destin d'Orphée* (Minard, 1972) make extensive reviews of recent criticisms and exegeses, and they themselves typify some of the modern approaches to Nerval.

3. Gautier, *Souvenirs Romantiques* (Garnier, 1929), p. 223.

4. *Œuvres complètes de Gérard de Nerval* (Gallimard), vol. 1, p. 86.

5. Dédéyan, *Gérard de Nerval et l'Allemagne.*

6. J. Schriffin, 1927.

7. Marcel Proust, *A La Recherche du temps perdu* (Gallimard, 1963), vol. 3, p. 919. Bibliothèque de la Pléïade.

8. G. LeBreton, "Nerval poète alchimique," *Fontaine,* nos. 44 and 45 (1945).

9. Jean Richer, *Gérard de Nerval et la doctrine esotérique* (Griffon d'Or, 1947).

10. Moulin, *Les Chimères.*

11. Marie-Jeanne Durry, *Gérard de Nerval et le mythe* (Flammarion, 1956).

12. Edouard Maynial, *Anthologie des poètes du XIXe siècle* (Hachette, 1935), p. 261.

13. Nerval, *Œuvres complètes* (Gallimard), vol. 1, p. 85.

EL DESDICHADO[1]

Je suis le ténébreux,—le veuf,[2]—l'inconsolé,
Le prince d'Aquitaine à la tour abolie:[3]
Ma seule *étoile* est morte,—et mon luth constellé[4]
Porte le *soleil* noir de la *Mélancolie.*[5]

Dans la nuit du tombeau, toi qui m'as consolé,[6]
Rends-moi le Pausilippe et la mer d'Italie,
La *fleur*[7] qui plaisait tant à mon cœur désolé,
Et la treille où le pampre à la rose s'allie.[8]

Suis-je Amour ou Phébus?... Lusignan ou Biron?[9]
Mon front est rouge encor du baiser de la reine;[10]
J'ai rêvé dans la grotte où nage la sirène...[11]

Et j'ai deux fois vainqueur traversé l'Achéron:[12]
Modulant tour à tour sur la lyre d'Orphée
Les soupirs de la sainte[13] et les cris de la fée.[14]

1. This poem, first in the collection of "Les Chimères" appended to the prose texts of *Les Filles du Feu* (1854), had appeared the previous year in the December tenth issue of the periodical *Le Mousquetaire*. It is one of the most often studied poems: in all sorts of ways, from its possible debt to other works of literature (such as the German novel *Heinrich von Ofterdingen*), to its possible significance in terms of the occult sciences, every line has been scrutinized and glossed. It is one of Nerval's most difficult poems. One will note, incidentally, that Nerval's obscurity is created by his allusions—syntax and vocabulary are perfectly normal. As Albert Béguin points out, in Nerval there is neither the conscious distillation of thought that one finds in Maurice Scève nor the deformation of language that one finds in Mallarmé (*La Poésie de Nerval*, Corti, 1945, p. 102). The problem with Nerval is strictly a problem of readings. The Pléiade edition lists the outstanding works of exegesis before 1945 (vol. 1, p. 1119). It is supplemented by the bibliographies in the more recent works cited here, but new studies continue to appear. *Desdichado* means unfortunate in Spanish, here in the sense of disinherited. The word is taken from *Ivanhoe* (chap. 8). It is the heraldic motto adopted by the knight in the novel who has been deprived of his property. One manuscript of the poem, which is in the Paul Eluard collection, bears the title "Le Destin."

2. Nerval may think of himself as being "widowed" by the death of his star, the actress Jenny Colon, or of the girl known as Adrienne (*Les Filles du Feu*).

3. Nerval fancied himself a descendant of the legendary Brunyer de la Brunie of Aquitania. The possible meanings for ruined tower are several: the tower of Brunyer long since destroyed; the literal sense of the family name, as Nerval indicated on his

genealogical chart (La Brunie = Brunn); the tower card of the tarot, which symbolizes exclusion from paradise.

4. On the seventeenth of the tarot pack, there is one large star surrounded by seven smaller ones.

5. Cf. Dürer's angel of melancholy. The expression *black sun* is not unusual in Nerval (see Moulin, *Les Chimères*, pp. 12–13).

6. This stanza evokes Nerval's trip to Naples, his visit to the nearby promontory, Posilipo, in the company of Octavie, as described in the story "Octavie" of *Les Filles du Feu*. Basing her opinion on the confidences Nerval makes in his story, Madame Moulin (*Les Chimères*, p. 14) believes that the first line means rescued from suicide, that the English girl saved him from *la nuit du tombeau*. The grammar does not seem to justify this interpretation. The phrase *dans la nuit du tombeau* modifies the verb in the next line. Now in *la nuit du tombeau*, he asks her who consoled him once to give him back the joys that they shared in southern Italy.

7. The Eluard manuscript bears notations in Nerval's hand. By the word *fleur* there is written in *ancolie*. The columbine, which is a symbol of sadness and of madness as well, is the richest possible rime with melancholy, as André Rousseaux points out, suggesting that it may have been deemed too rich to be stated otherwise than by allusion. I believe that the critic is here a bit carried away. See "Sur trois manuscrits de Gérard de Nerval," in *Le Monde classique* (Albin Michel, 1946), vol. 2, p. 157.

8. After this line, there is the notation *jardin du Vatican*. The image of trellis, vine, and rose occurs also in *Sylvie*.

9. The Greek gods are coupled with the legendary figures of the Valois region. Lusignan is the victimized lover of the fairy Melusina. Biron served Henry IV and died in the siege of Epernay. Cellier suggests that this line is structured on a contrast of light and dark. Cupid and Lusignan are associated with dark; Phoebus and Biron (see Biron of Shakespeare) are associated with light. Cellier reads the whole sonnet, in fact, as a combat of night and day. Léon Cellier, *Gérard de Nerval*, p. 236.

10. Madame Moulin interprets the queen to be Adrienne of *Les Filles du Feu*, who, "surgie aux lueurs rouges du couchant ..., marque le front de l'adolescent d'un ineffable baiser" (*Les Chimères*, p. 16). There is, however, the manuscript notation of "Reine Candace." André Rousseaux interprets this as a reference to the Queen of Sheba, who figures prominently in Nerval's private mythology (*Le Monde classique*, vol. 2, p. 158).

11. Grottoes, too, figure in Nerval's mythology. This line may allude to the grotto of Posilipo, where Octavie appeared as a siren. It may be an allusion to alchemy, as LeBreton believes ("Nerval poète alchimique," *Fontaine*, pp. 44–45). Madame Moulin considers it to be an allusion to the little undine of the folktale *La Reine des Poissons* that Nerval published in "Chansons et Légendes du Valois," a chapter of the *Filles du Feu*.

12. The two crossings are the two attacks of insanity (1841 and 1853). For the alchemic interpretation, see LeBreton, "Nerval poète alchimique."

13. Adrienne is the saint, for it is she who went into the convent.

14. Probably Mélusine (see Moulin, *Les Chimères*, pp. 18–19). The word *Mélusine* is written by the line on the Eluard manuscript.

MYRTHO[15]

Je pense à toi, Myrtho,[16] divine enchanteresse,
Au Pausilippe[17] altier, de mille feux brillant,
A ton front inondé des clartés d'Orient,
Aux raisins noirs mêlés avec l'or de ta tresse.[18]

C'est dans ta coupe[19] aussi que j'avais bu l'ivresse,
Et dans l'éclair furtif de ton œil souriant,
Quand aux pieds d'Iacchus on me voyait priant,[20]
Car la Muse m'a fait l'un des fils de la Grèce.

Je sais pourquoi là-bas le volcan s'est rouvert ...[21]
C'est qu'hier tu l'avais touché d'un pied agile,
Et de cendres soudain l'horizon s'est couvert.[22]

Depuis qu'un duc normand brisa tes dieux d'argile,[23]
Toujours sous les rameaux du laurier de Virgile,[24]
Le pâle hortensia s'unit au myrthe vert![25]

15. "Myrtho" appeared first in the magazine *L'Artiste*, 15 February 1854. There are two manuscripts both of which mix the verses of this poem with those of "Delfica." One of the prose pieces of the *Filles du Feu*, "Octavie," describes the circumstances that inspired these two poems. In Naples, after spending the evening with a certain Marquis de Gargallo, who shares Nerval's interest in the occult, Nerval encounters a girl who takes him to her room. There he is struck by the articles of magic and piety that the girl has about her. The next day, at dawn, he goes to meet the English girl Octavie, at the grotto of the Posilipo. His thoughts have been melancholy and confused since the night before—thoughts of past loves that dampen his present ardor, thoughts even of suicide. In the Temple of Isis among the ruins of Pompeii, he explains to Octavie the mysteries of the Egyptian cult. How much of this story is based on fact is hard to say, but, if not out of whole cloth, it is probably heightened considerably by Nerval's imagination. Octavie, for example, may well be an invention.

16. Myrtho is a woman's name in Greek, found notably in Theocritus. Associated with myrtle, the plant held sacred to Aphrodite, the name doubtless symbolizes for Nerval both love and ancient Greece. In the guise of the goddess, critics generally believe Nerval evokes the memory of Octavie, his real or imaginary companion in Naples. The poem reads very well, however, without seeing in it any allusion to the English girl at all.

17. Posilipo; a promontory to the west of Naples, site of an ancient Roman villa.

18. In view of the aggrandizement of the image, the apostrophe in this quatrain seems addressed not to a girl, but to Aphrodite herself, whose sublime countenance is of the

proportions of the landscape. Reference to the play of light and to the grapes is made in the prose piece "Octavie."

19. The sacred cup in the rites of Isis?

20. C. F. MacIntyre considers this line "an elegant euphemism for being drunk on the floor," *French Symbolist Poetry* (Berkeley: University of California Press, 1958), p. 117.

21. Allusion to the phenomenon of the hot and sulphurous air described in "Octavie"?

22. Notes 19 and 21 are suggested by Madame Moulin, but they may not be pertinent. The interpretation that she offers for this stanza is that Octavie's "initiation" in the Temple of Isis as described in the prose piece may have stirred up the forces of the volcano (*Les Chimères*, p. 27). Yet Nerval may not be alluding to Octavie at all, but simply offering a fanciful reason—a gigantic goddess treading near the crater.

23. This line may refer to the capture of Naples in 1139 by Roger, King of the Two Sicilies, who was a descendant of the Norman duke, Tancred.

24. Virgil was buried on the Posilipo. Petrarch was supposed to have planted a laurel on his tomb.

25. The final tercet may be understood as meaning the mingling of the modern Christian with the antique pagan. The hydrangea is a modern flower. This interpretation, justified by variants in one of the manuscript versions, ties in with the general theme of the poem and seems far more plausible than other possible readings listed by Madame Moulin. Since the hydrangea grows profusely in parts of the Normandy coast, the mingling may be also of north and south. Some of the obscurity of Nerval's verse is due just to his constant tinkering with it, not to any oblique intention. Even with its lines interchanged with those of "Delfica," this poem seems forthright; it must have been even more so in its first draft. Seeing it as just a verse version of "Octavie" may send us scurrying after irrelevant and over-subtle personal allusions. It is best read, I feel sure, as just a homage to Greece, with a twist of irony that anticipates Renan's prayer on the Acropolis.

DELFICA [26]

Ultima Cumaei venit jam carminis aetas

La connais-tu,[27] Dafné,[28] cette ancienne romance,
Au pied du sycomore, ou sous les lauriers blancs,
Sous l'olivier, le myrte, ou les saules tremblants,
Cette chanson d'amour qui toujours recommence? ...

Reconnais-tu le TEMPLE[29] au péristyle immense,
Et les citrons amers où s'imprimaient tes dents,
Et la grotte, fatale aux hôtes imprudents,[30]
Où du dragon vaincu[31] dort l'antique semence? ...

Ils reviendront, ces Dieux que tu pleures toujours!
Le temps va ramener l'ordre des anciens jours;
La terre a tressailli d'un souffle prophétique ... [32]

Cependant la sibylle au visage latin
Est endormie encor sous l'arc de Constantin ...
—Et rien n'a dérangé le sévère portique.[33]

26. This poem, dated from Tivoli in 1843 and dedicated to J. Y. Calonna (cryptogram for Jenny Colon), appeared in 1845 in the December twenty-eighth issue of *L'Artiste* under the title of "Vers Dorés." The definitive title refers to the sanctuary of Apollo at Delphi where oracles were pronounced. The epigraph is from Virgil, fourth Eclogue, and alludes to the return of the golden age predicted by the Sibyl of Cumae. Cumae is the name of an ancient Greek city on the Bay of Naples. The Sibyl is thought to be the author of a number of manuscripts of wisdom and prophecy.

Like "Myrtho," this poem may be considered a pendant to the "Octavie" story in *Les Filles du Feu* and is inspired by Nerval's visit to Naples. Octavie may be the model for Daphne, for not only do we note a grotto and a temple as in the prose piece which describes his adventure with the English girl, but in the sixth line of the poem we note mention of biting into a lemon, an item also to be found in "Octavie." The possible identification of Daphne with Octavie is only incidental, however, for it is the nymph who is apostrophized, a creature who has somehow survived beyond her times. Nevertheless, her times will return—such is Nerval's promise and the theme of his poem. This notion of the persistence of ancient cults is one of Nerval's occult beliefs. Professor Dédéyan sees in this poem an echo of the theme of the eternal return depicted in Goethe's *Faust* (*Gérard de Nerval*, vol. II, p. 564).

27. The opening words remind one of Goethe's *Kennst du das Land*. There is, moreover, a general affinity between these poems in their wistful nostalgia for a past of sensuous beauty. The device of alluding to an *ancienne romance* reminds one also of Verlaine's evocations. With Nerval as with Verlaine, the imagery is softened or blurred by veiling it with the past. Reminiscent of Goethe and anticipating Verlaine, a poem like this one also points the way to Parnasse. Here already is the pagan and pantheistic theme. But in form, Nerval's poem goes beyond mere plastic representation to the symbolic.

28. Daphne was the nymph loved by Apollo and metamorphosed into a laurel tree.

29. The Temple of the Vesta at Tivoli (called also the Temple of the Sibyl). Or else the Temple of Isis at Pompeii, spoken of in "Octavie."

30. The grotto may allude to the dragon-inhabited caverns that Mignon imagined in her trip across the Alps or to the various grottoes of sirens and sibyls.

31. The dragon is usually identified as the monster slain by Cadmus, the *antique semence* being its teeth. However, the source may be only a line devoid of symbolic meaning in Mignon's song, "Kennst du das Land" : "In Hohlen wohnt der Drachen alte Brut."

32. Presumably Nerval is thinking of nearby Vesuvius.

33. The idea may be that the Sibyl of Cumae, who represents paganism, has been asleep since the victory of Christianity was made decisive by the Edict of Constantine in 313. But she only waits to be awakened. Perhaps the severe portico (the Arch of Constantine) symbolizes for Nerval Christian insensitiveness to the beauties of paganism.

There seems to be another sibyl involved in this poem, the Sibyl of Tibur. Tibur is the ancient name of Tivoli, from where this poem was dated. Too, in "Octavie" there is specific mention of the Sibyl of Tibur. This prophetess is the one who showed the Emperor Augustus the Virgin holding the child Jesus. Nerval seems to be confusing—or combining—the images of the two sibyls in his juxtaposition of the Christian and pagan. If we think of the title, "Delfica," we have three prophetesses! He mixes up places in the same fashion, and we have Delphi, Rome, Tivoli, Naples and thereabouts as sites for the poem.

Le Centaure

"Le Centaure," *La Revue des Deux Mondes*, 15 May 1840. Appended are extracts from letters and an article by George Sand.

Reliquiae (Didier, 1861). Two volumes of Guérin's writings including *Le Centaure* collected and edited by his friend G. S. Trebutien. Notice by Sainte-Beuve.

Le Centaure, etc. (Mercure de France, 1909). Notice by Remy de Gourmont.

Œuvres (Divan, 1930). 2 vols. Introduction by Henri Clouard.

Œuvres complètes (Société Les Belles Lettres, 1947). 2 vols. Texte établi et présenté par Bernard d'Harcourt.

Readings

Arnold, Matthew. "Maurice de Guérin," in *Essays in Criticism* (London: Dent, 1964), pp. 60–86.

Bernard, Suzanne. *Le Poème en prose*, pp. 77–86.

Decahors, E. *Maurice de Guérin* (Bloud & Gay, 1932).

D'Harcourt, Bernard. *Maurice de Guérin et le poème en prose* (Les Belles Lettres, 1932).

Schärer-Nussberger, Maya. *Maurice de Guérin* (Corti, 1965).

Maurice de Guérin

1810–1839

In the history of the prose poem and in the line of poets that stretch from Sainte-Beuve to the Symbolists, a place must be made for Maurice de Guérin, author of *Le Centaure*. Aside from its intrinsic value, this minor gem of French literature has considerable interest on the basis of its derivations and the elements in it which seem to anticipate future trends: its historical importance explains Guérin's presence here. "Au-delà du Parnasse, il rejoint le symbolisme; au-delà des arts plastiques auxquels il emprunte ses inspirations premières, il découvre le monde vaporeux des correspondances, des musiques, des odeurs. Il est, après Rabbe et Aloysius Bertrand, avant Baudelaire, de ceux qui créèrent le poème en prose."[1]

Georges Maurice de Guérin was born in 1810 of a noble but not well-off family of Languedoc. His mother died when he was six years old, her duties in the family château of Le Cayla being taken over by his sister Eugénie. There Guérin, in the company of his bereaved father and sister, spent a rather gloomy and lonely childhood. But he was happier there than elsewhere. First at school in Toulouse and then in Paris at the Collège Stanislas and the Ecole de Droit, he felt his exile keenly and hoped that his father would let him one day return home to spend his life managing the estate.

He did return to Le Cayla, but only to die of tuberculosis at the age of twenty-eight. His few years of adulthood were passed mainly in Paris where he made a precarious living chiefly by private lessons. Off and on he studied law and tried his hand at journalism. For a brief period, he taught at Stanislas and thought some about preparing for the agrégation. But prolonged intellectual discipline and competitive examinations frightened Guérin. Probably his greatest enthusiasm for learning occurred at the time he spent away from Paris with Lamennais and his disciples at La Chesnaye in Brittany. Not knowing what really to do with his life and thinking he was perhaps destined for the church, he had gone there in 1832. The erudite discussions led by Lamennais inspired Guérin to undertake a vast program in languages and philosophy. But Guérin had no more an intellectual vocation than a religious one; and, when the little group disbanded the following year after Lamennais's trouble with Rome, Guérin did not pursue either for long.

Before he returned to Paris, however, he stayed for several weeks with a friend and fellow-poet, Hippolyte de la Morvonnais, who used to come often to La Chesnaye. The sojourn is important for the opportunity it afforded Guérin to become better acquainted with English writers, who were great favorites of his host; and for the inspiration of a platonic attachment for La Morvonnais's wife, Marie, who would die the following year. Back in the capital, Guérin took up with Barbey d'Aurevilly, who had been a student with him at Stanislas. Under Barbey's tutelage, Guérin, now aged twenty-four, blossomed out as a Parisian dandy and enjoyed the lighthearted pleasures of society. Barbey may have counted for something in Guérin's writing too. He says so: "C'est moi qui lui avais appris qu'il était beau, comme je lui avais appris qu'il avait du talent."[2] Moreover, the composition of *Le Centaure* belongs to this period of Guérin's life. The young "beau ténébreux," who, like Aloysius Bertrand and several others, acted out during a brief existence the part of a hero of romantic fiction, was to experience another unrequited passion for a married woman as well as to marry a young Creole beauty before being transported back to Le Cayla to die.

Throughout the various phases of his life in Paris and Brittany, Guérin had always remained close to his home through his beloved sister Eugénie. Eugénie served him as mother and friend; he wrote to her regularly confiding his hopes, ambitions, and frequent discouragements. These letters plus the famous *cahier vert*, the diary that he began keeping while in La Chesnaye, instruct us abundantly about this weak and wavering man, incapable of fending for himself in life yet magnificently strong in his faith in the world. The spinster sister may have done him as much harm as good: be that as it may, in literary history these two stand as one of the most famous examples of brother and sister relationships that exist.

It is George Sand who had the honor of first presenting *Le Centaure* to the public. She published parts of it, along with some extracts from letters and an introductory notice, in the *Revue des Deux Mondes* on 15 March 1840. The public did not react—as a matter of fact Eugénie's writings eclipsed her brother's for many years. Not until 1861 was *Le Centaure* published in its entirety. It came out in a volume entitled *Reliquiae* with an introduction by Sainte-Beuve, who had introduced another posthumous work, one will remember, that of Aloysius Bertrand. A second edition of *Reliquiae* the following year included the unfinished *Bacchante*.

Le Centaure is the story of Macarée, the oldest of the centaurs, the oldest of those creatures half-man, half-beast that symbolize the struggles of a double nature. Macarée tells of his early years in the cavern, his glorious youth, and his maturity. Sometimes he has exulted in his physical strength, in his free and ardent life, but he has known, too, moments of calm and eager curiosity about life. Dream and muse though he must, he has no hope of unraveling any mysteries, for the gods guard jealously their secrets. With melancholy gravity the ancient centaur reviews his life and gazes thoughtfully over the world. The unfinished poem *La Bacchante* is a sort of pendant to *Le Centaure*, pursuing through the voices of two Bacchantes, the theme of the acceptance of life.

Maurice de Guérin's inspiration is nature, and there breathes through *Le Centaure* a pantheism that early readers found difficult to reconcile with his Christianity in spite of Eugénie's indignant protest. Later readers like Remy de Gourmont and Ramuz, who introduced new editions, have had the same trouble. Henri Clouard likens Guérin to Goethe in his treatment of nature: "L'auteur du *Centaure* a exprimé la nature dans son unité et dans sa plénitude, il a surpris cette respiration de l'être universel que dégageait avant lui, par endroits, l'œuvre du seul Goethe, cette vie mystérieuse d'un organisme gigantesque, fait définitif et absolu, suprême divinité."[3] Indubitably there is in Guérin's poem the quality of *edle Einfalt und stille Grösse* that we associate with the latter Goethe.[4] Albert Béguin, too, remarks upon Guérin's feeling for cosmic life, which he finds almost unique in French Romantic writing, but prevalent in the German.[5] Maurice Pujo sees a resemblance to Novalis in the exalted fervor with which Guérin addresses himself to the mysteries of life and the universe.[6] Perhaps one can see influence as well as mere resemblance since Novalis was one of the authors discussed in Lammenais's group, and the cosmic evocations of the German poet would surely have interested Guérin.

But in trying to situate Guérin, we must consider his ties with the English poets as well as with the German. He is just as close to Wordsworth as to Novalis, Wordsworth with whom he shared the cult of nature and a philosophical optimism. Without being a serious student of the English poets (any more than of the German), Guérin did have a little firsthand knowledge of their writing, which he could, with difficulty, read in the text, and a great deal of secondhand knowledge (as of the German) through friends like La Morvonnais, who knew the English poets well. His principal guide in English was, however, Sainte-Beuve, who himself resembles Guérin in many ways like a brother and is without a doubt one of the chief sources of his inspiration. Here we can speak of affinities and influences without hesitation. There are remarkable parallels in their lives and spiritual evolution—similar childhood, moods and religious crises, preference for the meek and modest existence. Sainte-Beuve recognized in Guérin a kindred spirit, and Guérin could see in *Joseph Delorme* and *Volupté* his very own likeness. Moreover, he found in Saint-Beuve's books many lessons of craft. There he could study the technique of symbols, of fixing and generalizing personal experience in an art form. He could even have found in *Volupté* the symbol of the centaur itself, a volume which seems to be the source of numerous features of Guérin's style.[7]

There are several theories regarding where Guérin got the idea of the centaur. Whether it came from Sainte-Beuve or Alphonse Rabbe or from visits to museums is impossible to say, however, just as it is impossible to measure exactly how much he owes in style and theme to other writers. His concept of the universe surely owes something to Lamennais. If his affinities to foreign writers are stressed, it is because he seems so different from most of the French Romantic writers of his day. Apparently he disapproved of them on religious grounds, but his taste, too, seems to lead him away from his contemporaries back toward the classicists. The lesson of restraint and reconciliation which we find in *Le Centaure* is classical; the language is classical also. Abstract and lofty, rigorously limited in vocabulary, Guérin's style is closer to Fénelon than to Aloysius Bertrand. Unlike Bertrand, who is a great *visuel*, Guérin has no desire to make writing rival painting. Not only does he avoid the picturesque, the *couleur locale* that we see in the poet of Harlem, he systematically erases from his writing all that is concrete and specific. Whereas Bertrand exploits the adjective as the means par excellence of obtaining color, Guérin refuses to follow this nineteenth-century trend. He consistently plays down the adjective and retains the verb, even favoring some verbs expressly proscribed by his fellow poets.[8] In rhythm, too, Guérin seems reactionary. The long movements, stately and balanced, that characterize Guérin's rhythm hark back to the tradition of Bossuet and the masters of classic French prose. Deliberately Guérin avoided the transports of his contemporaries, never letting his inspiration take the bit in its teeth.

In spite of all in Guérin that seems to turn him toward the past, there are elements of modernity too. Pierre Moreau is not wrong in declaring that, beyond Parnasse, Guérin reaches out toward Symbolism. It is easy to see that in avoiding plastic effects he steps out of the line leading to Parnasse whereas by his sonorities he anticipates a school of poetry claiming kinship with music. It is also easy to see that in his representation of the cosmos he can be said to have discovered, before the Symbolists, "le monde vaporeux des correspondances, des musiques, des odeurs."[9] Suzanne Bernard points out that in spite of their abstract and general quality, Guérin's expressions are rich in suggestion and, by their repetition, operate the incantation which the Symbolists would demand of poetry. We must not, however, insist too much upon the presages of Symbolism in *Le Centaure.* It is a masterpiece standing rather much alone and without apparent succession. As Madame Bernard says, "Dans l'histoire du poème en prose, il n'y a pas de lignée guérinienne."[10]

Notes

1. Moreau, *Le Romantisme*, p. 243.
2. See Guérin, *Œuvres* (Divan, 1930), p. xi.
3. Henri Clouard, "Maurice de Guérin et le sentiment de la nature," *Mercure de France* (janvier-février 1909).
4. This is the expression that Winckelmann used to describe the beautiful. See *Erste Prägung der aesthetischen Kategorien.*
5. Albert Béguin, *Le Romantisme allemand et le Rêve* (Cahiers du Sud, 1937).
6. Maurice Pujo, *L'Idéalisme intégral, le règne de la grâce* (Alcan, 1894).
7. See D'Harcourt, *Maurice de Guérin*, p. 111.
8. See D'Harcourt, *Maurice de Guérin*, pp. 344–52.
9. Moreau, *Le Romantisme*, p. 243.
10. Suzanne Bernard, *Le Poème en prose*, p. 86.

LE CENTAURE

J'ai reçu la naissance[1] dans les antres de ces montagnes. Comme le fleuve de cette vallée, dont les gouttes primitives coulent de quelque roche qui pleure dans une grotte profonde, le premier instant de ma vie tomba dans les ténèbres d'un séjour reculé et sans troubler son silence. .... Mon accroissement eut son cours presque entier dans les ombres[2] où j'étais né. Le fond de mon séjour se trouvait si avancé dans l'épaisseur de la montagne que j'eusse ignoré le côté de l'issue, si, détournant quelquefois dans cette ouverture, les vents n'y eussent jeté des fraîcheurs et des troubles soudains. Quelquefois aussi, ma mère rentrait, environnée du parfum des vallées ou ruisselante des flots qu'elle fréquentait. Or, ces retours qu'elle faisait, sans m'instruire jamais des vallons ni des fleuves, mais suivie de leurs émana-tions, inquiétaient mes esprits, et je rôdais tout agité dans mes ombres. Quels sont-ils, me disais-je, ces dehors où ma mère s'emporte, et qu'y règne-t-il de si puissant qui l'appelle à soi si fréquemment? Mais qu'y ressent-on de si opposé qu'elle en revienne chaque jour diversement émue? Ma mère rentrait, tantôt animée d'une joie profonde, et tantôt triste et traînante et comme blessée.[3] La joie qu'elle rapportait se marquait de loin dans quelques traits de sa marche et s'épandait de ses regards. J'en éprouvais des communications dans tout mon sein; mais ses abattements me gagnaient bien davantage et m'entraînaient bien plus avant dans les conjectures où mon esprit se portait. Dans ces moments, je m'inquiétais de mes forces, j'y reconnaissais une puissance qui ne pouvait demeurer solitaire, et me prenant, soit à secouer mes bras, soit à multiplier mon galop dans les ombres spacieuses de la caverne, je m'efforçais de découvrir dans les coups que je frappais au vide, et par l'emportement des pas que j'y faisais, vers quoi mes bras devaient s'étendre et mes pieds m'emporter ... Depuis j'ai noué mes bras autour du buste des centaures, et du corps des héros, et du tronc des chênes; mes mains ont tenté les rochers, les eaux, les plantes innombrables et les plus subtiles impressions de l'air, car je les élève dans les nuits aveugles et calmes pour qu'elles surprennent les souffles et en tirent des signes pour augurer mon chemin; mes pieds, voyez, ô Mélampe, comme ils sont usés! Et cependant, tout glacé que je suis dans ces extrémités de l'âge, il est des jours où, en pleine lumière, sur les sommets, j'agite de ces courses de ma jeunesse dans la caverne, et pour le même dessein, brandissant mes bras et employant tous les restes de ma rapidité.

Ces troubles alternaient avec de longues absences de tout mouvement inquiet. Dès-lors, je ne possédais plus d'autre sentiment dans mon être entier que celui de la croissance et des degrés de vie qui montaient dans mon sein. Ayant perdu l'amour de l'emportement, et retiré dans un repos absolu, je goûtais sans altération le bienfait des dieux qui se répandait en moi. Le calme et les ombres président au charme secret du sentiment de la vie. Ombres qui habitez les cavernes de ces montagnes, je dois à vos soins silencieux l'éducation cachée qui m'a fortement nourri, et d'avoir, sous votre garde, goûté la vie toute pure et telle qu'elle me venait sortant du sein des dieux! Quand je descendis de votre asile dans la lumière du jour, je chancelai et ne la saluai pas, car elle s'empara de moi avec violence, m'enivrant comme eût fait une liqueur funeste soudainement versée dans mon sein, et j'éprouvai que mon être, jusque-là si ferme et si simple, s'ébranlait, et perdait beaucoup de lui-même, comme s'il eût dû se disperser dans les vents.

O Mélampe, qui voulez savoir la vie des centaures, par quelle volonté des dieux avez-vous été guidé vers moi, le plus vieux et le plus triste de tous? Il y a longtemps que je n'exerce plus rien de leur vie. Je ne quitte plus ce sommet de montagne où l'âge m'a confiné. La pointe de mes flèches ne me sert plus qu'à déraciner les plantes tenaces; les lacs tranquilles me connaissent encore, mais les fleuves m'ont oublié. Je vous dirai quelques points de ma jeunesse; mais ces souvenirs, issus d'une mémoire altérée, se traînent comme les flots d'une libation avare en tombant d'une urne endommagée. Je vous ai exprimé aisément les premières années, parce qu'elles furent calmes et parfaites; c'était la vie seule et simple qui m'abreuvait, cela se retient et se récite sans peine. Un dieu, supplié de raconter sa vie, la mettrait en deux mots, ô Mélampe.

L'usage de ma jeunesse fut rapide et rempli d'agitation. Je vivais de mouvement et ne connaissais pas de borne à mes pas. Dans la fierté de mes forces libres, j'errais, m'étendant de toutes parts dans ces déserts. ......
....

Je me délassais souvent de mes journées dans le lit des fleuves. Une moitié de moi-même, cachée dans les eaux, s'agitait pour les surmonter, tandis que l'autre s'élevait tranquille et que je portais mes bras oisifs bien au-dessus des flots. Je m'oubliais ainsi au milieu des ondes, cédant aux entraînements de leur cours qui m'emmenait au loin et conduisait leur hôte sauvage à tous les charmes des rivages. Combien de fois, surpris par la nuit, j'ai suivi les courants sous les ombres qui se répandaient, déposant jusque dans le fond des vallées l'influence nocturne des dieux! Ma vie fougueuse se tempérait alors au point de ne laisser plus qu'un léger sentiment de mon existence répandu par tout mon être avec une égale mesure, comme, dans les eaux où je nageais, les lueurs de la déesse qui parcourt les nuits. Mélampe, ma vieillesse regrette les fleuves; paisibles la plupart et monotones, ils suivent leur destinée avec plus de calme que les centaures, et une sagesse plus bienfaisante que celle des hommes. Quand je sortais de leur sein, j'étais suivi de leurs dons qui m'accompagnaient des jours entiers et ne se retiraient qu'avec lenteur, à la manière des parfums.[4]

Une inconstance sauvage et aveugle disposait de mes pas. Au milieu des courses les plus violentes, il m'arrivait de rompre subitement mon galop, comme si un abîme se fût rencontré à mes pieds, ou bien un dieu debout devant moi ....
....

Ainsi, tandis que mes flancs agités possédaient l'ivresse de la course, plus haut j'en ressentais l'orgueil, et, détournant la tête, je m'arrêtais quelque temps à considérer ma croupe fumante.[5]

La jeunesse est semblable aux forêts verdoyantes tourmentées par les vents: elle agite de tous côtés les riches présents de la vie, et toujours quelque profond murmure règne dans son feuillage. Vivant avec l'abandon des fleuves, respirant sans cesse Cybèle, soit dans le lit des vallées, soit à la cime des montagnes, je bondissais partout comme une vie aveugle et déchaînée. Mais lorsque la nuit, remplie du calme des dieux, me trouvait sur le penchant des monts, elle me conduisait à l'entrée des cavernes et m'y apaisait comme elle apaise les vagues de la mer, laissant survivre en moi de légères ondulations qui écartaient le sommeil sans altérer mon repos. ....

Mes regards couraient librement et gagnaient les points les plus éloignés. Comme des rivages toujours humides, le cours des montagnes du couchant demeurait empreint de lueurs mal essuyées par les ombres. Là survivaient, dans les clartés pâles, des sommets nus et purs. Là je voyais descendre tantôt le dieu Pan, toujours solitaire, tantôt le chœur des divinités secrètes, ou passer quelque nymphe des montagnes enivrée par la nuit.[6] Quelquefois, les aigles du mont Olympe traversaient le haut de ciel et s'évanouissaient dans les constellations reculées ou sous les bois inspirés. L'esprit des dieux, venant à s'agiter, troublait soudainement le calme des vieux chênes.

....

Pour moi, ô Mélampe, je décline dans la vieillesse, calme comme le coucher des constellations. Je garde encore assez de hardiesse pour gagner le haut des rochers où je m'attarde, soit à considérer les nuages sauvages et inquiets, soit à voir venir de l'horizon les hyades pluvieuses, les pléiades ou le grand Orion; mais je reconnais que je me réduis et me perds rapidement comme une neige flottant sur les eaux, et que prochainement j'irai me mêler aux fleuves qui coulent dans le vaste sein de la terre.[7]

The text used is in *Œuvres* (Divan, 1930).

1. In an appendix to his book *Maurice de Guérin et le poème en prose*, Bernard d'Harcourt comments on Guérin's use of the abstract term: "… son emploi est si fréquent, si habituel à Guérin, qu'il paraît inutile d'en citer des exemples. Il suffit d'ouvrir *Le Centaure* à la première page, d'en parcourir les premières lignes: 'J'ai reçu la naissance … Mon 'accroissement eut son cours … L'usage de ma 'jeunesse, etc.…''" (p. 338). Suzanne Bernard finds that these periphrases are poetic enrichments (*Le Poème en prose*, p. 84). They surely contribute to the lofty, Apollonian character of Guérin's style.

2. The use of plurals is just as typical, d'Harcourt suggests, as the use of abstractions: "Il faut joindre à ces tournures abstraites les pluriels dont Guérin use volontiers, comme 'les ombres', 'les nuits', 'les forêts', 'les campagnes', 'l'étendue des plaines', etc.…, car ils en sont parfois les équivalents." (p. 338) Guérin thus generalizes or intellectualizes an image, turns sensation into concept, in the classical manner. Hugo used abstractions, too, but in an opposite manner and for an opposite effect. He makes his description more vivid by animating the noncorporeal in the most incongruous of images. It will be Hugo's manner, not Guérin's, that the nineteenth century will follow: "Un des éléments les plus intéressants du vocabulaire artistique au XIXe siècle a été le mot abstrait, employé comme productif de couleur et de vision," says Gustave Lanson in his *Art de la Prose* (Librairie des Annales, 1909), p. 239.

3. Guérin's treatment of verb and adjective is as much at variance with the trend as his treatment of the substantive. The nineteenth century will increasingly stress the adjective and weaken the verb. Note that in the prose poem already Bertrand and Baudelaire may omit it entirely. Not so Guérin, who prefers participles to adjectives and depends greatly upon the verb to "animate" his narrative. (See d'Harcourt, pp. 344–52.)

4. The "psychoanalysis" of the elements of nature as advocated by Gaston Bachelard finds an ideal subject in *Le Centaure*, with its earth and water symbolism. Needless to say the classical Freudian analysis is also well served.

5. Throughout the poem the double nature of the centaur is emphasized. It extends as a theme into contrasts between the senses and the spirit; instinct and intelligence; movement and repose; youth and old age. We have here a dialectical pattern which constitutes a structural feature of the poem.

6. The image of the centaur in repose watching the spectacle of the shadows may be taken as a symbol of the poet inspired. The agitation of the day has given way to peaceful contemplation in the pale light from the summits in the distance where Pan, choirs of divinities, or woodland nymphs may be seen descending.

7. This final sentence of the poem, stately and gracefully articulated, is typical of Guérin's rhythm. Such a long, undulating line is quite different from the syntax of a Bertrand who seems rather to be splashing paint on canvas as he creates the brief stanzas of his poems in prose. Matthew Arnold was sure that the magic of Guérin lay in his rhythm. He is haunted by a line occurring in a portion of the poem not included here: "Les dieux jaloux ont enfoui quelque part les témoignages de la descendance des choses:

mais au bord de quel océan ont-ils roulé la pierre qui les couvre, ô Macarée?" (*Essays in Criticism*, p. 60) In accounting for this "magic," Bernard d'Harcourt and Suzanne Bernard emphasize what they call a technique of suspension which breaks the rhythm but by so doing, sets it off. D'Harcourt notes how suspension operates in the instance of past participles not followed by complements (which one would normally expect). Bernard mentions the apostrophe, adverbs in apposition, the use of the dash (*Le Poème en Prose*, p. 85). To return to the line that delighted Arnold, we may note an example of suspension in the odd break in rhythm effected by placing "ô Macarée" at the end of the line. For a detailed analysis of the rhythm patterns of *Le Centaure*, see d'Harcourt, *Maurice de Guérin*, appendix 4, pp. 353–56.

Les Fleurs du Mal

Les Fleurs du Mal (Poulet-Malassis, 1857).

Les Fleurs du Mal (Poulet-Malassis, 1861). Omission of the six poems deemed offensive and addition of thirty-five other poems.

Œuvres complètes (Lévy, 1868–1869). Preface by Théophile Gautier. *Les Fleurs du Mal*, vol. 1.

Œuvres complètes (Conard, 1922–1953). Sous la direction de Jacques Crépet. *Les Fleurs du Mal*, vol. 1 (1922).

Les Fleurs du Mal (Corti, 1942). Edition critique établie par Jacques Crépet et Georges Blin.

Œuvres complètes (Gallimard, 1964). Texte établi par Le Dantec. Edition présentée par Claude Pichois. Bibliothèque de la Pléiade.

Readings

Blin, Georges. *Baudelaire* (Gallimard, 1939).

Chérix, R. B. *Commentaire des Fleurs du Mal* (Droz, 1962).

Hubert, J. D. *L'Esthétique des Fleurs du Mal* (Geneva: Cailler, 1953).

Peyre, H. *Connaissance de Baudelaire* (Corti, 1951).

Quennell, P. *Baudelaire and the Symbolists* (London: Chatto and Windus, 1929).

Rhodes, S. A. *The Cult of Beauty in Baudelaire* (New York: Institute of French Studies, Columbia University, 1929).

Ruff, Marcel. *Baudelaire* (Pauvert, 1957).

Charles Baudelaire

1821–1867

The first great modern poet, Charles Baudelaire, was born in Paris and educated first at the Collège of Lyon and then at the Lycée Louis-le-Grand. His formative years were troubled by his hatred of his stepfather. As a young man unruly and sullen, interested only in literature and bad company, in 1841 he was sent on a trip to India by his mother and stepfather who had hopes of straightening him out. He did not go so far as India, however; after spending some time on Mauritius and Réunion, the memory of which introduced an exotic element into some of his later poetry, he returned to Paris. There, with an inheritance he had just come into, he took up the life of a fashionable dandy. His spending became so extravagant that the family placed a control upon his income: the dandy became a bohemian. He shared his lodging with the mulattress Jeanne Duval, wrote verse, and associated with the artists and writers also working in the capital.

His friends were Gautier, Banville, Gérard de Nerval, Louis Ménard, and others the most of whom are important names in the history of the arts. With them he socialized in the cafés and the drawing rooms of the demimondaines who served often as mistress and muse as well as hostess to the artists they received. Such was Madame Sabatier, the "Venus blonde," whose Sunday dinner parties included many notables and who inspired sculpture and painting as well as verse. Another woman in Baudelaire's life was Marie Daubrun, an actress appearing at La Gaîté. But there was always Jeanne, companion of misery and debauchery, in later years ugly and hateful but from whom Baudelaire—out of habit, perhaps, or pity—never separated. Even when they were living apart, Jeanne called regularly to ask for money. Her morning calls were followed by his mother's. Madame Aupick never abandoned her ungrateful and dissolute son, visiting him in the sordid little hotels where he hid from his creditors, helping him as she could. There was not much actually that she could do, for Baudelaire, from the first, seemed doomed to destruction. Abuse of alcohol and drugs aggravated his bad health; professional frustration undermined his morale. It is remarkable that he could work at all or feel the enthusiasm of which we know he was capable throughout his life.

One of his great enthusiasms was painting. In 1845, he began writing reviews of art exhibits. They would be collected in the posthumous *Curiosités esthétiques*. As an art critic, Baudelaire did not believe that art should be the application of any system. His views are generally approved today, and he is given a high place among the art critics of his age. As a literary critic Baudelaire also enjoys high esteem; some would call him France's greatest. One of his remarks, "la critique doit être partiale et passionnée," became the slogan of the school of critics prominent during the 1940s and 1950s. His literary criticism was collected, like his art criticism, in a posthumous volume. It is titled *L'Art Romantique*. Although present-day fashions in criticism may have made professors incline too favorably toward Baudelaire's critical writing as opposed to more academic critics, in the field of literary theory his position can scarcely be challenged.

It is Baudelaire's formulation of ideas garnered from Poe, Hoffmann, Coleridge, and some philosophers that laid the basis for modern poetry. First in importance is the concept of the imagination as the queen of the faculties, that power given man, Baudelaire believed, to perceive secret analogies in nature. The poem is then less invented than deciphered, for it already exists in the cosmos. The word is sacred and the true poet is a seer rather than merely a sensitive soul capable of touching others by the outpourings of his feelings. Not a sweet singer, the poet is not a preacher either, who uses his verse to teach a moral. But if he is a seer he is also a craftsman, giving to his vision the most perfect material form of which he is capable and thereby serving beauty. His means to his end are not the conventional. To achieve totality of effect, he will keep the poem short. To obtain musical appeal, he will stress rhythm and diffused suggestivity. By including thematic elements that are modern, novel, and strange, he will give piquancy and enlarge the scope of poetry. Much of Baudelaire's *ars poetica* is close to Anglo-American and German statements. In the French tradition, one can see how much it differs from the practice of the major Romantic poets and how much it resembles what Parnassians, Symbolists, and more recent poets will do. Marcel Raymond plots the development of French poetry from Baudelaire like this: the line of the "artists" through Mallarmé to Valéry;·the line of the "seers" through Rimbaud to the Surrealists (*De Baudelaire au Surréalisme*, Corti, 1933).

Baudelaire's importance as a theorist would be inadequately summarized if his article on Richard Wagner were left out. Wagner's notion of the *Gesamtkunstwerk* was endorsed by Baudelaire, and his music filled him with enthusiasm. He was one of the first to hail the German composer who would play a great role in the Symbolist movement later on in the century.

Although he had been writing criticism, verse, and diverse pieces for years and widely publishing in periodicals, Baudelaire did not appear in volume until the second half of the 1850s. His first translation of Edgar Allan Poe, *Les Histoires extraordinaires*, was published in 1856; he had discovered Poe in 1847 and, with the zeal of a disciple, had been working all the intervening years on his translations of the American. In 1857 appeared *Les Fleurs du Mal*. For this work Baudelaire was brought to trial and fined on the grounds of immorality. He replied by publishing a second edition in 1861; it contained thirty-five additional poems but lacked the six of the first edition judged offensive. *Les Fleurs du Mal*, in implementing and illustrating Baudelaire's poetic theory, may be said to have oriented the trends that poetry has followed since their publication. By their formal ornateness, they may be associated with Parnasse; their transcendental implications put them in the line that will lead to Symbolism.

During the first few years of the 1860s, Baudelaire published considerably, especially in reviews. Many of the prose poems appeared now, but they would not be collected into a volume until after the poet's death. The last of his great articles on art came out in 1863, occasioned by the death of Delacroix. In spite of his activity, Baudelaire felt increasingly discouraged by public indifference or hostility. He had submitted his candidacy for the French Academy but the gesture met with such a reception in the press that, advised to do so by Sainte-Beuve and others, he had withdrawn it. In 1864, he left Paris for Brussels where he hoped to find a more sympathetic public, a publisher, and, incidentally, a haven from his creditors. Belgium was less than he expected, however. He gave some lectures, visited the principal cities, but found in Belgium a country with all the bad features of his own. Along with his spirits, his health worsened. In 1866, paralyzed and very ill, Baudelaire was taken back to Paris. He died the following year.

Although too late for him to find much satisfaction in it, recognition did come to Baudelaire before his death. Leconte de Lisle praised his work, Verlaire admired him, and Sainte-Beuve acknowledged that Baudelaire was becoming an important figure. Perhaps even his mother, in whose arms he died, finally recognized in her son the genius that he was. After his death, his reputation accelerated. Baudelaire's first admirers were attracted by his art. Théophile Gautier was one of the earliest to point out the mastery of prosody that Baudelaire exhibited. The generation of 1880 shifted the emphasis from his art to his thought. He became, moreover, a personality due to the portraits published by Huysmans and Bourget, and *Les Fleurs du Mal* seemed to the Decadents the Bible of youth and revolt. His reputation as a literary artist, a theorist, and as a personality has since never ceased to grow. Known throughout the world and translated in all the literary languages, Baudelaire stands today with the greatest poets of all times.

In sketching Baudelaire's life and career, we have paused to mention particularly his criticism and theory. The reason for this emphasis is merely that we are less concerned here with literary appreciation than literary history, the direction of which is most explicitly indicated by an artist's statements. *Les Fleurs du Mal* is, of course, the work that has assured Baudelaire's fame and all else, however excellent, is of secondary importance. But before turning to these poems, let us complete a review of his work.

In order of publication, first there are his translations of Poe, which came out in five volumes between 1856 and 1865. If Baudelaire had done nothing else, he would have merited a place in the history of French Symbolism so important is Poe for poets from Mallarmé to Valéry. Next are *Les Paradis Artificiels*, which were published as a volume first in 1860. They are a series of essays made up of personal observations, anecdotes, relation of visions—all with the professed intention of demonstrating that, in having recourse to drugs the "chercheurs de paradis font leur enfer." [1] A considerable part of the work is devoted to analyzing DeQuincey's *Confessions of an Opium Eater*. No doubt *Les Paradis Artificiels* added something in creating the public image of Baudelaire as a scandalous author.

Intended to complement and supplement the poems in verse, Baudelaire's prose poems are far more than mere sketches to be reworked as poems. In the preface that he wrote for *La Presse* (1862), he explains what ambition possessed him: "Quel est celui de nous qui n'a pas, dans ses jours d'ambition, rêvé le miracle d'une prose poétique, musicale sans rythme et sans rime, assez souple et assez heurtée pour s'adapter aux mouvements lyriques de l'âme, aux ondulations de la rêverie, aux soubresauts de la conscience?"[2] Baudelaire studied very carefully the example of Bertrand and hoped to be able to adapt the genre to the subject of modern life. For modern life, a modern form of poetry is what he was seeking, a form supple enough to express the contrasts and contradictions that he found all around him as he walked through the streets of Paris. It is impossible to separate in the case of Baudelaire the idea of modern and of metropolis. Perhaps the alexandrine verse was too closely associated with the classic ideal to be a suitable vehicle for the vignettes of modern urban life he wished to paint—neither prosy enough nor directly brutal enough. Baudelaire was very much interested in the theme Sainte-Beuve had approached in "Les Rayons Jaunes," and Gautier in "Paris." He may have seen here an example of the unsuitability of the French classic verse.[3] Even Bertrand's prose was too formal for what Baudelaire was seeking, and in his own prose poems he moved increasingly away from pattern and external poetic effects.

In spite of Baudelaire's enthusiasm and the care which he lavished upon them, his prose poems were not very well received when they appeared in magazines, and his idea of publishing a volume of them was not realized while he lived. Posterity would, of course, make up for the incomprehension of contemporaries; the greatest poets of France to come after Baudelaire would emulate his achievement in the poetic prose genre.

Victor Hugo's comment that *Les Fleurs du Mal* created a "frisson nouveau" probably best describes the particular quality that the poems possess. We have already alluded to the gulf between them and most of the Romantic poetry. Baudelaire called Théophile Gautier and Théodore de Banville his masters and shared with them a repugnance for Romantic sentimentality and a respect for craftsmanship. Yet, in spite of certain affinities, there are wide differences between Baudelaire and poets who, formed by the masters of Art for Art's sake, will be known as Parnassian. He does not usually affect either the aristocratic impassivity or the cult of antique beauty that are associated with that group, and a classical evocation as in "La Beauté" with its plastic beauty and its implication of emotional and moral detachment is exceptional. Rather is he drawn to the modern—the modern city with its ugliness, vice, and misery, the modern temperament with its taste for the morbid, the unnatural, and the eccentric. Other than an occasional manifestation as in "La Beauté," there is little in *Les Fleurs du Mal* of the *edle Einfalt und stille Grösse* that characterize the classical or Apollonian mood. The mood of *Les Fleurs du Mal* seems the more typically modern longing after the unattainable mingled with despair of ever attaining it, the basic conflict between the urge upward and the push downward, the eventual crushing and anni-hilation—spleen and ideal. These poems suggest little of the pagan spirit but rather are profoundly Christian in their preoccupation with good and evil, their moral anxiety. Rather than in "La Beauté," it is in the "Hymne à la Beauté," where beauty is mingled with voluptuousness and death, that we find the typical Baudelairian statement.

The technical achievement of *Les Fleurs du Mal* was already pointed out by Théophile Gautier, who noted that in addition to having adopted the metrical innovations of the Romantics, Baudelaire used devices that were wholly personal. He cited, by way of example, the crossed rimes, the polysyllabic words, and several other features. What Gautier did not show was the musicality of Baudelaire's verse and the suggestivity of his images, which combine to produce the *sorcellerie évocatoire* that, from Rimbaud on, would be recognized as the mark of his genius.

The basic artistic unity of *Les Fleurs du Mal* is assured by the ambivalent themes indicated by the title of the first and main section—Spleen and Ideal. The poems gravitate toward one pole or the other, reacting to Baudelaire's *horreur* or *extase de la vie*. On all levels this thematic polarity is maintained, whether the subject is the personal situation of the poet, human kind, or world order. Baudelaire is not a simple lyricist, and his tendency is to move rapidly from the personal into the general or the cosmic. We may therefore be justified in seeing in *Les Fleurs du Mal* a conscious grouping of the poems under abstract headings, such as R. B. Chérix specifies: namely, an *ars poetica*, a definition of the artistic vocation, the nature of beauty, the universal order of correspondences, etc., fol-lowing in order through the original section of "Spleen et Idéal" and the added sections of "Tableaux parisiens" and the final pieces. Baudelaire, we know from letters to his mother and to Alfred de Vigny, insisted that his book was not just a collection of various lyrical pieces. Barbey d'Aure-villy, cited by Chérix,[4] would have us read the poems only in the order in which they are placed. We are aware, however, that no matter how real or conscious the organization is, it was done after the poems were written, so despite Baudelaire's own claims and those of many of his critics, it does not seem very important. The significant architecture of *Les Fleurs du Mal* is in the personality and talent of Baudelaire rather than in the sorting and grouping of individual poems.

Notes

1. Baudelaire, *Œuvres complètes*, p. 463.
2. Ibid., p. 229.
3. See Bernard, *Le Poème en prose*, p. 111.
4. Chérix, *Commentaire des Fleurs du Mal*, p. xv.

L'ALBATROS[1]

Souvent, pour s'amuser, les hommes d'équipage
Prennent des albatros, vastes oiseaux des mers,
Qui suivent, indolents compagnons de voyage,
Le navire glissant sur les gouffres amers.

A peine les ont-ils déposés sur les planches,
Que ces rois de l'azur, maladroits et honteux,
Laissent piteusement leurs grandes ailes blanches
Comme des avirons traîner à côté d'eux.

Ce voyageur ailé, comme il est gauche et veule!
Lui, naguère si beau, qu'il est comique et laid!
L'un agace son bec avec un brûle-gueule,
L'autre mime, en boitant, l'infirme qui volait!

Le Poète est semblable au prince des nuées
Qui hante la tempête et se rit de l'archer;[2]
Exilé sur le sol au milieu des huées,
Ses ailes de géant l'empêchent de marcher.

---

1. The basis for this emblem of the artist in society may be an incident of Baudelaire's Indian voyage. The third stanza, not in the original composition, was added to give concrete emphasis to the misfortunes of the bird out of his element.

Charles Mauron, whose "psychocriticism" deals with an author's obsessions, notes in Baudelaire recurring images of weight which impedes forward movement. The albatros recalls the chimera's mount ("Chacun sa Chimère"), the monster with the appendage on his head (Baudelaire's letter to Asselineau, 13 March 1856), the women whose heavy hair seems to drag them backwards, and the windowpane vendor with his wares on his back ("Le Mauvais Vitrier"). *Des Métaphores obsédantes au Mythe personnel* (Corti, 1963), pp. 58ff. There is, of course, more obvious thematic similarity between this poem and other poems of the sea, of the voyage, of poets and great birds in alien surroundings.

2. Allusion to classical antiquity?

CORRESPONDANCES[3]

La Nature est un temple où de vivants piliers
Laissent parfois sortir de confuses paroles;
L'homme y passe à travers des forêts de symboles
Qui l'observent avec des regards familiers.

Comme de longs échos qui de loin se confondent
Dans une ténébreuse et profonde unité,
Vaste comme la nuit et comme la clarté,
Les parfums, les couleurs et les sons se répondent.

Il est des parfums frais comme des chairs d'enfants,
Doux comme les hautbois, verts comme les prairies,
—Et d'autres, corrompus, riches et triomphants,

Ayant l'expansion des choses infinies,
Comme l'ambre, le musc, le benjoin et l'encens,
Qui chantent les transports de l'esprit et des sens.

3. With its title evoking Hoffmann, Swedenborg, and many other poets and thinkers throughout the centuries who sought universal unity in analogies, this poem summarizes the transcendental point of view in art and philosophy, presenting a world in which natural phenomena all refer to spiritual counterparts, a world in symbolic relationship to an ideal or absolute world and organized in such a way that it can be grasped only through poetic intuition. The mysterious affinities which tie the material world are suggested by synesthesia, the association of the senses. This poem is, moreover, the key to Baudelaire's poetry, for the figures of allegory and symbolism that characterize it are the processes by which the affinities in nature can be demonstrated and the unity of the universe proclaimed.

Anna Balakian sees, however, a certain contradiction in the poem. Although using the Swedenborgian term *correspondence*, Baudelaire does not link abstract qualities with concrete objects. Rather than link heaven and earth, he merely mingles sense perception. See Balakian, *The Symbolist Movement*, p. 36. Perhaps Miss Balakian's distinction is over-subtle and there are, as we have always thought, spiritual implications in the earthly associations. Baudelaire seems to think so, to judge from numerous comments (in *Art Romantique*, for example). Jean Prévost explains the "myth" of affinities on the basis of perception. If a color and a sound call forth the same affective response in the poet, he is inclined to think that he has discovered a real affinity in nature. The image by which he represents this subjective identification is a further bond. According to Prévost, then, the only universe that the poet is describing is his own. This may be rather self-evident for some readers or a little too simplistic for others, who may be inclined to see the poet's experience a real intuition. *Baudelaire* (Mercure de France, 1953), pp. 73–77. In occult matters one may note finally that the attitudes of Baudelaire and Nerval are quite different, Baudelaire believing that revelation came to the poet directly, whereas Nerval believed that it came only through intuition and deciphering. Of the two, Baudelaire would seem more modern, the examples of Mallarmé and of Rimbaud notwithstanding.

Later nineteenth-century poets did not have the reservations expressed by present-day critics; they considered this sonnet an authoritative statement of the esthetic and metaphysic to which they adhered. Moréas is said to have been moved by it to change the name of his group from Les Décadents to Les Symbolistes.

LA VIE ANTERIEURE[4]

J'ai longtemps habité sous de vastes portiques
Que les soleils marins teignaient de mille feux,
Et que leurs grands piliers, droits et majestueux,
Rendaient pareils, le soir, aux grottes basaltiques.

Les houles, en roulant les images des cieux,
Mêlaient d'une façon solennelle et mystique
Les tout-puissants accords de leur riche musique
Aux couleurs du couchant reflété par mes yeux.

C'est là que j'ai vécu dans les voluptés calmes,
Au milieu de l'azur, des vagues, des splendeurs
Et des esclaves nus, tout imprégés d'odeurs,

Qui me rafraîchissaient le front avec des palmes,
Et dont l'unique soin était d'approfondir
Le secret douloureux qui me faisait languir.[5]

---

4. I suppose that there can be no doubt that Baudelaire took the idea of universal palingenesis quite seriously, quite literally. It fits in with his general views and could have been a help in putting up with the miseries of his present life. At any rate, it is an important feature of his poetic mythology.

The voluptuous evocation of contours, colors, sounds, and perfumes combines Classical grandeur with Romantic color and exoticism. One might think first of Claude Lorrain, then of Gauguin or Delacroix, finally of Théophile Gautier, whose *Mademoiselle de Maupin* contains imaginary landscapes of similar beauty and splendor.

5. The painful secret alluded to here has, I believe, unduly puzzled commentators. It is probably just a device for mood, and has no more ulterior significance than the pillars and grottoes of the first stanza. On the other hand, the pillars and grottoes may have, as René Galand suggests, the sense of Plato's cave, and the secret may be the poet's longing to turn from the shadows to behold the real world. See Galand, *Baudelaire: Poétiques et Poésie* (Nizet, 1969), p. 268.

HARMONIE DU SOIR [6]

Voici venir les temps où vibrant sur sa tige
Chaque fleur s'évapore ainsi qu'un encensoir;
Les sons et les parfums tournent dans l'air du soir;
Valse mélancolique et langoureux vertige!

Chaque fleur s'évapore ainsi qu'un encensoir; [7]
Le violon frémit comme un cœur qu'on afflige;
Valse mélancolique et langoureux vertige!
Le ciel est triste et beau comme un grand reposoir. [8]

Le violon frémit comme un cœur qu'on afflige,
Un cœur tendre, qui hait le néant vaste et noir!
Le ciel est triste et beau comme un grand reposoir;
Le soleil s'est noyé dans son sang qui se fige.

Un cœur tendre, qui hait le néant vaste et noir,
Du passé lumineux recueille tout vestige!
Le soleil s'est noyé dans son sang qui se fige ...
Ton souvenir en moi luit comme un ostensoir! [9]

6. The Romantic bombast and posturing which make some of *Les Fleurs du Mal* rather ridiculous seem banished from this poem, a marvel of mood. Its musical character made it a favorite of the Symbolists. With only two rimes repeated throughout the poem, it has the quality of the waltz alluded to, turning and turning until coming to the halt suggested by the last two lines. There is a noticeable lack of concrete descriptive detail, in its stead a suave harmony of forms, colors, sounds, and perfumes evoking a past love. The personal and affective experience hinted at broadens, as the poem progresses, into vast nature frescoes of evening and sunset, still, of course, a "soulscape" rather than a

landscape, not description of things, but of the effect that things produce—Mallarmé's objective is already realized by Baudelaire. Anna Balakian uses this poem to demonstrate effectively the qualities that make Baudelaire a precursor of Symbolism. Instead of the direct statement of the poet's emotions, characteristic of Romantic technique, the indirect discourse of imagery; instead of parallels between physical and spiritual, mingling of the subjective state into nature. In the use of nature, pathetic fallacy gives way to the "objective correlative."

René Galand, in keeping with the general thesis of his book, underlines the archetypal aspect of the poem—the dread of darkness falling, the anguish caused by the sun's setting (*Baudelaire*, p. 302).

Although interpreted liberally, this poem is an example of the Malayan pantoum. In France the form was made famous by Victor Hugo. It was also used by Banville and by Leconte de Lisle. Characteristically in stanzas of four verses, the second and fourth recur as first and third in the succeeding stanza.

7. Cf. Vigny, "La Maison du Berger:" ... "Balance les beaux lys comme des encensoirs."

8. The sky may suggest its red and gold drapery, flowers, and incense associated with the altar.

9. The golden receptacle can look like a stylized representation of the sun. In fact, sometimes the monstrance is called a sun. Madame Sabatier inspired this poem.

L'INVITATION AU VOYAGE[10]

Mon enfant, ma sœur,
Songe à la douceur
D'aller là-bas vivre ensemble!
Aimer à loisir,
Aimer et mourir
Au pays qui te ressemble!
Les soleils mouillés
De ces ciels[11] brouillés
Pour mon esprit ont les charmes
Si mystérieux
De tes traîtres yeux,
Brillant à travers leurs larmes.

Là, tout n'est qu'ordre et beauté,
Luxe, calme et volupté.[12]

Des meubles luisants,[13]
Polis par les ans,
Décoreraient notre chambre;
Les plus rares fleurs
Mêlant leurs odeurs
Aux vagues senteurs de l'ambre,
Les riches plafonds,
Les miroirs profonds,
La splendeur orientale,
Tout y parlerait
A l'âme en secret
Sa douce langue natale.

Là, tout n'est qu'ordre et beauté,
Luxe, calme et volupté.

Vois sur ces canaux
Dormir ces vaisseaux
Dont l'humeur est vagabonde;
C'est pour assouvir
Ton moindre désir
Qu'ils viennent du bout du monde.
—Les soleils couchants
Revêtent les champs,
Les canaux, la ville entière,
D'hyacinthe et d'or;
Le monde s'endort
Dans une chaude lumière.[14]

Là, tout n'est qu'ordre et beauté,
Luxe, calme et volupté.

---

10. The actress with the golden hair and the green eyes, Marie Daubrun, is said to have inspired this poem on the land-of-milk-and-honey theme, one of Baudelaire's most perfect. The landscape, which is doubtless Holland, reflects her sweet and level disposition and possibly Baudelaire's feelings for her—an affection without violence or strong passion. Dutch paintings, the accounts of the country by Baudelaire's friends Nerval and Esquiros, Bernardin de Saint-Pierre's *Observations sur la Hollande* may all have been drawn upon.

The lovely vision of distant places is set in an exquisitely musical form, which even suggests the roll or toss of a ship. Unique in its combination of verses chiefly of five and seven syllables, this poem may have been in Verlaine's mind when he extolled the *vers impair*. For an interesting discussion of a possible alteration of the rhythm scheme, see Jean Prévost, *Baudelaire* (Mercure de France, 1953), p. 329. Following Paul Valéry's recommendations, Prévost changes certain lines from seven syllables to eight. The instability and fleeting nature of the uneven lines, instead of being brought under control only in the refrain is thus counteracted repeatedly throughout the stanza itself.

· 11. *Ciels* is a term in painting.

12. The refrain applies to the country depicted in paintings rather than the actual country itself.

13. The scenes depicted here are common to Dutch painting, this interior described could be a Vermeer.

14. Are we to see here, as René Galand does, a difference from the dread of night described in *Harmonie du Soir?* Here they go to sleep while it is still light. See Galand, *Baudelaire*, p. 310.

LA CLOCHE FELEE [15]

Il est amer et doux, pendant les nuits d'hiver,
D'écouter, près du feu qui palpite et qui fume,
Les souvenirs lointains lentement s'élever
Au bruit des carillons qui chantent dans la brume.

Bienheureuse la cloche au gosier vigoureux
Qui, malgré sa vieillesse, alerte et bien portante,
Jette fidèlement son cri religieux,
Ainsi qu'un vieux soldat qui veille sous la tente!

Moi, mon âme est fêlée, et lorsqu'en ses ennuis
Elle veut de ses chants peupler l'air froid des nuits,
Il arrive souvent que sa voix affaiblie

Semble le râle épais d'un blessé qu'on oublie
Au bord d'un lac de sang, sous un grand tas de morts,
Et qui meurt, sans bouger, dans d'immenses efforts. [16]

15. The horror of the last stanza seems quite out of keeping with the homeliness of the first and the pathos that comes close to the ridiculous of the second and third. The

first and, especially, the last stanza are in themselves, however, very fine. The poem presents a curious succession of mood, moving from the coziness of "bittersweet memories" before a winter fire, to the pathos of a doughty old soldier and a poet whose soul can muster only the feeble sound of a cracked steeple bell, finally to the horror of the battlefield with its heaps of dead.

16. The archetypal significance of the poem is emphasized by René Galand. He sees it as representing the basic conflict of the urge upward and the push downward, the eventual crushing and annihilation. For Galand there is a factor of guilt in the fate of the poet. I am not sure that the poem implies that the poet is responsible at all for his fate. See Galand, *Baudelaire*, pp. 330–31.

SPLEEN[17]

Quand le ciel bas et lourd pèse comme un couvercle
Sur l'esprit gémissant en proie aux longs ennuis,
Et que l'horizon embrassant tout le cercle
Il nous verse un jour noir plus triste que les nuits;

Quand la terre est changée en un cachot humide,
Où l'Espérance, comme une chauve-souris,
S'en va battant les murs de son aile timide
Et se cognant la tête à des plafonds pourris;

Quand la pluie étalant ses immenses traînées
D'une vaste prison imite les barreaux,
Et qu'un peuple muet d'infâmes araignées[18]
Vient tendre ses filets au fond de nos cerveaux,

Des cloches tout à coup sautent avec furie
Et lancent vers le ciel un affreux hurlement,
Ainsi que des esprits errants et sans patrie
Qui se mettent à geindre opiniâtrement.

—Et de longs corbillards, sans tambours ni musique,
Défilent lentement dans mon âme; l'Espoir,
Vaincu, pleure, et l'Angoisse atroce, despotique,
Sur mon crâne incliné plante son drapeau noir.[19]

17. As a protest to the complicated exegesis often practiced upon Baudelaire, one is tempted to read this poem as nothing more than an expression of boredom on a rainy day, interrupted for a moment by the startling sound of steeple bells. But that would take away a great deal of its interest. The mood itself, the Romantic version of *acedia*, deserves comment, and so does the art of the poet, who has structured the piece like a five-act play, the first three stanzas depicting a rising tension which reaches a climax in the fourth and a dénouement in the fifth. In projecting his mood, the poet develops a remarkable series of parallels between spirit and matter. Furthermore, he moves less precisely but in a remarkable fashion nonetheless, back and forth inside his skull and outside in the landscape to accomplish a fusion of the inner and outer worlds.

18. "Bats in the Belfry," the English expression, is offered by J. D. Hubert as a possible source of the image in stanza two (*L'Esthétique des 'Fleurs du Mal'*), p. 138. This image of spiders may have a similar source, the French equivalent to "Bats in the Belfry" being "avoir une araignée au plafond" (Galand, *Baudelaire*, p. 337).

19. The orchestration of the final stanza is particularly fine: first a funeral march, then a jerky line carrying out the idea of sobs, finally the resolution, the ceasing of sound and the fixing into the everlasting.

RECUEILLEMENT[20]

Sois sage, ô ma Douleur, et tiens-toi plus tranquille.
Tu réclamais le Soir; il descend; le voici:
Une atmosphère obscure enveloppe la ville,
Aux uns portant la paix, aux autres le souci.

Pendant que des mortels la multitude vile,
Sous le fouet du Plaisir, ce bourreau sans merci,
Va cueillir des remords dans la fête servile,
Ma Douleur, donne-moi la main; viens par ici,

Loin d'eux. Vois se pencher les défuntes Années,
Sur les balcons du ciel, en robes surannées;
Surgir du fond des eaux le Regret souriant;

Le Soleil moribond s'endormir sous une arche,
Et, comme un long linceul traînant à l'Orient,
Entends, ma chère, entends la douce Nuit qui marche.

20. One of the best known of Baudelaire's poems, it did not figure in *Les Fleurs du Mal* until the 1868 edition. It is to many a faultless specimen with its unity of design assured through the personification sequence and the transition between the two parts of the poem brilliantly executed by an enjambement that separates as well as connects the quatrains with the tercets. Paul Valéry, however, limits his admiration to the first and last stanzas (*Situation de Baudelaire*). Perhaps they do contain all that is great of the poem and are free from the bombast and the commonplace which deface the center stanzas. Yet it would be hard to sacrifice stanza three. Jean Prévost has an emended version, one corrected of all of the flaws of pleonasm, etc., which carping critics have found in the poem. The result of his mischievous attempt is a monument of nullity, in spite of retaining the theme and images. See *Baudelaire*, p. 333. Bernard Weinberg believes that this poem is basically about death. His explications in *The Limits of Symbolism* (University of Chicago Press, 1966) present clearly and methodically the layered meanings of Baudelaire's poetry.

Poetry of Mallarmé

Œuvres Complètes de Stéphane Mallarmé (Gallimard, 1945). Bibliothèque de
la Pléïade.

Readings

Chassé, Charles. *Les Clefs de Mallarmé* (Montaigne, 1954).
Chisholm, A. R. *Mallarmé's L'Après-midi d'un Faune* (Melbourne, Australia: Melbourne University Press, 1958).
Cohn, Robert Greer. *Mallarmé's Un Coup de dés* (New Haven: Yale University Press, 1949); *Mallarmé's Masterwork* (The Hague: Mouton, 1966).
————. *Toward the Poems of Mallarmé* (Berkeley: University of California Press, 1965).
Mauron, Charles. *Introduction à la Psychanalyse de Mallarmé* (Neuchâtel: Baconnière, 1950).
Michaud, Guy. *Mallarmé l'homme et l'œuvre* (Hatier-Boivin, 1953).
Noulet, Emilie. *Vingt Poèmes de Stéphane Mallarmé* (Droz, 1967).
Richard, Jean-Pierre. *L'Univers imaginaire de Mallarmé* (Seuil, 1961).
Thibaudet, Albert. *La Poésie de Stéphane Mallarmé* (Gallimard, 1913).

Stéphane Mallarmé

1842–1898

Mallarmé, the man behind the work, seems at first more enigmatic than any other of the major Symbolist poets. Even though it may not be an exact likeness, the image that we conjure up of Baudelaire, Rimbaud, or Verlaine is a clear one. Of Mallarmé the series of pictures that we get tends rather to blur the features: Mallarmé the schoolmaster, the fashion editor, the bourgeois, the lover, the metaphysician, the poet. The enigma may be stated thus: is the poetry that he produced mathematical formulas of human experience lifted to the highest power, the naive lucubrations of a man inspired by secondhand knowledge of metaphysics and esthetic theory, or verbal needlework executed by a fussy and terribly mannered person? If we do not think of them as a judgment (which should be made only on the basis of his poetry as poetry) but as a means of understanding his motivation, actually these descriptions of Mallarmé's poetry are all admissible and point back to a personality far more coherent than we first supposed. All the pictures of Mallarmé can be absorbed into the first, that of the schoolmaster. He was the classic type of schoolmaster, almost a caricature. Slight and mousy in appearance, he endured the rowdiness of his pupils in class and, with a paper *bonhomme* pinned on his back, went home every night to correct a mountain of English compositions. His health was fragile and his finances paltry. Neither his fame as a poet nor his public life nor his love affair alters the picture: a professor with a shawl and a goatee, a wife and family in a modest Paris flat and a rural retreat for the holidays. The looks of a schoolmaster, the life of a schoolmaster, the character of a schoolmaster. The features of his poetry which seem to indicate an extraordinarily faceted personality may have their source merely in the finickiness, the intellectualism, and the escape drive common to members of the teaching profession.

He had been born, in 1842, into a family of government employees. Losing his mother at the age of five, he was put in the charge of a grandmother. His early schooling was obtained in a religious college in Auteuil, then in another, a snobbish school where Mallarmé disguised his family name under a very aristocratic sounding one to keep up with his classmates. The invention did not keep him from feeling lonely and inferior. In 1856, he moved to Sens, where his father had been transferred, and attended the Lycée de Sens. His tendency toward withdrawal was increased by the death of his sister when he was fifteen. He found comfort in reading and composing verses and stories in imitation of the Romantic authors. With hindsight one can see indications of his future vocation in these pieces inspired by Béranger and Hugo. However, it is not until 1861, when Mallarmé, with the baccalauréat behind him and employed as a government clerk in Sens, made a decisive literary encounter. The *Fleurs du Mal* had everything to enchant the young man: sensuality and emotional struggles which seemed to express his own psyche. He wrote poems now that are almost pastiches of Baudelaire. Baudelaire's influence was soon tempered by a new discovery, Banville, who may have been introduced by one Emmanuel des Essarts, a young teacher in Sens who had taken Mallarmé under his wing. The whimsy of the *Odes Funambulesques* is discernible in "Placet," the sonnet which through des Essarts's good offices, Mallarmé published in the little Parisian review *Le Papillon*. It may have been Banville who kindled a fondness in Mallarmé for rich rime. Not only do his occasional poems testify to this fondness but some of his more serious pieces as well. The earlier period is, however, less marked by tour de force effects than the latter, when Mallarmé tended to view poetry as the "ultimate game" and Baudelaire has the upper hand in the next poem, "Guignon," which appeared in 1862 in *L'Artiste*. Other influences besides Banville's challenged the domination of Baudelaire, chiefly that of Théophile Gautier and that of Edgar Allan Poe, who both made important contributions to the philosophy of poetry that Mallarmé was formulating at the time. Baudelaire led him to prefer poetic distillation over sentimental outpourings and gave him the vision of art as a sacred function, Gautier encouraged his longing for the ideal, Poe showed him the part of craftsmanship in art. By the age of twenty, Mallarmé was clear as to what poetry meant to him. Poetry is a sacred art. It should be deliberately difficult, veiled from the profane. Its practice is a means to knowledge. As he would explain to Edmond de Goncourt, a poem is a "mystère dont le lecteur doit chercher la clef." He had already discovered that such a philosophy of art could be crippling to his inspiration, yet he knew that without it what sublime accomplishments of which he dreamed were impossible.

At the same time that he stabilized his esthetic position, he settled his future as to career and private life. With a German girl named Maria Gerhard, whom he had met in Sens, he went to England to prepare himself for a teaching position in English. The year in London (1862–1863), with its bad weather and uncomfortable accommodations was not a very happy one, but Mallarmé's real life was in his dreams. A poem that he composed at this time, "Les Fenêtres," demonstrates that, in basic pattern at least, Mallarmé's philosophy of life is already as fixed as his philosophy of art. It postulates the existence of an ideal world above the real one, in which the imperfections of the here below are all corrected. There the poet can find refuge and consolation. He married Marie and, late in the autumn of 1863, took a teaching position in Tournon. If London had not been pleasant, Tournon was worse. Mallarmé was badly housed, in poor health, and unable to find inspiration for his work. Doubts concerning his vocation brought him to the point of apostasy. But ultimately his ideal triumphed and in the spring he wrote the "Pitre châtié," the terse statement of all his longings, hopes, and fears for his artistic career, and three prose poems that extol his masters: Gautier, Baudelaire, and Banville ("Symphonie Littéraire"). During the following winter, as he meditated before his lamp, unmindful of the schoolboys who had tried his patience during the day and of the baby squalling in the next room, he worked out a subject that would suitably express the theme of the pure ideal. "Hérodiade" states this theme in terms of cold gems and a girl's virginity. Entirely free of subjective evocation or personal confession, the poem shows how increasingly mindful Mallarmé was of Poe's teaching summarized as "peindre non la chose mais l'effet qu'elle produit."

The work gave him great difficulty. Doubtless he wanted too much of it, and his high ideal made him easily discouraged. After a good beginning, it was laid aside. It would be taken up from time to time throughout Mallarmé's life, but never completed. With "Hérodiade" on the shelf, the table is clear for "Brise Marine" and the "Faune." Suggesting a rebellion of the flesh, these poems oppose the "Hérodiade" in theme. Yet they are nonetheless continuations of that work, further explorations on the subject of reality and dream, reality and flight. The "Faune," like "Hérodiade," is a poem for recitation. Mallarmé esteemed the dramatic form highly and hoped that his works could be presented on the stage.[1]

When Mallarmé resumed his school duties after the summer holidays of 1865, he seemed in the best of spirits. But soon, while working again on "Hérodiade," he was assailed by the same old doubts. As he composed, his discouragement increased: his poetry, which verbalized his meditations and visions, was not revealing to him the other side of the glass. On the contrary, it was making him suspect that the meaning man gives to life is just an invention of his fancy. The discovery of Hegel in 1866 seems to have helped Mallarmé out of his despair. It gave strength at a needed moment to his belief in a world of absolutes behind that of appearances, a world of universal harmony which could be revealed by poetry. In addition, to a man already given to escape in ideality, the notion of salvation through "impersonality," identification with *weltseele* was heartwarmingly compatible. Three poems, although not published until twenty years later, are thought to have been composed at this time. "Tout Orgueil fume-t-il du soir," "Surgi de la croupe et du bond," "Une Dentelle s'abolit" all demonstrate Mallarmé's technique of suggesting an absent object by describing a present one. By linking phenomena thus, the poet exposes the abstract quality that they have in common, reaches the pure idea. From Besançon where he transferred in 1866, from Avignon where he was sent the next year, Mallarmé's letters give us glimpses of his activities and the trend of his thinking. He wrote to his friends of a treatise on the subject of beauty, of "Hérodiade," and of four prose poems that may have evolved into "Igitur." More than ever he seems to regard his work as a means of transcendental attainment, as a "work," one might say, in the alchemical sense. "Igitur" is indeed a sort of wizard's book depicting mankind, the world, and the poet.

In May 1871, Mallarmé took leave of Avignon and the provincial life that he hated to have a desperate try for Paris. The move was foolhardy but successful. By November he had settled his wife and two children in an apartment and was teaching in the Lycée Condorcet. Three years later he moved to the rue de Rome, the site of his famous Tuesdays. The same year he found a rural retreat at Valvins, near Fontainebleau. It was there that he composed the first issue of his review *La Dernière Mode*. Before the periodical failed, eight numbers had appeared, Mallarmé writing all the columns.

"Igitur" remained in manuscript, *La Dernière Mode* ceased publication, but "L'Après-midi d'un Faune," laid aside for ten years, came out as a plaquette (1876). Mallarmé continued working, produced the "Tombeau d'Edgar Poe" and the "Toast funèbre," puttered with various other literary projects, and dreamed of the master work that he hoped to write one day. He was firmly established now in the literary world of Paris to which he had so long aspired. His appearance in Huysmans's novel *A Rebours* and in Verlaine's gallery of *Poètes Maudits*, both of 1884, made him a notorious figure. He thanked Verlaine by letter and Huysmans by the poem "Prose pour des Esseintes," which drew to his side a group of young admirers. Jean Moréas, Louis le Cardonnel, Teodor de Wyzewa, Félix Fénéon, René Ghil, Maurice Barrès are among those who forsook the cafés of the Left Bank to attend the Tuesday evenings in the rue de Rome. Mallarmé read them the "Vierge, le vivace," the "Hommage à Wagner," the "Victorieusement fui." While he was composing his sonnets and teaching his English classes (Lycée Janson de Sailly in 1884, Collège Rollin the next year), the Symbolist revolution gathered momentum. By 1891, the triumph of the new school was generally admitted and Mallarmé, although still going his own way, was considered its leader. He accepted the obligations of fame with good grace, writing letters, receiving disciples, attending functions. From all sides came invitations to make speeches, toasts, statements on an absurd range of subjects from bicycles to Scandinavian literature. Around him his disciples clamored for his attention and quarreled among themselves. He had got out several collections of verse and prose (1887, 1891, 1893), but the work that he longed to give himself to demanded a leisure that he did not have. Even after his retirement in 1894, it was only at Valvins that he could find some peace and quiet. There he took up "Hérodiade" again with the resolve to finish it. Only the "Cantique de Saint-Jean" materialized. However, in 1897 *Divagations* appeared in volume and the "Coup de dés" in the review *Cosmopolis*. The extraordinary physical appearance of the poem, with the variety of lettering and spacing, plus the obscurity of the text made even the most faithful hesitate to applaud. The following year Mallarmé died suddenly. He had time only to scribble a request that his manuscripts be burned. No one else, he felt sure, could put them in shape and for him it was now too late. What a pity, he said, since "ce devait être très beau."

From his early twenties on, it is clear that for Mallarmé poetry was a means of metaphysical knowledge, of apprehending the universe. Behind phenomena he glimpsed a cosmos organized under the sign of beauty. The poet alone by his intuition of analogies can perceive this world and suggest it to the chosen few. Grasping its inner organization, its profound meaning, the decipherer who is also a magician effects a reduction of the universe by verbal symbolism.

To make of language such an instrument, the poet must turn it away from its habitual role as a vehicle of direct expression or communication. Distorting the syntax by putting the object before the verb and the subject after it and by separating parts of the sentence normally found close together is the most obvious way of throwing the switch on language. Mallarmé likes also to change the normal voice of the verb, introduce Latin structures and Anglicisms. Critics have defined poetry recently as an "abuse of language." Mallarmé is a perfect example: the normal discursive function of language is arrested first by syntax, then by image. In the poem "Toute l'âme résumée" Mallarmé asserts that the material of the poem should fall like the ash from a cigar, that is to say, that the first term of the comparison must disappear. Rather than the illustrative simile or comparison, Mallarmé uses the shortcut metaphor which presents a subject directly in terms of something else far removed. Often the form is the precious epithet, a periphrase extremely subtle and delicate in nature. Absence of punctuation, unconventional punctuation, curious spacing, and use of various type further remove the poem from the prose vehicle.

Mallarmé's concept of poetry as a verbal mystery from which the profane are excluded implies a certain amount of mystification. "Donner un sens plus pur aux mots de la tribu" may mean first of all destroying the pattern of linguistic conventionality so that poetic evocation can replace prosy communication. Distorting syntax and using words in rare or special senses may also be just a means of confounding the reader, prankish games to force him to work if he hopes to extract the "substantificque moelle." Charles Chassé has emphasized this aspect of Mallarmé, demonstrating much to the discomfort of lovers of Mallarmé who would see him exclusively on a high plane of poetic ambiguity, that Mallarmé's muse was often the dictionary and that his poems, particularly after 1876, were puzzles whose hidden meaning was quite specific, often erotic and even scatological. We remember the anecdote concerning the pompous young fan who asked concerning a poem, "Is it a synthesis of the absolute, Maître?" "No indeed, it is the description of a chest of drawers." Clearly with the many who parodied Mallarmé, such as the authors of the *Déliquescences d'Adoré Floupette*,[2] we must include Mallarmé himself.

For a foreign language teacher the dictionary is, of course, an object of constant reference. Mallarmé's lexigraphic interest is patently attested to by his *Petite Philologie à l'usage des classes et des gens du monde*. There is no doubt that for Mallarmé it was more than just whimsy, the literal value that he attributed to the sound of a word, the classifications and relationships that he worked out on the basis of initial letters. The fanciful interpretations that we observe here spilled over, as we have seen, into his poetry. Before "Igitur" and "Un Coup de dés" there is the evidence of "L'Après-midi d'un Faune," where, among others, one may remember the example of the word *lys*. Lily = male, with phallic symbol reinforced by exclamation mark that follows. The physical properties of a word like *lys* offer Mallarmé a treasure of inspiration. The appearance of the word itself, narrow and upright, intensifies the symbolism suggested by the form of the object represented. The sound of the word is the acute *i*. Closely allied with Mallarmé's etymological interests is the attention that he paid to folk mythology. In 1880, he published *Les Dieux antiques*, an adaptation of an English work by George W. Cox. He shared the common interest of his day in tracing the diverse languages back to an original one and in finding in mythological or religious topoi archetypal sources such as the course of the sun, one of Mallarmé's favorite themes. In his early poems, the rising and the setting sun appears without disguise. In the latter, it is not easy to recognize, although in "Une dentelle s'abolit" the "jeu suprême" probably means the sunrise just as in "Victorieusement fui ..." the "suicide beau" is the setting of the sun. The single metaphor which structures the "Cantique de Saint Jean" is doubtless based on the association Saint John's Day = summer solstice. The trajectory of the head at the moment of decollation is identified with that of the sun. As the sun halts at the highest point in its course, so the head pauses in its flight. Incidentally, for the moon Mallarmé felt no interest and referred contemptuously to it as "ce fromage."

Actually Mallarmé was essentially *un homme d'intérieur* and nature as such appealed to him very little. If he enjoyed himself at Valvins and even took pleasure in sitting in his boat out on the river, it was more for the peace that his refuge brought him than for the contact with the earth or the contemplation of the skies. His long residence in the south of France elicited from him no enthusiasm for the luminous beauty of that landscape; his preference went to the dark and foggy northern climates. Of the seasons he preferred winter, preferred landscape covered with a shroud of snow. He was more at ease inside, in any case, and behind drawn shutters. Huysmans depicted Mallarmé in *A Rebours* as the exquisite of civilization, and we see that everything in the man and his poetry elaborate this image. Mallarmé's habitat is the parlor and the dining room, under the suspension lamp or before the coal fire, occasionally the boudoir. The poems calligraphed on fans seem natural products of this setting, but no less so than the poems of barbaric splendor, of sailing the seven seas, or of idyllic antiquity. These are escape motifs all presented without realism. "Igitur," "Hérodiade," and the "Faune" are the dreams of a schoolmaster.

Mallarmé's drab existence can probably be counted (along with his lofty concept of art) as a factor in the obsession of sterility that tormented him always. It is, of course, hard to say whether it was his notion of art that gave him his complex or his complex that gave him his notion of art or even the sort of existence that he led. They are, however, all tied together and sterility is a key word in understanding Mallarmé's poetic theory and practice. We know that he was able to turn the very fear of having nothing to say into an inspiration itself, since artistic sterility is the latent theme in some of his greatest poems. In some of his minor works too, for in his fallow moments he could give himself over to verbal games, creating the tours de force of rich rime that we have in "Ses purs ongles." Some, like "Surgi de la croupe," exemplify the baroque with its heavy decoration over something empty, others more rococo like the exquisite trivialities that he inscribed on fans. Such diversions may also be considered therapeutic; they are frequently indulged in by artists whose essential ambition is far more pretentious.

Mallarmé has seemed to recent avant-garde writers in France like a kindred spirit and a precursor. They do not speak of his transcendental concept of art, his predication of a world of truth and beauty that could be attained through art, but remember only the famous remark to Degas, "Ce n'est pas avec des idées mais avec des mots que l'on fait un poème." They interpret his preoccupation with language in modern structuralist terms and delight that he, no more than Raymond Roussel, was concerned with mimesis or self-expression. Following Foucault, they place Mallarmé, along with other artists born out of their own time, back in the pre-seventeenth century world where words and things were not separate. Doubtless it matters very little if Mallarmé loses some of his identity in being modernized. That is the price of significance and relevance in an age that is not one's own.

Notes

1. For a thorough study of Mallarmé and the theater, see Haskell Block, *Mallarmé and the Symbolist Drama* (Detroit: Wayne State University Press, 1963). Particularly rewarding is the discussion of Wagner, the nature and extent of his influences upon Mallarmé, the points upon which they differ.

2. A spoof on decadent writing by Gabriel Vicaire and Henry Beauclair (1885).

HERODIADE[1]

I. Ouverture Ancienne d'Hérodiade[2]

> La Nourrice
> (*Incantation*)

> Abolie,[3] et son aile affreuse dans les larmes
> Du bassin, aboli, qui mire les alarmes,
> Des ors nus fustigeant l'espace cramoisi,
> Une Aurore a, plumage héraldique, choisi
> Notre tour cinéraire et sacrificatrice,
> Lourde tombe qu'a fuie un bel oiseau, caprice
> Solitaire d'aurore au vain plumage noir ...[4]
> ....

II. Scène[5]

> La Nourrice—Hérodiade
> H.

> ....
> Oui, c'est pour moi, pour moi, que je fleuris, déserte!
> Vous le savez, jardins d'améthyste, enfouis[6]
> Sans fin dans de savants abîmes éblouis,
> Ors ignorés, gardant votre antique lumière
> Sous le sombre sommeil d'une terre première,[7]
> Vous, pierres où mes yeux comme de purs bijoux
> Empruntent leur clarté mélodieuse, et vous
> Métaux qui donnez à ma jeune chevelure
> Une splendeur fatale et sa massive allure!
> Quant à toi, femme née en des siècles malins
> Pour la méchanceté des antres sibyllins,
> Qui parles d'un mortel! selon qui, des calices
> De mes robes, arôme aux farouches délices,
> Sortirait le frisson blanc de ma nudité,
> Prophétise que si le tiède azur d'été,
> Vers lui nativement la femme se dévoile,
> Me voit dans ma pudeur grelottante d'étoile,
> Je meurs!

J'aime l'horreur d'être vierge et je veux
Vivre parmi l'effroi que me font mes cheveux[8]
Pour, le soir, retirée en ma couche, reptile
Inviolé sentir en la chair inutile
Le froid scintillement de ta pâle clarté
Toi qui te meurs, toi qui brûles de chasteté,[9]

....
....

1. The idea of doing a "Hérodiade" came to Mallarmé early in his career and stayed with him until his death. Yet the poem was never actually completed.

Mallarmé's choice of subject may have been dictated by Flaubert's *Salammbô*. Or possibly by a sonnet on the Queen of Judea in a collection by Théodore de Banville (*Les Princesses*). Hérodiade is the queen who will have her daughter, Salomé, ask for the head of John the Baptist. Mallarmé retains little of the biblical story, although there is some intimation of the tragic role that she is destined to play. She is here just a young princess living alone with her nurse in a lonely fortress. The landscape, the building, and the princess herself all belong to some desolate dream world in which, despite reference to the past and omens of the future, time seems to stand still. The over-all static impression serves the sterile and useless theme which is all that Mallarmé wants the story for. He uses this legendary princess to allegorize sterility, purity, virginity, or the fascination and the beauty implied in these words. Here too, Banville may have inspired Mallarmé. Or Baudelaire. For a very thorough analysis of this poem and for the "Faune," see Robert Greer Cohn, *Toward the Poems of Mallarmé*.

In spite of the conventional appearance of the verses, the alexandrines follow neither the pattern of hemistich or ternary division, but one so novel in grouping and in en-jambement that they seem no longer alexandrines. Professor St. Aubyn notes that the first eight lines have the following syllabic arrangement: 3-6-3, 3-3-6, 3-9, 4-6-2, 6-6, 6-4-2, 6-6, 1-8-3. See *Stéphane Mallarmé* (Boston: Twayne, 1969), p. 53.

2. The presentation of "Hérodiade" as a triptych, is a posthumous assembly of Mallarmé's unfinished work. The "Ouverture ancienne," consisting of ninety-six lines in which Hérodiade's old nurse describes the scene, sets the mood, and prepares for the appearance of her mistress, was called by Mallarmé, "Incantation."

3. *Aboli*, a word heavy with poetic meaning since Nerval's poem, is here used twice. Such repetition creates an internal rime, a device habitual to Mallarmé. The word is chosen to state the dispersion of night and the passing of dawn into day.

4. The scene that she has described is one at dawn on a day of autumn. Its colors streaked with the lingering shadows conjure up the image of the black wing of a golden bird beating against something crimson. The colors reinforce the figurative epithets to sug-gest opulence, violence, and impending tragedy.

5. This part is a dialogue between Hérodiade and the nurse. There are 134 lines.

6. Metals and precious stones, which express the sterility theme, were exploited by the Parnassians before the Symbolists.

7. The classic purity of this verse contrasts with the broken rhythm that Mallarmé often uses.

8. Another very classical line. St. Aubyn notes that in this couplet the liquid *r*'s, fricative *f*'s and *v*'s, the *eux* rimes create an impression of menace (*Stéphane Mallarmé*, pp. 66–67).

9. Throughout this poem Mallarmé uses devices of antinomy that recall poets of the baroque tradition.

L'APRES-MIDI D'UN FAUNE[10]

Eglogue

Le Faune

Ces nymphes, je les veux perpétuer.
                                    Si clair,
Leur incarnat léger, qu'il voltige dans l'air
Assoupi de sommeils touffus.
                                    Aimai-je un rêve?
Mon doute, amas de nuit ancienne, s'achève.
En maint rameau subtil, qui, demeuré les vrais
Bois mêmes, prouve, hélas! que bien seul je m'offrais
Pour triomphe la faute idéale de roses.[11]
Réfléchissons..
                        ou si les femmes dont tu gloses
Figurent un souhait de tes sens fabuleux!
Faune, l'illusion s'échappe des yeux bleus
Et froids, comme une source en pleurs, de la plus chaste:
Mais, l'autre tout soupirs, dis-tu qu'elle contraste
Comme brise du jour chaude dans ta toison?
Que non! par l'immobile et lasse pâmoison
Suffoquant de chaleurs le matin frais s'il lutte,
Ne murmure point d'eau que ne verse ma flûte
Au bosquet arrosé d'accords; et le seul vent
Hors des deux tuyaux prompt à s'exhaler avant
Qu'il disperse le son dans une pluie aride,
C'est, à l'horizon pas remué d'une ride,

Le visible et serein souffle artificiel
De l'inspiration, qui regagne le ciel.

O bords siciliens d'un calme marécage
Qu'à l'envi[12] de soleils ma vanité saccage,
Tacite[13] sous les fleurs d'étincelles,[14] CONTEZ
"Que je coupais ici les creux roseaux domptés
"Par le talent; quand, sur l'or glauque de lointaines
"Verdures dédiant leur vigne à des fontaines,
"Ondoie une blancheur animale au repos:[15]
"Et qu'au prélude lent où naissent les pipeaux[16]
"Ce vol de cygnes, non! de naïdes se sauve
"Ou plonge.."
    Inerte, tout brûle dans l'heure fauve[17]
Sans marquer par quel art ensemble détala
Trop d'hymen souhaité de qui cherche le *la:*
Alors m'éveillerai-je à la ferveur première;
Droit et seul, sous un flot antique de lumière,
Lys! et l'un de vous tous pour l'ingénuité.[18]

Autre[19] que ce doux rien par leur lèvre ébruité,
Le baiser, qui tout bas des perfides assure,
Mon sein, vierge de preuve, atteste une morsure
Mystérieuse, due à quelque auguste dent;
Mais, bast! arcane tel élut pour confident
Le jonc vaste et jumeau dont sous l'azur on joue:
Qui, détournant à soi le trouble de la joue,[20]
Rêve, dans un solo long, que nous amusions
La beauté d'alentour par des confusions
Fausses entre elle-même et notre chant crédule;
Et de faire aussi haut que l'amour se module
Evanouir du songe ordinaire de dos
Ou de flanc pur suivis avec mes regards clos,
Une sonore, vaine et monotone ligne.[21]

Tâche donc, instrument des fuites, ô maligne
Syrinx,[22] de refleurir aux lacs où tu m'attends!
Moi, de ma rumeur fier, je vais parler longtemps
Des déesses; et par d'idolâtres peintures,
A leur ombre enlever encore des ceintures:

Ainsi, quand des raisins j'ai sucé la clarté,
Pour bannir un regret par ma feinte écarté,
Rieur, j'élève au ciel d'été la grappe vide
Et, soufflant dans ses peaux lumineuses, avide
D'ivresse, jusqu'au soir je regarde au travers.

O nymphes, regonflons des SOUVENIRS divers.
"Mon œil, trouant les joncs, dardait chaque encolure
"Immortelle, qui noie en l'onde sa brûlure
"Avec un cri de rage au ciel de la forêt;
"Et le splendide bain de cheveux disparaît
"Dans les clartés et les frissons, ô pierreries!
"J'accours; quand, à mes pieds, s'entrejoignent (meurtries
"De la langueur goûtée à ce mal d'être deux)
"Des dormeuses parmi leurs seuls bras hasardeux;
"Je les ravis, sans les désenlacer, et vole
"A ce massif, haï par l'ombrage frivole,
"De roses tarissant tout parfum au soleil,
"Où notre ébat au jour consumé soit pareil."
Je t'adore, courroux des vierges, ô délice
Farouche du sacré fardeau nu qui se glisse
Pour fuir ma lèvre en feu buvant, comme un éclair
Tressaille! la frayeur secrète de la chair:
Des pieds de l'inhumaine au cœur de la timide
Que délaisse à la fois une innocence, humide
De larmes folles ou de moins tristes vapeurs.
"Mon crime, c'est d'avoir, gai de vaincre ces peurs
"Traîtresses, divisé la touffe échevelée
"De baisers que les dieux gardaient si bien mêlée:
"Car, à peine j'allais cacher un rire ardent
"Sous les replis heureux d'une seule (gardant
"Par un doigt simple, afin que sa candeur de plume
"Se teignit à l'émoi de sa sœur qui s'allume,
"La petite, naïve et ne rougissant pas:)
"Que de mes bras, défaits par de vagues trépas,
"Cette proie, à jamais ingrate se délivre
"Sans pitié du sanglot dont j'étais encore ivre."

Tant pis! vers le bonheur d'autres m'entraîneront
Par leur tresse nouée aux cornes de mon front:

Tu sais, ma passion, que, pourpre et déjà mûre,
Chaque grenade éclate et d'abeilles murmure;
Et notre sang, épris de qui le va saisir,
Coule pour tout l'essaim éternel du désir.
A l'heure où ce bois d'or et de cendres se teinte
Une fête s'exalte en la feuillée éteinte:
Etna! c'est parmi toi visité de Vénus
Sur ta lave posant ses talons ingénus,
Quand tonne un somme triste ou s'épuise la flamme.
Je tiens la reine!

       O sûr châtiment..

               Non, mais l'âme
De paroles vacante et ce corps alourdi
Tard succombent au fier silence de midi:
Sans plus il faut dormir en l'oubli du blasphème,
Sur le sable altéré gisant et comme j'aime
Ouvrir ma bouche à l'astre efficace des vins!

Couple, adieu; je vais voir l'ombre que tu devins.

10. A "summer" work for Mallarmé, in contrast to "Hérodiade" which is associated with the more laborious tasks of winter, "L'Après-midi d'un Faune" is, notwithstanding, the author's most famous poem. The reason may be that here Mallarmé's special qualities are all in evidence, but in amounts moderate enough to keep the poem quite comprehensible. Its beginnings promised anything but success. It had been started during the spring of 1865, while Mallarmé was still at Tournon, and the first version was a dramatic monologue which he hoped to have presented at the Comédie Française. He held the same hope for "Hérodiade." He hoped in vain, however. According to his friends in the national theater, his plots were too thin to permit either to qualify as theatrical material and Mallarmé, without bitterness, did not insist. Ten years later, just as he reworked "Hérodiade," he set about shaping the "Faune" into a poem. It appeared finally as a plaquette de luxe embellished by the illustrations of Edouard Manet. In the early 1890s, Debussy composed his musical adaptation of the poem and in 1912, at the Ballets Russes, Nijinski presented his choreographed version.

The story of what Verlaine described as an "adorable poème cochon" (see Chassé, *Les Clefs de Mallarmé*, p. 74) is that of a faun drowsing on a hot afternoon and trying to recall the events of the morning, whether he had really captured two nymphs who subsequently escaped or whether the whole episode was a hallucination. The italicized passages record the lucid recollections that break through the general somnolence. But fact and fancy blend just as the past with the present. By alternating the tenses, Mallarmé further blurs his picture and prevents our reading the poem as just an anecdote. Bernard Weinberg's commentary (*The Limits of Symbolism*) is a helpful guide through the poem stanza by stanza. Incidentally, Weinberg considers this poem "impressionistic" rather than symbolistic on the grounds that the faun does not symbolize anything. Such a distinction which Weinberg repeats throughout his book does not seem justified since what a symbolist poem "symbolizes" is not specific or precise. If the faun interests us, it is because he transcends his status as a mythological creature.

A. R. Chisholm distinguishes four themes in this poem that Mallarmé composed as if he were writing music, what Chisholm calls the themes of sensuality, of the dream, of art, and of memory. The faun's lust, his befuddled consciousness, the consolation of his pipes, his efforts to reconstruct the past are all stated in their place, then modulated as they combine with one another harmonically. (See *Mallarmé's L'Après-midi d'un Faune.*)

11. Faute=fault, error, or lack (absence)

Idéale=fancied but not real

De roses=based on color, confusion between flowers and nymphs.

12. Rivaling with.

13. Antecedent is *marécage*.

14. Image based on sunlight playing over the reeds.

15. The nymphs.

16. The faun is making pipes from the reeds.

17. Fauve=wild, as wild beast, here reinforcing the statement of heat=tawny color, as of a hot summer landscape.

18. Lys! Lily = male, with phallic symbol reinforced by exclamation mark. Rose = female.

19. Anticipates *morsure*.

20. The swelling and contracting involved in playing the double pipes.

21. Typical broken syntax . . . the reed . . . which dreams . . . that we . . . and dreams of letting escape . . . a sonorous line (melody). . . .

Robert Greer Cohn points out the affective quality of the letter sounds in the poem: bright, lucid *i*'s, dark *ou*'s, flat, mat *a*'s, etc. (*Toward the Poems of Mallarmé*, p. 21 and pass.). Mallarmé himself believed in letter values. Here the symbolism based on the form of the object named is reinforced by the appearance of the word: *lys* is narrow and upright, its sound is the acute *i*.

22. Syrinx, a nymph changed into a reed to escape Pan. She fled, just as the faun's nymphs have fled.

UN COUP DE DES[23]

JAMAIS

QUAND BIEN MEME LANCE DANS DES
CIRCONSTANCES ETERNELLES

DU FOND D'UN NAUFRAGE

SOIT

    que

          l'Abîme

  blanchi

     étale

      furieux

        sous une inclinaison

         plane désespérément

            d'aile

           la sienne

             par

avance retombée d'un mal à dresser le vol
et couvrant les jaillissements
coupant au ras les bonds

très à l'intérieur résume

l'ombre enfouie dans la profondeur par cette voile alternative

jusqu'adapter
à l'envergure

sa béante profondeur en tant que la coque

d'un bâtiment

penché de l'un ou l'autre bord

LE MAÎTRE

surgi
    inférant

        de cette conflagration

        que se

       comme on menace

    l'unique Nombre qui ne peut pas

           hésite
         cadavre par le bras
plutôt
    que de jouer
      en maniaque chenu
        la partie
        au nom des flots

            un

      naufrage cela

hors d'anciens calculs
où la manœuvre avec l'âge oubliée

jadis il empoignait la barre
à ses pieds
de l'horizon unanime

prépare
s'agite et mêle
au poing qui l'étreindrait
un destin et les vents

être un autre

Esprit
pour le jeter
dans la tempête
en reployer la division et passer fier

écarté du secret qu'il détient

envahit le chef
coule en barbe soumise

direct de l'homme

sans nef
n'importe
où vaine

ancestralement à n'ouvrir pas la main

crispée

par delà l'inutile tête

legs en la disparition

à quelqu'un ambigu

. . . .

23. Robert Greer Cohn (*Mallarmé's Un Coup de dés* and *Mallarmé's Masterwork*) has revealed the particularity of *Coup de dés* in Mallarmé's work. Whereas "Igitur" anticipates it most patently, in a sense all his previous poems lead to this one. Mallarmé conceived of it as nothing less than "l'explication orphique de la terre" (letter to Verlaine, 16 November 1885, *Autobiographie*). To obtain this ultimate achievement, Mallarmé called upon all the resources that he could muster, exploiting the sister arts and all aspects of language in an elaborately contrived scheme of relationships. Doubtless he had in mind Wagner's *gesamtkunstwerk*, the ideal of the times, for he thought of the poem as a symphony with recurring motifs. It is indeed a score, but a score that belongs also to the plastic arts, with its type various in size and sort and the ideographic grouping on each page. Position on the page itself has significance, with a median division separating the upper half from the lower. The direct sense of the words is enhanced by sound and anagrammatic association. Like de Saussure (see Jean Starobinski's presentation of the notebook of anagrams in *Les Mots sous les mots*, Gallimard, 1971), Mallarmé heard in words echoes of many others which he grouped into families or clusters. With the help of Littré, he explored origins and alternate definitions; where philology left off, Mallarmé's own imagination took over.

The poem springs from a blank page, nothingness, upon which is engendered the first words of the title and the central phrase: "Un coup de dés." Each page contains the seeds of what is to appear and develop upon the succeeding page, until the cycle is complete and the poem recedes into the oblivion from whence it came. Typographically and symbolically, the pattern of the Wave and all that is implied in this elemental form, is basic to the work's structure. The Wave is a rhythmic force inherent in all life, and in that source of all life, the Sea (*mer-mère*). Its crests and troughs are identified with the male-female polarity of human life, with the periodicity of history, the rise and fall of cultures and civilizations.

In the syntax of the poem, the page is taken as the unit, rather than the line. In the spatial relationships which arise, horizontally and vertically, on the page and between pages, various paradoxes are involved. For example, the crest is, Cohn tells us, "positive in relation to its trough on a vertical scale, negative on a horizontal scale, since the trough follows it and has the positive aspect of future (vs. past)" (*Un Coup de dés*, p. 17). Paradox is essentially involved in the metaphysical concept of dual polarity upon which the poem is constructed, a concept that advances the poem dialectically. A chain of proportions is generated, starting with the parent terms A^1 and A^2: positive:negative = synthesis: analysis = stasis:kinesis = male:female = unity:multiplicity = One:Two = concavity:

convexity, etc. Each page corresponds roughly to a level in the hierarchy of sciences, the correspondence being shown by examination of the textual content and by its ideogram.

For a detailed analysis of the poem, one should consult Cohn's exegesis. However, a word concerning the title. Critics following Albert Thibaudet have interpreted this poem as the disillusioned contradiction of "Igitur"—that the absolute is unattainable after all. Cohn and some others see the poem as merely the elaboration of the first, emphasizing the paradox implied in the title. *Hasard* may have the meaning of *coup de dés* itself, since the word stems from an Arabic word meaning dice. Thus we have a self-cancelling element already in the title which will develop in the poem into the chain of paradoxes that summarize all thought and the history of the world. One might also see in the word *dés* a suggestion of the word *deity*, suggesting an equally interesting interpretation.

Poetry of Verlaine

Œuvres Complètes de Paul Verlaine (Vanier, 1900). 5 vols.
Œuvres Poétiques Complètes (Gallimard, 1940). Texte établi et annoté par
    Y.-G. Le Dantec. Bibliothèque de la Pléïade.
Œuvres Complètes (Club du Meilleur Livre, 1959–1960). 2 vols. Texte
    établi par Bouillane de Lacoste, notes de Jacques Borel.

Readings

Adam, Antoine. Verlaine (Hatier, 1953). Translated by Carl Morse as The
    Art of Paul Verlaine (New York: New York University Press, 1963).
Carter, A. E. Verlaine (Boston: Twayne, 1971).
Cuénot, Claude. Le Style de Paul Verlaine (C.D.U., 1963).
Lepelletier, Edmond. Paul Verlaine, sa vie, son œuvre (Mercure de France,
    1907).
Richardson, Joanna. Verlaine (New York: Viking, 1971).
Underwood, Vernon P. Verlaine et l'Angleterre (Nizet, 1956).
Zayed, Georges. La Formation littéraire de Verlaine (Droz, 1962).

Paul Verlaine

1844–1896

Paul Verlaine was born in Metz in 1844. His father was an army officer who moved his wife and son around with him on his tours of duty. In 1851, however, Captain Verlaine had enough of the nomadic life in the provinces and, resigning his commission, went to settle in Paris. Paul grew up in a happy and indulgent home; as a young boy he was charming but very much spoiled. In school his work was quite uneven; worsening during adolescence to the point of getting his baccalauréat degree only by desperate cramming. A basic ambivalence seems to have taken hold of his personality from the age of fourteen on. Stronger even than with most adolescents, the urges toward wickedness and virtue disputed Verlaine's character. To look at his face, one would say that wickedness was winning out—the boy had become very ugly.

After his diploma, Verlaine was supposed to study law; but, spending his time in the cafés instead of the classrooms, he was put to work. Apparently an undistinguished but not very tiring job at the Hôtel de Ville satisfied him well enough, for there he stayed until his political posture at the time of the Commune forced him out. In the meantime, his father had died. Verlaine lived with his mother, who continued to treat him like a child, until he got married. The only dramatic aspect of this common-place story is Verlaine's drinking. It began as early as 1862 and soon thereafter became very serious because, under the influence of alcohol, this mild, sweet-natured man became violent. He would come home drunk and explode in fits of temper. In alarm, his mother consulted the relatives. They counseled marriage. Verlaine was agreeable and, in 1870, married the seventeen-year-old Mathilde Mauté. His drinking did not stop, however, and the young husband often made scenes and abused his wife.

In 1871, Rimbaud came into the picture. To the bad boy of Charleville, Verlaine had written "Venez, chère grande âme!" He came, and trouble started in earnest for Verlaine. The years that followed are ones of the separations and temporary reconciliations between Verlaine and Mathilde before the final estrangement; of the sojourns in Belgium and England that Verlaine made with Rimbaud—wretchedness and debauchery culminating in a prison sentence for Verlaine. Then additional years of expatriation, teaching in England. Lucien Létinois replaced Rimbaud as Verlaine's companion. Lucien got into trouble over a girl and the two Frenchmen left England in a hurry. They tried farming in France and failed. Lucien died suddenly of typhoid. At the same time, 1883, Verlaine's petition to be reinstated in the civil service was rejected. Misfortune seemed to have Verlaine hopelessly trapped. Ill, debauched, squandering whatever money came his way, "poor Lélian" [1] played out the rest of his life in the Bohemia of the Left Bank.

But as Verlaine the man sank lower and lower, the poet Verlaine began to win wide recognition and respect. During the latter 1880s, Verlaine occupied a place of high honor in the world of poetry. Young poets sat at his feet. When he died in 1896, several thousands of persons followed the hearse, and, at the graveside, the most eminent writers of the day pronounced orations.

Verlaine's career as a poet began while he was a high-school pupil. His first inspiration was Victor Hugo, then Baudelaire. That a boy should know *Les Fleurs du Mal* in 1861 is somewhat surprising, for at that date Baudelaire was not likely reading for a *lycéen*. In his *Confessions*, we learn that Verlaine had helped himself to a copy that a teaching assistant had left in a classroom. After graduation, Verlaine began to make literary contacts. He first joined the group around Louis-Xavier de Ricard, then met Catulle Mendès, Sully-Prudhomme, and Anatole France. In 1866, Verlaine felt ready to put together his first volume of verse, the *Poèmes Saturniens*. In it the evidence of a debt to Leconte de Lisle is less certain than has formerly been presumed. Baudelaire was Verlaine's real master, and the Parnassian virtues Verlaine professed were those that he found first in the author of *Les Fleurs du Mal*. There already Verlaine could observe the effects of artistic control and craftsmanship that he admired above all else. Among the influences on the young poet, Leconte de Lisle's place is secondary, shared with Banville and Gautier—even with Aloysius Bertrand.

The mood of Verlaine's first collection is one of plaintive melancholy. Baudelaire's spleen and Leconte de Lisle's aristocratic despair are reduced, attenuated, just as the grand style that characterizes the former poets turns with Verlaine into something intimate and humble. In place of sumptuous orchestration we find a light and graceful musical form— muted sounds, often just a murmur. In verse form, subject, mood, and in general treatment, Verlaine's originality and independence from his models is apparent throughout the volume. The little scenes of Paris and the fog-shrouded landscapes that we find there are products of restraint, but of a restraint due as much to a native inhibition or delicacy as to the Parnassian ideal of impassivity to which Verlaine subscribed at the time.¹ The *Poèmes Saturniens* were brought out by Lemerre of the Passage Choiseul, where Parnassian poets gathered and where, until recent years, one could still see in the dusty window the familiar little volumes of the firm. Verlaine's poems met with no success. The press, on the whole, ignored them, and, of the fellow poets to whom Verlaine sent copies, only Mallarmé realized their importance.

The *Fêtes Galantes* (1869) were somewhat more successful. Perhaps their admirers were taken by the remarkable unity of tone. Whereas the *Poèmes Saturniens* were something of a miscellany, this collection projected a consistent universe, the charming eighteenth century made popular by the Goncourts. Elegant figures from Watteau or Fragonard move about through formal gardens. Faded pastel colors, halftones, velvety textures, and wistful sentiments are evoked in the most delicate of rhythms. Verlaine plays with images and rimes, vying with Baudelaire's sense mingling and Parnassian metrical feats. His musical effects complement the pictures, help create the mood of melancholy and tender languor, typical of Verlaine.²

Shortly after the *Fêtes Galantes* appeared, Verlaine made the acquaintance of Mathilde, who would become his wife. Their engagement inspired his next collection, *La Bonne Chanson*. Verlaine is ready to put his life in order; he is going to marry a proper young woman and expects to find joy in bourgeois domesticity. These sentiments, which dominate the collection, are often expressed so directly that the impression is prosy. In his virtuous mood, the poet avoids artifices and feats of skill. For some critics this is good, the sign that Verlaine had broken with Parnasse and found his calling in an ingenuous and natural poetry. For others, this represents a blind alley and a mistake. But even for those who think thus, there are places in the volume where suggestive image and rhythm transpose, as formerly, raw sentiment into poetry of remarkable purity. Here, for example, is "La Lune blanche," utterly devoid of direct expression, but in which his love emanates through the landscape drenched in moonlight. The volume was printed in June of 1870. Again luck was against Verlaine: publicity for the book was started when war broke out and publication was deferred. When the book finally appeared in 1872, it passed unnoticed.

Already moving away from Parnasse with *La Bonne Chanson*, Verlaine made the definitive break before his next volume appeared. Initially it was more of a banishment, actually, than a repudiation—and on nonliterary grounds. After the war and the Commune, Leconte de Lisle, Coppée, and France would have nothing more to do with a man who had not been with them politically. Verlaine, accordingly, turned to other friends, in particular to the group which was founding a new review, *La Renaissance Littéraire et Artistique*. They had rejected the Parnassian doctrine for something more human and modern. Verlaine's *Romances Sans Paroles* (1874) demonstrate the esthetic convictions of the "Groupe des Vivants," the anti-Parnassians. Unlike the poems of *La Bonne Chanson*, the ones here depend entirely upon suggestion. Argument and description are extremely reduced; little remains but images and sonorities to evoke those landscapes that translate the soul-states of the poet. The poems were composed during years of emotional turmoil for Verlaine. They were the years of his marriage, his encounter with Rimbaud, his sojourn in Belgium and in England. In many instances it is easy to relate a poem to a given event or occurrence, thus explaining the soul-state depicted. It is with this volume also, that one may study the effect of Verlaine's contacts with the Impressionist painters. Manet, Fantin-Latour, and others were personal acquaintances; Verlaine adopted for poetry the ideas that the new painters were formulating for their own art. Although not published until eight years later, the celebrated "Art poétique" calling for nuance and nonchalance dates from 1874.

During the 1870s, Verlaine's concept of poetry continued to evolve. His head was full of ideas of new undertakings such as grandiose word paintings depicting things with no human presence involved. But nothing came of this idea which would have made Verlaine a precursor of Francis Ponge and Robbe-Grillet. He carried out his ambition, however, of taking up the old Romantic practice of narrative poems and told the story of the madly Promethean quest that he had engaged upon with his companion who aspired to be God or the Devil. Rimbaud was the greatest influence upon Verlaine and was doubtless the one who encouraged

Verlaine to push beyond simple impressionism toward the zones of the poetic absolute. Already adept at painting soul-states in terms of landscape, Verlaine now would approach the allegory directly. As to the specific form of some of his allegorical verse, one may see a similarity with the English tradition. And as to content, there are suggestions of other contacts in the poems written after Verlaine was sent to prison at Mons and after his conversion: Spanish mystics and modern Catholic thinkers like Joseph de Maistre. Verlaine's newly found faith led him, moreover, to the Middle Ages "énorme et délicat," as described in one of his sonnets. Several times during the 1870s, Verlaine made plans to publish collections of his verse. Not until 1881 did *Sagesse* appear, however. It was a miscellany, made up of poems of different years and different moods. The dominating inspiration is religious, and this is strong enough to give the impression of unity and coherence. It has often been considered Verlaine's masterpiece. The public of 1881 did not recognize it as such, however, for it met with no success at all. If Verlaine had counted on the Catholic faction to support him and counteract the hostility of the Parnassians, he was mistaken. His publisher stacked the copies of *Sagesse* in his cellar.

Paul Verlaine's success came in the mid-eighties. Toward the end of 1882, when the "Art poétique" first appeared in the periodical *Paris-Moderne*, young poets began to take notice. They saw the "Art poétique" as the reply to "L'Art" of Théophile Gautier, and rejection of sculpture in favor of music, of plasticity in favor of fluidity, of eloquence in favor of irony met with their full endorsement. The following year they hailed the *Poètes maudits*. Verlaine was particularly acclaimed by the "Décadents" of the Left Bank; the leader of the "Symbolistes" was Stéphane Mallarmé. For awhile, in spite of self-deprecatory remarks, Verlaine took his role seriously. He held "Wednesdays" and preached a new idealism to replace the fin-de-siècle pessimism that had given the group its name and to counteract Naturalism and Parnassianism as well. In the matter of poetic expression, Verlaine developed the points made already in the "Art poétique." Young poets gravitated either toward Verlaine and his "poésie de la vie" or toward Mallarmé and his "poésie métaphysique." In the quarrels that ensued between the two factions, Verlaine was obliged to take part and for several years he became quite involved in issues that mingled politics, personalities, and poetic theory. By 1890, however, he was alone again.

Perhaps because of the recognition that was coming his way during the 1880s, Verlaine was stirred to new creative efforts. In 1885, he published *Jadis et Naguère*, a miscellany of pieces left over from earlier publications along with some new ones. His young followers could read here the latest chapter in the Verlaine drama of spirituality and abjection expressed in verses of remarkable power. Less given to suave harmonies than formerly, Verlaine created here poetry of greater density and sophistication. It is clear that, in spite of personal miseries, Verlaine still had a good supply of courage and hope. He went to work on two great projects, the first continuing *Sagesse* and illustrating the divine theme, the second dealing with the theme of the flesh. *Amour, Bonheur,* and *Liturgies intimes* make up the first group, which was finished by 1892. *Parallèlement* and some other volumes constitute the second. These volumes stretch over all the rest of Verlaine's life, the last one, *Chair,* appearing posthumously. They are unequal, marred by didacticism, personal rancors, and dubious sincerity and taste. But if the pieces that make up these volumes show the weakening of Verlaine's powers, they show also his ability, on occasion, to muster his faculties and create beautiful, moving verse.

Precisely because he never lost that ability, his popularity as a poet has always been assured. And the scandal of his personal life to which it relates has added the factor of great human appeal. But for some critics, Verlaine is just an unfortunate man and a sweet, melancholy singer. He is just the author of lovely mood poems, poems of sustained sadness or dreamy nostalgia through which we can follow the poet's life and his desires, errors, repentances. But he is not a seminal force in the development of poetry. It is true that in spite of his association with Parnasse, Impressionism, Symbolism, and other *isms* of the period, Verlaine never seemed to take theory very seriously and never stayed long in any group that he joined. Did he not say, "L'art, mes enfants, c'est d'être absolument soi-même?" Too personal to subscribe to Parnassian ideals, too little of a philosopher to embrace the Symbolist point of view, too optimistic to be a Decadent, Verlaine was never wholly committed to any doctrine. Yet it is not right to see in him only a spontaneous lyricist. If theory interested him little, poetic technique was his constant concern and, to achieve the muted, musical effects that he sought, he suppressed the logical order of words, used words in strange senses, let rhythms take over for rime. His role in the gradual liberation of French verse, his innovations in rhythm and diction cannot be denied. And since these metrical changes were created to serve not only personal expression but evolving concepts of poetry, Verlaine deserves a place among the shapers of literary history. The concept of poetry as inner revelation and cosmic communication, as a means of crossing the barrier of reason, had been the great discovery of Romanticism and the stimulus for the greatest poetic accomplishments of the century. Yet neither Baudelaire nor Nerval departed very much from traditional forms. Only Verlaine created in language and prosody something really new, eminently adapted to the inspiration of the day. For this, the younger generation treated him as a master and attributed to him even, as in the matter of free verse, a revolutionary intention greater than he actually possessed. They were not wrong, however, in the widest sense, for Verlaine represents a link in the chain that leads to today and, on the way, to Symbolism.

Notes

1. "Pauvre Lélian," an epithet created out of the anagram of Paul Verlaine.
2. The mood had, however, already been struck by Victor Hugo. Certain of his poems influenced Verlaine directly. See Verlaine, *Œuvres Poétiques Complètes*, pp. 893–95. Bibliothèque de la Pléïade.

MON REVE FAMILIER[1]

Je fais souvent ce rêve étrange et pénétrant
D'une femme inconnue, et que j'aime, et qui m'aime,
Et qui n'est, chaque fois, ni tout à fait la même
Ni tout à fait une autre, et m'aime et me comprend.

Car elle me comprend, et mon cœur, transparent
Pour elle seule, hélas! cesse d'être un problème
Pour elle seule, et les moiteurs de mon front blême,
Elle seule les sait rafraîchir, en pleurant.

Est-elle brune, blonde ou rousse?—Je l'ignore.
Son nom? Je me souviens qu'il est doux et sonore
Comme ceux des aimés que la Vie exila.[2]

Son regard est pareil au regard des statues,
Et, pour sa voix, lointaine, et calme, et grave, elle a[3]
L'inflexion des voix chères qui se sont tues.

---

1. "Mon Rêve familier" was published in Verlaine's first volume, the *Poèmes Saturniens*, 1866. Saturnine, which has here the sense of gloomy, morose, may have been picked up from Baudelaire, for it appears in "Epigraphe pour un livre condamné," *Parnasse Contemporain*, 1866, as an epithet used by Baudelaire to describe his *Fleurs du Mal*. J. Bornecque, musing over the incantatory quality of this poem, suggests that it might be caused by the ambivalent character of the word *rêve*, which never defines itself clearly, being now literal now figurative in the sense of nostalgia. Professor Bornecque also reports a touching episode in which the old poet, mellowed by a few absinthes, begins a beautiful recital of this poem in a café. The charm is broken when his companion, the harridan Marie Krantz, bursts in and leads Verlaine off. See *Les Poèmes Saturniens de Paul Verlaine* (Nizet, 1952); pp. 158–60.

2. Who are already dead.

3. For André Gide's commentary on this enjambement, see *Les Cahiers d'André Walter* (Gallimard, 1952, 18th ed.), pp. 140–41. The narrator observes that the violated caesuras give an extraordinary rhythm to the line, dragging it on to what seems like fourteen syllables. With its tempo and alliteration, it gives "l'impression de pas lents qui s'en vont dans un éloignement immuable."

CHANSON D'AUTOMNE[4]

Les sanglots longs
Des violons[5]
   De l'automne
Blessent mon cœur
D'une langueur
   Monotone.

Tout suffocant
Et blême, quand
   Sonne l'heure,
Je me souviens
Des jours anciens
   Et je pleure;

Et je m'en vais
Au vent mauvais
   Qui m'emporte
Deça, delà,
Pareil à la
   Feuille morte.

4. From the *Poèmes Saturniens*, one of the best known of Verlaine's poems. Although it is strongly a mood poem, we have it on the testimony of Edmond Lepelletier that Verlaine is not expressing his own feelings but performing an artistic exercise (see Verlaine, *Œuvres Poétiques Complètes*, p. 890). Be that as it may, it is a remarkable example of fusion (season, landscape, mood) that, since Baudelaire, is a pattern for poetry. It is, one might add, the pattern of the Japanese poem, the haiku.

The rhythm pattern is 4+4+3, with each sequence ending on a feminine rime. Such originality seems all the more remarkable when one remembers that at the time the poem was composed, 1864, the Parnassian ideal of rigid formality prevailed.

The musicality of this poem is analyzed schematically by Guy Michaud (*L'Œuvre et ses techniques*, Nizet, 1957). Verlaine's recourse to alliteration and to the nasals which suggest the sound of violins, to daring run-over lines and resonant rimes has always been noted as contributing to the particular charm of the poem. Here Michaud makes a complete census of its vowel and consonantal sonorities. Among vowels, the *o* sound is recognized as dominant and responsible for over-all tonality. It is seconded by the variations of *o* circumflex and *o* nasal. The contrasting vowel theme is *eu* and *è* which, with the *o*'s, gives the poem a distinct vowel pattern. Consonants, on the other hand, lack importance and create merely a sort of blurred background for the liquids and nasals.

In conclusion, Michaud ties up the vocalic themes of the *o*'s and *e*'s and the auditory theme of the violins with the topic theme of autumn, concretely represented only by one item—the dead leaf. He notes, furthermore, that all these themes combine to establish the affective quality of the poem.

5. The "sobbing violins" are usually understood as an epithet for winds. Actually they need not be defined so specifically. The poem is free from explicit description as it is free from meditation or discourse.

CLAIR DE LUNE[6]

Votre âme est un paysage choisi[7]
Que vont charmant masques et bergamasques,[8]
Jouant du luth, et dansant, et quasi
Tristes sous leurs déguisements fantasques.

Tout en chantant sur le mode mineur
L'amour vainqueur et la vie opportune,
Ils n'ont pas l'air de croire à leur bonheur
Et leur chanson se mêle au clair de lune,

Au calme clair de lune triste et beau,
Qui fait rêver les oiseaux dans les arbres
Et sangloter d'extase les jets d'eau,
Les grands jets d'eau sveltes parmi les marbres.[9]

6. From the collection *Fêtes Galantes*. This poem originally bore the title later given to the volume. It appeared under that title in *La Gazette Rimée*, 1867. C. F. MacIntyre says that it is perhaps Verlaine's first purely Symbolist achievement. The lady's soul is the real subject, but the trope makes the poem. See *Paul Verlaine: Selected Poems* (Berkeley: University of California Press, 1970), p. 208.

7. *Choisi* meaning composed, a composed landscape as if on canvas, suggests immediately that the poem is based on a painting. As a matter of fact, Watteau is mentioned in the manuscript.

8. In *Midsummer Night's Dream*, Bottom speaks of a Bergomask dance (act 5, scene 2), and one might think that Shakespeare is Verlaine's source. But here the word refers to a person. The characters of the *Commedia dell'Arte* are each associated with a certain

city in Italy, Brighello and Harlequin being from Bergamo. *Vont charmant* must mean that the masks and Bergamasks are rendering the landscape delightful, *charmant*.

9. J. P. Weber, who "psychoanalyzes" the works that he studies, finds that in many of Verlaine's poems there is symbolic representation of peeling statues in a park. It crops up here in the reference to marbles. See *Genèse de l'Œuvre Poétique* (Gallimard, 1960), p. 318.

> Il pleut doucement sur la ville.
> (Arthur Rimbaud)[10]

Il pleure dans mon cœur[11]
Comme il pleut sur la ville.
Quelle est cette langueur
Qui pénètre mon cœur?

O bruit doux de la pluie
Par terre et sur les toits!
Pour un cœur qui s'ennuie,
O le chant de la pluie!

Il pleure sans raison
Dans ce cœur qui s'écœure.
Quoi! nulle trahison?
Ce deuil est sans raison.

C'est bien la pire peine
De ne savoir pourquoi,
Sans amour et sans haine,
Mon cœur a tant de peine.

10. The epigraph is doubtless taken from a poem that is lost, because the lines do not figure in any known work of Rimbaud.

11. The poems of *Romances sans paroles*, Verlaine's fourth volume of verse, were for the most part written in 1872 and are the first to be affected by Verlaine's association with Arthur Rimbaud. Rimbaud's influence is here apparent in the metrical innovations such as the assonance and the uneven lines. The poem was set to music by Debussy and by Fauré.

Guy Michaud performs on this poem the same sort of schematic analysis as on the
"Chanson d'automne" (*L'Œuvre et ses techniques*, pp. 75–79). The two poems, separated
by eight years, resemble each other in tone and musical suggestivity. Yet Michaud's
analysis reveals clear differences in sonorous make-up. Here the *o* theme has almost
entirely disappeared in favor of what was the counter theme in the earlier poem, the *eu*
and *è*. Michaud finds consonants more important in this poem, particularly *p*, *k*, and *s*,
which combine with the vowel themes to establish a sonorous pattern. As for the plastic
and affective themes, the rain here replaces the wind, but the landscape remains vague
and imprecise. There is, moreover, the same translation of mood into external nature.
Michaud's analysis concludes with the tracing through each stanza what he calls a drama
—in other words, the progressive stages in the psychological crisis that the poem records.
Thus he has treated one by one the poem's pattern of sonorities, of allusion to natural
phenomena, of mood and finally its story content. All the thematic material is mutually
supporting and all contributes to the total effect of the poem.

ART POETIQUE[12]

De la musique avant toute chose,
Et pour cela préfère l'Impair[13]
Plus vague et plus soluble dans l'air,
Sans rien en lui qui pèse ou qui pose.

Il faut aussi que tu n'ailles point
Choisir tes mots sans quelque méprise :
Rien de plus cher que la chanson grise[14]
Où l'Indécis au Précis se joint.

C'est des beaux yeux derrière des voiles,
C'est le grand jour tremblant de midi,
C'est, par un ciel d'automne attiédi,
Le bleu fouillis des claires étoiles !

Car nous voulons la Nuance encor,
Pas la Couleur, rien que la nuance !
Oh ! la nuance seule fiance
Le rêve au rêve et la flûte au cor !

Fuis du plus loin la Pointe[15] assassine,

L'Esprit cruel et le Rire impur,
Qui font pleurer les yeux de l'Azur,
Et tout cet ail de basse cuisine!

Prends l'éloquence et tords-lui son cou!
Tu feras bien, en train d'énergie,
De rendre un peu la Rime assagie,
Si l'on n'y veille, elle ira jusqu'où?

O qui dira les torts de la Rime!
Quel enfant sourd ou quel nègre fou
Nous a forgé ce bijou d'un sou
Qui sonne creux et faux sous la lime?

De la musique encore et toujours!
Que ton vers soit la chose envolée
Qu'on sent qui fuit d'une âme en allée
Vers d'autres cieux à d'autres amours.

Que ton vers soit la bonne aventure
Eparse au vent crispé du matin
Qui va fleurant la menthe et le thym ...[16]
Et tout le reste est littérature.[17]

---

12. Although written in 1874, this poem was not published until 1882 when it appeared in the periodical *Paris-moderne*. It found its permanent place in 1884 in the volume *Jadis et Naguère*. Some critics have questioned how seriously Verlaine took the precepts he formulates here, suggesting that he may have been spoofing a bit since, for example, he himself never abandoned rime. Moreover, in the preface that Verlaine wrote for a new edition of some poems in 1890, he declared that the "Art poétique" should not be taken literally—"n'est qu'une chanson, après tout." (See *Œuvres Poétiques Complètes*, p. 888.) It is difficult to believe, notwithstanding, that he was anything but serious. Although his poetry does not go to the limits of the direction in which he points, it goes a long way —farther, in fact, than most writers' work goes in the direction of their theory. It might be correct, however, to look at this poem more as a protest against poetry of the past rather than as a blueprint for poetry of the future. The barbs directed at Romanticism and Parnassianism are very apparent. Théodore de Banville, in his *Petit Traité de la Poésie Française*, published only two years before, had summed up the Parnassian ideal, empha- sizing more than ever the importance of rime. This work, along with the Leconte de Lisle preface to *Poèmes antiques* (1852) is surely among Verlaine's principal targets. The Symbolists of the eighties hailed the "Art poétique" as the reply to "L'Art" of Théophile Gautier. Although Verlaine may have intended his poem partly as just a means of settling personal scores with former colleagues, the Symbolists made it a credo and considered

its author the "grand patron," exactly as the Impressionists were considering Edouard Manet, who had advocated similar reforms for painting. Rejection that the poem advocated of sculpture in favor of music, of plasticity in favor of fluidity, of eloquence in favor of irony met with their full endorsement. Abroad, the fame of the "Art Poétique" was enormous—poets like Rubén Darío would paraphrase it to foment revolution in their native literature.

13. Verse of three, five, seven, nine, or eleven syllables. Here Verlaine is using a nine-syllable line.

14. The adjective doubtless is intended to suggest vagueness.

15. Contrived witticism, epigram.

16. Poetry should be like the careless song of a vagabond gypsy girl running gaily along at dawn. See C. F. MacIntyre, *Paul Verlaine: Selected Poems*, p. 222.

17. This poem is so well known that the use of the word *literature* in this derogatory sense is widely understood. Thus the Surrealists, to show their contempt for conventional writing, called their review *Littérature*.

Les Amours Jaunes

Les Amours Jaunes (Glady Frères, 1873).
Les Amours Jaunes (Crès, 1920). Notice by René Martineau.
Les Amours Jaunes (Gallimard, 1973). Preface by Henri Thomas.
Œuvres complètes de Tristan Corbière (Gallimard, 1970). Edited by P. O. Walzer. Bibliothèque de la Pléïade.
The Centenary Corbière. Poems and Prose of Tristan Corbière (Chester Springs, Pa.: Dufour Editions, 1975). Translated and with an introduction by Val Warner.

Readings

Burch, Francis F. Tristan Corbière, L'Originalité des "Amours Jaunes" et leur influence sur T. S. Eliot (Nizet, 1970).

Grin, Micha. Tristan Corbière, poète maudit (Evian: Nant d'Enfer, 1971).

Laforgue, Jules. "Notes sur Baudelaire, Corbière, Mallarmé, Rimbaud," Entretiens Politiques et Littéraires 11 (1891): 20–32.

Lindsay, Marshall. Le Temps Jaune, Essais sur Corbière (Berkeley: University of California Press, 1972).

Martineau, René. Tristan Corbière (Divan, 1925).

Sonnenfeld, Albert. L'Œuvre Poétique de Tristan Corbière (Presses Universitaires de France, 1960).

Thomas Henri. Tristan le dépossédé (Gallimard, 1972).

Edouard-Joachim Corbière, known as "Tristan Corbière"

1845–1875

Revealed by Verlaine, who included him in his *Poètes maudits* (1884), Tristan Corbière fully merits the epithet of poet accursed. He died at the age of thirty after a life of illness and failure. Two years before, his single volume of poems appeared, the testament of an unhappy man. Yet in a gallery of unhappy poets, the place of Corbière is somewhat distant from that of patient sufferers like Verlaine himself and others associated with the Symbolist movement. Corbière struck back at life with a sneer. His place is near Rimbaud's, both rebels one hundred percent, who refused to adjust and comply, who could not be satisfied with anything short of death itself.

Corbière was born near Morlaix in Brittany, the son of a swashbuckling ship captain who had become famous as an author of novels about the sea. Edouard Corbière elder was already past fifty when he married a girl of eighteen and settled down to a life of retirement and domestic felicity. Of their three children, Edouard-Joachim was the oldest. Both father and mother were apparently overindulgent toward their frail and precocious firstborn, whose affectionate, cajoling ways got him generally what he wanted. At the age of twelve, however, he was sent off to boarding school, and the happy part of his life was over. Lonely and sickly and painfully aware that he was not at all good-looking, the boy knew profound misery. The worsening state of his health delivered him ultimately from the prison of school. At the age of fifteen, rheumatism took him out for a time; two years later he was out for good. His mother took him south to

Provence, but he did not seem to improve. They returned to Morlaix. Finally, on the advice of the family doctor, he was settled in the nearby port of Roscoff, where his father owned a summer place. Corbière's bad health had got him out of school, but had dashed forever his dreams of the future. The boy who idolized his father and dreamed of rivaling his life of seafaring adventure was an invalid and a cripple.

In Roscoff, famous for its mild weather, Corbière remained most of every year, all by himself, reading his books, sailing his boat, riding bareback on his horse with his dog following along behind. He dragged his boat into the parlor and used it for a bed; he spread his nets to dry in the bedroom. When the need for company overtook him, he went off to the local restaurant-bar, where he could chat with the sailors or the old fishermen who frequented the place. They called him *ankou*, which means "specter of death," and he was a grotesque figure indeed. Alexandre Arnoux describes him after the pencil-sketch caricature that Corbière had made of himself: "Rugueux, disloqué, craquant de toutes ses jointures, il pousse contre le vent du large, sa carcasse mal lubrifiée, ses vastes oreilles, son nez, pareil à une burlesque étrave."[1] Corbière's reaction to his uncomely appearance was to exaggerate it; to his good-for-nothing existence, to playact. He called himself Tristan and, in rags and pirate boots, he played the absurd roles that he invented for himself; entertaining the yokels of Morlaix and Roscoff with his practical jokes—and shocking the good burghers.

The winter of 1868–69 Corbière spent in Italy travelling with a friend. The land so dear to the Romantics disappointed him, as he plainly states in his verses, and he returned to Roscoff to take up his old life of carousing and playing the enfant terrible. There he passed the months of the war. Not long after the armistice Corbière met the love of his life, "Marcelle," who had accompanied one Count Rodolphe de Battine to Roscoff on a holiday. The Count seems not to have taken offense at Corbière's infatuation with his mistress and tolerated his persistent company. For the few years that Corbière would have left to live, this curious triangle continued, Corbière following his friends to Paris in the winter and leading them back to Brittany in the summer. His unrequited affection deepened his bitterness. In love as in all else he had failed, and his insufficiencies were to him all the more painful since they revealed how different he was from his brilliant and dashing father. He did not like Paris and remained there only to be near the Battine couple. When not with them, he was with a couple of painters that he had known in Roscoff, or alone, writing his verses. A few he placed in *La Vie Parisienne*, and toward the end of 1873, he brought out a collection, calling the volume *Les Amours Jaunes*.

What is meant by the *jaune* of the title is moot. Ordinarily it is taken in the sense of *rire jaune*, an epithet which suggests Corbière's typical sarcasm and self-mockery. However, Albert Sonnenfeld, chiding French critics for not using their dictionary enough, declares that yellow is given by Littré as being Judas's color and therefore the word should mean betrayed.[2] Anna Balakian reminds us that yellow standing for mourning goes back to Swedenborg.[3] Whatever Corbière had in mind precisely, the title expresses marvelously well the mood of the poems.

As for the presentation of the poems, the collection is framed by a prologue and an epilogue, both parodying *La Cigale et la Fourmi*. The poems themselves are grouped in six main divisions, the first three dealing with Paris and Marcelle, the second with Brittany and the sea. Organization is entirely thematic, chronology of composition being utterly ignored. The poems are sonnets, songs, ballads, rondels, and other recognizable forms, but the genre is usually just approximate and the metrical scheme adapted to suit the author's purpose. Uneven lines abound and there are alexandrines with thirteen syllables. The language is racy and slangy, conversational rather than poetic, appropriate to the wry humor of the pieces. In addition to the oral quality of the language, word play and the free association of images do much to establish this mood, Corbière's trademark. Needless to say, when *Les Amours Jaunes* appeared, the volume was not widely appreciated. The ideal of the day, one must remember, was the Parnassian: lofty beauty and perfection of form. Corbière's rough verse had no more of either than of the mellifluous harmony of some of the Symbolists.

Apparently Corbière was not unduly affected by the indifferent reception that his book was given. After sending copies to his family and friends, he set to work on a new collection that he intended to call *Mirlitons*. But he did not have time to finish it. In December 1874, his health broke completely. His mother took him home to Morlaix, where he lingered only a short time. It is said that on the evening before his death, he had his room filled with great sheaves of heather gathered on the moors that he loved.

Works like *Les Amours Jaunes* cannot be separated from the tragic lives that lie behind them. If Corbière's life is a sort of allegory of the life of a poet, his poetry is but the expression of that life, to the point where one becomes merely an aspect of the other. It is not that he was a "primitive" in the sense of being untutored or naive, as some of his contemporaries supposed. He knew his poets very well and had definite ideas concerning matters of technique and art. The faults that were ascribed to him by Laforgue, Gourmont, and other critics were conscious liberties, as can be proved by the number of poems in which the versification is impeccable. To think him incapable of counting syllables is an absurdity, as subsequent critics such as René Martineau and Jean Rousselot have indignantly remarked. His line long or short, smooth or broken, is deliberately struc-tured so and, if here and there it limps, it does so for an effect. The same may be said for his diction, which ignores categories of style, and for his images, which justify Breton's remark about Corbière having an "écriture en éclairs et en ellipses."[4] Poetry for Corbière was not technique, not art, but "dans *la chose*."[5] Poetry is the cry from the heart—in his case, a raucous, rough cry cut short by sarcasm—what Jules Laforgue referred to as his old "crincrin."[6] As poetry, it may rasp like an old fiddle or the bagpipes of Brittany, but *Les Amours Jaunes* may well be the most beautiful, notwithstanding, collection of verse to place between *Les Fleurs du Mal* and *Romance sans Paroles*.

Although somewhat outside the mainstream of French poetry, it con-stitutes a link between the Romantic school and the Symbolists. In theme and attitude, its association with Romanticism is evident, an association of course underlined by allusion and imitation of Romantic poets. One thinks of "Le Crapaud," which recalls Hugo's famous poem of the same title. Hugo's poem and Corbière's offer interesting comparison in that each is typical of its author. As for technique, in Corbière there is nothing of the bombast, heavy effects, and moralizing anecdote that characterize Hugo. A scene is evoked by a few brief strokes, sentiments expressed by epithets, movement obtained by fragmentary monologue. As for theme, Corbière reduces the scope to his own person, the disgust and horror that he inspires in himself. Georges-Emmanual Clancier speaks of Corbière being "un Narcisse muré dans la haineuse contemplation de sa laideur."[7] The scorn for Hugo, which Corbière expresses here and there in *Les Amours Jaunes*, does not, of course, preclude influence. In general, Corbière is less hard on the Romantics than on the Parnassians, because sentimen-tality was less inimical to him than the plastic ideal of impersonal form, but he seems to have been truly fond only of Musset and Baudelaire.[8] In its turn, *Les Amours Jaunes* has made a mark in French poetry from the Symbolists to the present day. Brought to Verlaine's attention almost ten years after its publication, it may have inspired some of that poet's latter verse—particularly in the matter of syntax. The influence of *Les Amours Jaunes* on Laforgue is notorious, Laforgue being drawn to Corbière at first but then retreating because of comparison with his own work. Yet he owed this "country cousin" more than he would admit. After Symbolism one may trace evidence of Corbière's influence all along the way from Apollinaire (sentimental themes mitigated by irony, typography and punctuation) to Raymond Roussel and André Breton. Breton could admire in Corbière his technique of free association and his humor black enough to merit a place in Breton's anthology.

Notes

1. Preface to *Les Amours Jaunes* (Librairie Celtique, 1947), p. 13.

2. Sonnenfeld, *L'Œuvre Poétique de Tristan Corbière*, p. 48.

3. Balakian, *The Symbolist Movement*, p. 25. See also Sainte-Beuve, "Les Rayons Jaunes."

4. *Anthologie de l'humour noir* (1940).

5. The expression is from Corbière's cousin, who is stating Corbière's position. Cited by René Martineau, *Tristan Corbière*, p. 93.

6. Jules Laforgue, "Tristan Corbière," *Entretiens Politiques et Littéraires* (July 1891).

7. Clancier, *De Rimbaud au Surréalisme* (Seghers, 1953), p. 80.

8. See Sonnenfeld, *L'Œuvre Poétique*, chap. 8.

LE POETE CONTUMACE

Sur la côte d'ARMOR. — Un ancien vieux couvent.[1]
Les vents se croyaient là dans un moulin à vent,
        Et les ânes de la contrée,
Au lierre râpé venaient râper leurs dents
Contre un mur si troué que, pour entrer dedans,
        On n'aurait pu trouver l'entrée.

— Seul — mais toujours debout avec un rare aplomb,
Crénelé comme la mâchoire d'une vieille,
Son toit à coups de poing sur le coin de l'oreille,
Aux corneilles bayant, se tenait le donjon,

Fier toujours d'avoir eu, dans le temps, sa légende ...
Ce n'était plus qu'un nid à gens de contrebande,
Vagabonds de nuit, amoureux buissonniers,
Chiens errants, vieux rats, fraudeurs et douaniers.

— Aujourd'hui l'hôte était de la borgne tourelle,
Un poète sauvage, avec un plomb dans l'aile ;
Et tombé là parmi les antiques hiboux
Qui l'estimaient d'en haut. — Il respectait leurs trous,
Lui, seul hibou payant, comme son *bail* le porte :
Pour vingt-cinq écus l'an, dont : remettre une porte. —[2]

Pour les gens du pays, il ne les voyait pas :
Seulement, en passant, eux regardaient d'en bas,
        Se montrant du nez sa fenêtre ;
Le curé se doutait que c'était un lépreux ;
Et le maire disait : — Moi, qu'est-ce que j'y peux,
        C'est plutôt un Anglais ... un *Etre.*

Les femmes avaient su — sans doute par les buses —
Qu'il *vivait en concubinage avec des Muses !* ...
Un hérétique enfin ... Quelque *Parisien*
De Paris ou d'ailleurs — Hélas ! on n'en sait rien. —
Il était invisible ; et, comme *ses Donzelles*
Ne s'affichaient pas trop, on ne parla plus d'elles.

— Lui, c'était simplement un long flâneur, sec, pâle ;
Un ermite-amateur, chassé par la rafale ...

Il avait trop aimé les beaux pays malsains.
Condamné des huissiers, comme des médecins,
Il avait posé là, soûl et cherchant sa place
Pour mourir seul ou pour vivre par contumace ...

Faisant, d'un à peu près d'artiste,
Un philosophe d'à peu près,
Râleur de soleil ou de frais,
En dehors de l'humaine piste.[3]

Il lui restait encore un hamac, une vielle,
Un barbet qui dormait sous le nom de *Fidèle ;*
Non moins fidèle était, triste et doux comme lui,
Un autre compagnon qui s'appelait l'Ennui.

Se mourant en sommeil, il se vivait en rêve,
Son rêve était le flot qui montait sur la grève,
                    Le flot qui descendait ;
Quelquefois, vaguement, il se prenait attendre...
Attendre quoi ... le flot monter — le flot descendre —
                    Ou l'Absente ... Qui sait ?

Le sait-il bien lui-même ! ... Au vent de sa guérite,
A-t-il donc oublié comme les morts vont vite ?
Lui, ce viveur vécu, revenant égaré,
Cherche-t-il son follet, à lui, mal enterré ?

— Certes. Elle n'est pas loin, celle après qui tu brâmes,
O Cerf de Saint-Hubert ! Mais ton front est sans flammes.[4]
N'apparais pas, mon vieux, triste et faux déterré ...
Fais le mort si tu peux... Car Elle t'a pleuré !

— Est-ce qu'il pouvait, Lui ! ... n'était-il pas poète ...
Immortel comme un autre ? ... Et dans sa pauvre tête
Déménagée, encore il sentait que les vers
Hexamètres faisaient les cent pas de travers.

— Manque de savoir-vivre extrême — il survivait —
Et — manque de savoir mourir — il écrivait :

"C'est un être passé de cent lunes, ma Chère,
En ton cœur poétique, à l'état légendaire.
Je rime, donc je vis ... ne crains pas, c'est *à blanc,*

— Une coquille d'huître en rupture de banc! —
Oui, j'ai beau me palper; c'est moi! Dernière faute —
En route pour les cieux — car ma niche est si haute! —
Je me suis demandé, prêt à prendre l'essor:
Tête ou pile ... — Et voilà — je me demande encor ... "

"C'est à toi que je fis mes adieux à la vie,
A toi qui me pleuras, jusqu'à me faire envie
De rester me pleurer avec toi. Maintenant
C'est joué, je ne suis qu'un gâteux revenant,
En os et ... (j'allais dire en chair). — La chose est sûre.
C'est bien moi, je suis là — mais comme une rature."

"Nous étions amateurs de curiosité:
Viens voir *le Bibelot*. — Moi j'en suis dégoûté. —
Dans mes dégoûts surtout, j'ai des goûts élégants;
Tu sais: j'avais lâché la Vie avec des gants;
L'*Autre* n'est pas même à prendre avec des pincettes ...
Je cherche au mannequin de nouvelles toilettes."

"Reviens m'aider: Tes yeux dans ces yeux-là! Ta lèvre
Sur cette lèvre! ... Et, là, ne sens-tu pas ma fièvre
— Ma *fièvre de Toi?* ... — Sous l'orbe est-il passé
L'arc-en-ciel au charbon par nos nuits laissé?
Et cette étoile? ... — Oh! va, ne cherche plus l'étoile
                    Que tu voulais voir à mon front;
                    Une araignée a fait sa toile,[5]
                    Au même endroit — dans le plafond."

"Je suis un étranger. — Cela vaut mieux peut-être ...
— Et bien! non, viens encore un peu me reconnaître;
Comme au bon saint Thomas, je veux te voir la foi.
Je veux te voir toucher la plaie et dire: — Toi! —
"Viens encore me finir — c'est très gai. De ta chambre,[6]
Tu verras mes moissons — Nous sommes en décembre —
Mes grands bois de sapins, les fleurs d'or des genêts,
Mes bruyères d'Armor ... — en tas sur les chenêts.
Viens te gorger d'air pur — Ici j'ai de la brise
Si franche! ... que le bout de ma toiture en frise.

Le soleil est si doux ... — qu'il gèle tout le temps.
Le printemps ... — Le printemps, n'est-ce pas tes vingt ans?
On n'attend plus que toi, vois: déjà l'hirondelle
Se pose ... en fer rouillé, clouée à ma tourelle. —
Et bientôt nous pourrons cueillir le champignon ...
Dans mon escalier que dore ... un lumignon.
Dans le mur qui verdoie existe une pervence
Sèche. — ... Et puis nous irons à l'eau *faire* la planche
— Planche d'épave au sec — comme moi — sur ces plages.
La Mer roucoule sa *Berceuse pour naufrages;*
Barcarolle du soir ... pour les canards sauvages."

"En *Paul et Virginie*, et virginaux — veux-tu? —
Nous nous mettrons au vert du paradis perdu ...
Ou *Robinson avec Vendredi* — c'est facile —
La pluie a déjà fait, de mon royaume, une île."

"Si pourtant, près de moi, tu crains la solitude,
Nous avons des amis, sans fard — un braconnier;
Sans compter un caban bleu, qui, par habitude
Fait toujours les cent pas et contient un douanier ...
Plus de clercs d'huissier! J'ai le clair de la lune,[7]
Et des amis pierrots amoureux sans fortune."

— "Et nos nuits! ... *Belles nuits pour l'orgie à la tour!*
Nuits à la Roméo! — Jamais il ne fait jour. —
La Nature au réveil — réveil de déchaînée —
Secouant son drap blanc ... éteint ma cheminée.
Voici mes rossignols ... rossignols d'ouragans —
Gais comme des pinsons — sanglots de chats-huans!
Ma girouette dérouille en haut sa tyrolienne
Et l'on entend gémir ma porte éolienne,
Comme chez saint Antoine en sa tentation ...
Oh viens! joli Suppôt de la séduction!"

— "Hop! les rats du grenier dansent des farandoles!
Les ardoises du toit roulent en castagnoles![8]
Les Folles du logis...
                    Non, je n'ai plus de Folles!"

... "Comme je revendrais ma dépouille à Satan
S'il me tentait avec un petit Revenant ...
— Toi — Je te vois partout, mais comme un voyant blême.
Je t'adore ... Et c'est pauvre: adorer ce qu'on aime!
Apparais, un poignard dans le cœur! — Ce sera,
Tu sais bien, comme dans *Inès de La Sierra* ...[9]
— On frappe ... oh! c'est quelqu'un ...
                    Hélas, oui, c'est un rat.

— "Je rêvasse ... et toujours c'est *Toi*. Sur toute chose,
Comme un esprit follet, ton souvenir se pose:
Ma solitude — *Toi!* — Mes hiboux à l'œil d'or:
— *Toi* — Ma girouette folle: Oh *Toi!* ... — que sais-je encor ...
— Toi! mes volets ouvrants les bras dans la tempête ...
Une lointaine voix: c'est Ta chanson! — c'est fête! ...
Les rafales fouaillant Ton nom perdu — c'est bête —
C'est bête, mais c'est *Toi!* Mon cœur au grand ouvert
                    Comme mes volets en pantenne,
                    Bat, tout affolé sous l'haleine
                    Des plus bizarres courants d'air."

"Tiens ,.. une ombre portée, un instant, est venue
Dessiner ton profil sur la muraille nue,
Et j'ai tourné la tête ... — Espoir ou souvenir —
Ma Sœur Anne, à ta tour, voyez-vous pas venir? ...

— Rien! — je vois ... je vois, dans ma froide chambrette,
Mon lit capitonné de *satin de brouette;*
Et mon chien qui dort dessus — Pauvre animal —
... Et je ris ... parce que ça me fait un peu mal."

"J'ai pris, pour t'appeler, ma vielle et ma lyre,
Mon cœur fait de l'esprit — le sot — pour se leurrer ...
Viens pleurer, si mes vers ont pu te faire rire;
                    Viens rire, s'ils t'ont fait pleurer ..."

"Ce sera drôle ... Viens jouer à la misère.
D'après nature: — *Un cœur avec une chaumière.* —
... Il pleut dans mon foyer, il pleut dans mon cœur feu.[10]
Viens! Ma chandelle est morte et je n'ai plus de feu."

Sa lampe se mourait. Il ouvrit la fenêtre.
Le soleil se levait. Il regardait sa lettre,
Rit et la déchira ... Les petits morceaux blancs,
Dans la brume semblaient un vol de goélands.

Penmarc'h — jour de Noël[11]

1. In Brittany, in the dead of winter, Corbière is longing for his absent friends the Count and Marcelle. But he turns each pathetic outburst into a joke and each lyrical evocation into something unexpectedly grotesque. The process amounts to systematic depoeticization. For the inspiration of the building described here, see *Les Amours Jaunes* (Gallimard, 1953), ed. Yves-Gérard Le Dantec, p. 247. Note the characteristic descriptive technique "en éclairs et en ellipses" as André Breton described it.

2. These two lines may recall Villon, with whom Corbière is often compared. See Sonnenfeld, p. 143.

3. The regularity of the alexandrines is broken by the introduction of eight-syllable lines. There is no real pattern in rime or length of line in this poem. See Lindsay, "The Versification of Corbière's *Les Amours Jaunes*," *PMLA* (September 1963), pp. 358–68.

4. Ironic reminiscences of "Les Djinns"? See Sonnenfeld, page 135.

5. Of the poets to whom Corbière was indebted, perhaps Baudelaire is first. Here the allusion to a spider recalls "Spleen." See Sonnenfeld, p. 150.

6. This stanza particularly displays Corbière's depoetizing procedure, with each pretty evocation dispelled and replaced by an image of harsh reality. As the succession of burlesque antitheses develops, the tears seem increasingly apparent through the mockery.

7. Note here the associative mechanism in Corbière's inspiration. The words of the old song remain in his thoughts to erupt again in the last lines of the poem.

8. "Castagnoles may be the fish called pomfrets (Brama raii), which skip vigorously when stranded on a beach; or wooden billets of the kind used to tighten awning-ropes on a vessel." Corbière, *Les Amours Jaunes* (Berkeley: University of California Press, 1954). Translated with an Introduction and Notes by C. F. MacIntyre. P. 208. Could Corbière be merely taking liberties with the word *castagnette* in the interest of his rime? The association with dancing strengthens this supposition.

9. Gautier has a poem, "Inès de las Sierra," (*Emaux et Camées*) which derives from Charles Nodier's novel by the same name. See MacIntyre, p. 208.

10. The similarity to Verlaine's poem is striking, but there seems no possibility of influence one way or the other.

11. This poem was actually composed in Morlaix at Christmas, 1871. Penmarc'h refers to the Tristan legend with which Corbière liked to associate himself. The legendary Tristan "se fit porter sur la falaise de Penmarc'h ..." See the last lines of *Tristan et Iseut* in the Bédier edition.

A word concerning the numerous ironic devices used throughout the poem: parody of various sorts from legal language to provincialisms, verbal effects of alliteration, etc., parallels, antitheses and other types of word play such as diaphora and anadiplosis.

RONDEL [12]

Il fait noir, enfant, voleur d'étincelles! [13]
Il n'est plus de nuits, il n'est plus de jours;
Dors ... en attendant venir toutes celles
Qui disaient: Jamais! Qui disaient: Toujours!

Entends-tu leurs pas? ... Ils ne sont pas lourds:
Oh! les pieds légers!—l'Amour a des ailes ...
Il fait noir, enfant, voleur d'étincelles!

Entends-tu leurs voix? ... Les caveaux sont sourds.
Dors: il pèse peu, ton faix d'immortelles:
Ils ne viendront pas, tes amis les ours,
Jeter leur pavé sur tes demoiselles: [14]
Il fait noir, enfant, voleur d'étincelles!

---

12. The group of rondels purporting to be lullabies for a dead child, seem to plunge us into the world of misty Celtic folklore. The identification of the poet himself with the dead child becomes clear in subsequent poems. Corbière becomes softer and more tender in these poems written as a sort of farewell to life and an anticipation of death. The earlier harshness is replaced by a "sweet airiness." Alexandre Arnoux says that Verlaine himself never moved with such ease and weightlessness (Preface to *Les Amours Jaunes*, 1947 edition).

A rondel is a "poème à structure fixe, fort pratiqué aux XIVᵉ, XVᵉ et XVIᵉ siècles, et comprenant treize vers construits sur deux rimes. Il se compose de trois strophes, savoir: un quatrain à rimes embrassées, un quatrain à rimes alternées, un quintil formé d'un quatrain à rimes embrassées et de la reprise du premier vers du poème; en outre, les deux derniers vers du second quatrain répètent les deux premiers vers du rondel" (Henri Morier, *Dictionnaire de Poétique et Rhétorique*, PUF, 1961, p. 366). Although the genre permits a certain variety, Corbière's poems do not seem to follow any one formula strictly. This, of course, is typical of his attitude toward matters of prosody. For an analysis of the versification of Corbière's rondels, see Lindsay.

13. MacIntyre says, "Childish, almost without meaning, this little poem has a magic, indefinable, light as thistledown, evanescent as a bubble." (p. 235) Sonnenfeld calls the epithet *voleur d'étincelles* hallucinatory.

14. La Fontaine has a fable concerning the bear who accidentally kills his friend the gardener. With a heavy cobblestone he smashes a fly on the gardener's nose.

PETIT MORT POUR RIRE[15]

Va vite, léger peigneur de comètes!
Les herbes au vent seront tes cheveux;
De ton œil béant jailliront les feux
Follets, prisonniers dans les pauvres têtes ...

Les fleurs de tombeau qu'on nomme Amourettes
Foisonneront plein ton rire terreux ...
Et les myosotis, ces fleurs d'oubliettes ...

Ne fais pas le lourd; cercueils de poètes
Pour les croque-morts sont de simples jeux,
Boîtes à violon qui sonnent le creux ...
Ils te croiront mort—Les bourgeois sont bêtes—
Va vite, léger peigneur de comètes!

---

15. The Surrealists delighted in the magic meaningless quality of Corbière, in his images that spring from the subconscious and succeed one another in patterns that have little to do with plain statement. To such "sorcellerie verbale" the critics also present their homage. MacIntyre says about the rondels: "Here we have a plaintive and far-away piping, frail as the soughings of the *mirliton* (reed-pipe) itself. These are songs without words, *chansons sans paroles*, as much as anything ever written. They are elegiac zephyrs blowing over a grave on which grows the *myosotis*, the forget-me-not ... These rondels are what Arnoux (pp. 21–22) considers a 'naked cry, the twisted heart, the words torn from their natural meaning, in a frenzy which evades both language and grammar.' There is something in that line, 'Va vite, léger peigneur de comètes,' which haunts me, and it is by this phrase—the comet-comber—that I always think of Tristan." (p. 237).

Poetry of Lautréamont

Les Chants de Maldoror, par le comte de Lautréamont (Lacroix, 1869).
Poésies (Gabrie, 1870).
Œuvres Complètes (Corti, 1953). With prefaces from earlier editions by
Gourmont, Jaloux, Breton, Soupault, Gracq, Caillois, Blanchot, and
two imaginary portraits by Dali and Valotton.
Œuvres Complètes (Gallimard, 1970). Lautréamont and Germain Nouveau.
Bibliothèque de la Pléiade.

Readings

Bachelard, Gaston. *Lautréamont* (Corti, 1939).
Blanchot, Maurice. *Lautréamont et Sade* (Minuit, 1949).
Caradec, François. *Isidore Ducasse* (Table Ronde, 1970).
Fowlie, Wallace. *Lautréamont* (Boston: Twayne, 1973).
Gourmont, Remy de. *Livre des Masques* (Mercure de France, 1891).
Montal, Robert. *Lautréamont* (Editions Universitaires, 1973).
Peyrouzet, Edouard. *Vie de Lautréamont* (Grasset, 1970).

Isidore Ducasse, known as "Lautréamont"

1846–1870

Genius or madman, infernal spirit or rebel without a cause, Isidore Ducasse has perplexed the critics ever since *Les Chants de Maldoror* first came to their attention. Léon Bloy and Remy de Gourmont, who were the first to notice the work, decided that the self-styled Comte de Lautréamont was a genius but quite insane. This was in the early 1890s, twenty years after the work had first been printed. The original edition had never been distributed out of fear of censorship; only the previously published first canto had circulated at all. Bloy and Gourmont read *Les Chants de Maldoror* in a new edition that was brought out in 1890. The work would then be put back on the shelf for twenty more years until taken down by Valery Larbaud. However, to the Surrealists of the early 1920s must go the credit for really "discovering" Ducasse; their enthusiasm set him out in the window and compensated richly for the neglect that he had previously suffered. For André Breton, the discovery of Ducasse amounted to "l'apparition de l'esprit infernal sous les traits d'un admirable jeune homme nu aux ailes cramoisies, les membres pris dans l'orbe des diamants sous un souffle antique de roses, l'étoile au front et le regard empreint d'une mélancolie farouche."[1]

Since that time, writers and critics have generally permitted the adulation of the Surrealists to go unchallenged. Judging from the example of Philippe Sollers, the advance-guard of the 1960s and 1970s regard Ducasse as highly as did the advance-guard of the 1920s and 1930s. He has been generally granted a place among the major French poets, with new studies and commentaries accompanying each successive edition of his work. Those of Gaston Bachelard (1939) and Maurice Blanchot (1949) rank with Léon Pierre-Quint's essay, *Lautréamont et Dieu* (1927), as the classic criticism on Ducasse. The anniversary of the poet's death occasioned a spurt of activity; new editions of the works plus new scholarship appeared around 1970. Twenty years earlier only Albert Camus sounded a note of protest in referring to *Maldoror* as "le livre d'un collégien presque génial."[2] Today among the new critics only Robert Faurisson refuses to treat the work with the reverent seriousness that has become the tradition; he considers it an enormous hoax.[3] There is nothing yet really to tell us how to interpret the life and works of Isidore Ducasse, and the objective contribution of recent work amounts to the correction of previous minor errors of detail. If his standing is now assured, what sort of person he was and what actually he was trying to do remain a matter of opinion. We still know so little that we may speculate as we please. After all, no one knows even what the man looked like.

This poet of whom we have only imaginary portraits was born in Montevideo, 4 April 1846, of French parents. His father was in the consular service there, reportedly well-off, something of a dandy and a Don Juan, but actually no better known by posterity that Isidore's mother, who apparently committed suicide within two years of her son's birth. The boy was eventually sent to France to be educated, to Tarbes, near where his father had been born. The records show him to have been a student there between 1859 and 1862, then at Pau until 1865. He did rather well in his studies, to judge from the *palmarès*, although his intelligence does not seem to have impressed his classmates. They remember him as rather an odd sort, keeping to himself, capricious in what he studied, and given to the wildest sort of writing in his compositions. One suspects considerable hindsight in testimony gathered years later, but there is no reason other than its appropriateness to believe that Isidore Ducasse was not as they remember him even to the physical appearance—a tall and slender young man, somewhat stooped, with his hair falling over a pallid brow.

The years 1866 and 1867 remained for long blank in the life of Ducasse. It seems likely now that he lived mainly in Tarbes and made a trip back to Uruguay for a visit. By the end of 1867, however, he was in Paris, possibly preparing for the Ecole Polytechnique. Our picture of Ducasse at this time depends on the meager testimony passed on from Albert Lacroix, the original publisher of *Maldoror*, to Louis Genonceaux, who incorporated it in his preface to the work. The young man had moved into a room near the Bourse with two trunks of books and a piano. He spent his time alone—reading, writing, or roaming over the city. It was at night that he labored over his literary compositions, declaiming as he wrote and striking long chords on the piano. In August of 1868, he published the first of the *Chants*. The other five were printed the next year, but, as previously mentioned, their distribution was cancelled. Ducasse went to work on the enigmatic *Poésies*, which appeared a few months before his death. In November 1870, Paris was under siege, threatened by famine and revolution. The death of the lonely student at number 7, rue du Faubourg Montmartre passed unnoticed.

Les Chants de Maldoror is a long prose poem of which only the first six cantos were written. Ducasse signed it Comte de Lautréamont, a name perhaps borrowed from Eugène Sue. As for *Maldoror*, it lends itself to several interpretations involving paronomasia, the essential factor being evident from the first syllable. Maldoror is the Devil, the Anti-Christ, God's everlasting foe.

The six cantos are divided into a varying number of strophes, each strophe an entity in itself yet, in spite of breaks and shifts in narrative voice, giving the impression of unity. This is due in part to the existence of a rudimentary story line. The strophes seem to form a succession of episodes in which Maldoror is usually the hero. Thus we have Maldoror luring an adolescent away from his family, Maldoror doing battle with an angel in the form of a lamp; Maldoror raping a little girl and leaving her to be finished off by a bulldog, Maldoror coupling with a female shark. At times, however, the prodigious Maldoror seems to shrink to the size of an ordinary mortal, a young man identifiable with the author perhaps, whose role is that of observer rather than of protagonist. As such he recounts the episode of the beetle rolling about the ball of excrement that turns out to be a woman, the man on the gibbet being tormented by his mother and his wife. Alternating with the narrative parts are passages of discourse in which the reader is called upon to witness the abomination that is the world, the cruel comedy of life, the triumph of evil. It is as if a narrative is interrupted by outbursts of rage and hysterical laughter. There is, however, no real justification for supposing that Ducasse ever conceived of his work as a single piece of fiction. As it stands, it is not only incomplete but lacking in the connecting and articulating devices that would make it a structural whole. And apparently Ducasse was satisfied to leave it a succession of sketches or virtuosity pieces, many of which are frankly imitations or parodies, such as the enticement episode based on the *Erlkönig*. Marcelin Pleynet has compiled a list of all the sources that critics have noted for *Les Chants de Maldoror;*[4] it is clearly one of the most derivative works in literature. The fragments and pieces in their totality create, however, a pattern in theme and tone and this, as well as the story line, helps explain the impression of unity that the work gives.

It can be said that the cry of revolt often heard in France since the early Romantic days has never sounded more pure, more total than in *Les Chants de Maldoror*. All the *mal du siècle* readings of a schoolboy of the times poured out in it, and all the history of the times, too, perhaps— developments in the natural sciences which gave a brutal new image of life, the course of society under Napoleon III which attested to the law of struggle-for-life and survival-of-the-fittest. But beyond being a tardy expression of Romanticism and a reaction to the Second Empire, it is a cry of youth. Whether to praise or to belittle, the word *collégien* applied to Ducasse is well chosen. One must be young to be as violent, as uncompromising as the author of the *Chants*. The shock of realizing for the first time the plight of all living beings reverberates throughout. In addressing himself to them all, he makes to the Creator as poignant a reproach as has ever been uttered: "Le mal que vous m'avez fait est trop grand, trop grand le mal que je vous ai fait, pour qu'il soit volontaire ..."[5] Evil, the author is saying, goes beyond the will, is just in the nature of things. Perhaps, as has been suggested, Ducasse planned his work as a sort of allegory—Evil, incarnate in Maldoror, overcomes in succession God, Conscience, then Hope. What is certain is that Ducasse's despair is total, as is possible only with a young man, and the rage that it provokes is the reaction of one who possesses the strength of youth.

The palliative that the German Romantics found for their chagrin was irony; in Ducasse it is present in its most truculent form, student humor. The preposterous incongruities, burlesque heroics, and poker-face put-ons evoke the *canular*.[6] It may be, as some affirm, that Ducasse was insane and that he demonstrates the cold humor of the schizophrenic. It is, nonetheless, the sort engendered in the schools. There, with all the problems of the universe constantly before one's eyes, seriousness (out of a perfectly healthy reflex) sometimes turns into levity, awe into derision. With the voices of all the great in science and literature thundering in one's ears, a cry from the heart can resound like a plagiarism. The subject matter of *Les Chants de Maldoror* is quite patently based on readings; the style, combining the grandeur of a Bossuet sermon with the triviality of everyday speech is typical of the *fort-en-thème*. Suzanne Bernard has analyzed the prose of the cantos, pointing out the typical rhetorical procedures such as apostrophe, repetition, parallel, interrogation, exclamation, that students learn along with their Latin.[7] These are turned into vehicles for burlesque and elaborated with all the prolixity that young writers delight in.

It is, however, Ducasse's imagery that shocks the most and best illustrates his ferocious humor. The world of Hieronymus Bosch is no more fantastic than that of Ducasse, full of monsters that disgust or terrify. Psychoanalytical critics have made much of it, Gaston Bachelard suggesting that in Ducasse's imagery we have a subconscious recapitulation of the whole biological past of the human species. Whether inspired by the subconscious collective or individual, or consciously invented, his creatures are selected from the most unlovely in nature and altered in size or prodigiously multiplied to make them even more terrible. The louse described in Chant II is an outstanding example. Furthermore, in the universe of Isidore Ducasse, natural laws are suspended and everything becomes susceptible to marvelous transformation. Abstractions turn into objects, things from the most widely separate categories come violently together in comparisons, the world of everyday perception and common sense turns into a phantasmagoria or a fun house in Luna Park. Either a madman or an undergraduate with tongue in cheek (or both) concocted the following: "la rencontre fortuite sur une table de dissection d'une machine à coudre et d'un parapluie."[8] It is this image which enchanted the Surrealists and insured Ducasse's fame in the twentieth century. But since Baudelaire it has been recognized that beauty in metaphor is sometimes in proportion to the disparity of its terms.

The supplemental publication, the *Poésies*, which Ducasse hastened to get ready while the *Chants de Maldoror* were locked up in a storeroom, has been no help in solving the enigma of this young poet. Rather have the *Poésies* complicated the problem of what he was like and what he was trying to do. They came out under the name Ducasse instead of Lautréamont, a fact which may or may not have significance. They comprised two unbound fascicles constituting sixteen pages in all and bore the subtitle *Préface à un livre futur*. In subject matter, the *Poésies* are a sort of literary manifesto, airing the author's views on writing and writers, scoring the literary great of his day. Such a farrago of invective and paradoxical assertion it is that even critics hesitant to call Ducasse insane are likely to concede that, before he died, he was going quite out of his head. On the surface he seems here to repudiate *Maldoror* and, as a rebel reformed, to preach law and order and middle-class morality. This is, of course, highly suspect. The about-face seems too sudden, the views that he expresses too easily interpreted as irony.. But one cannot be sure just what his ravings mean; and certain passages, such as the one denouncing the "grandes-têtes molles" of literature and the one that speaks of his own folly in having believed that revolution by the pen was effective revolution, certainly sound sincere. Since it is doubtful that outside support can ever be found for arguments on the subject, Ducasse will probably remain ambiguous enough to fit each reader's notion of him, and his work will remain (according to the reader) a book of seven seals, a treasury of rhetorical forms, a metaphysical protest, a social protest, or a case history. However understood, Isidore Ducasse has had a great impact on the twentieth century. Léon Pierre-Quint puts him in company with Gérard de Nerval, Baudelaire, Mallarmé, and Rimbaud as having given to the contemporary trend its "impulsion, son contenu, sa coloration."[9]

Notes

1. Preface to the G. L. M. edition of *Les Chants de Maldoror*, 1938.
2. Camus, "Lautréamont et la banalité," *Cahiers du Sud*, no. 307 (1951), pp. 399–401.
3. Robert Faurisson, *A-t-on lu Lautréamont?* (Gallimard, 1972).
4. See Pleynet, *Lautréamont par lui-même* (Seuil, 1967), pp. 98–99.
5. Lautréamont, Chant I.
6. This point of view is systematically sustained by Faurisson, who studies each successive piece as a schoolboy farce. (*A-t-on lu Lautréamont?*)
7. Bernard, *Le Poème en Prose*.
8. Lautréamont, Chant VI.
9. Pierre-Quint, *Le Comte de Lautréamont et Dieu* (new ed., Fasquelle, 1967), p.21.

CHANT QUATRIEME[1]

Je suis sale. Les poux me rongent. Les pourceaux, quand ils me regardent, vomissent. Les croûtes et les escarres de la lèpre ont écaillé ma peau, couverte de pus jaunâtre. Je ne connais pas l'eau des fleuves, ni la rosée des nuages. Sur ma nuque, comme sur un fumier, pousse un énorme champignon, aux pédoncules ombellifères. Assis sur un meuble informe, je n'ai pas bougé mes membres depuis quatre siècles. Mes pieds ont pris racine dans le sol et composent, jusqu'à mon ventre, une sort de végéta-tion vivace, remplie d'ignobles parasites, qui ne dérive pas encore de la plante et qui n'est plus de la chair. Cependant mon cœur bat. Mais com-ment battrait-il, si la pourriture et les exhalaisons de mon cadavre (je n'ose pas dire corps) ne le nourrissaient abondamment? Sous mon aisselle gauche, une famille de crapauds a pris résidence et, quand l'un d'eux remue, il me fait des chatouilles. Prenez garde qu'il ne s'en échappe un, et ne vienne gratter, avec sa bouche, le dedans de votre oreille: il serait ensuite capable d'entrer dans votre cerveau. Sous mon aisselle droite il y a un caméléon qui leur fait une chasse perpétuelle, afin de ne pas mourir de faim: il faut que chacun vive. Mais quand un parti déjoue complète-ment les ruses de l'autre, ils ne trouvent rien de mieux que de ne pas se gêner, et sucent la graisse délicate qui couvre mes côtes: j'y suis habitué. Une vipère méchante a dévoré ma verge et a pris sa place: elle m'a rendu eunuque, cette infâme. Oh! si j'avais pu me défendre avec mes bras paralysés; mais, je crois plutôt qu'ils se sont changés en bûches. Quoi qu'il en soit, il importe de constater que le sang ne vient plus y promener sa rougeur. Deux petits hérissons, qui ne croissent plus, ont jeté à un chien, qui n'a pas refusé, l'intérieur de mes testicules: l'épiderme soig-neusement lavé, ils ont logé dedans. L'anus a été intercepté par un crabe; encouragé par mon inertie, il garde l'entrée avec ses pinces, et me fait beaucoup de mal! Deux méduses ont franchi les mers, immédiatement alléchées par un espoir qui ne fut pas trompé. Elles ont regardé avec attention les deux parties charnues qui forment le derrière humain, et, se cramponnant à leur galbe convexe, elles les ont tellement écrasées par une pression constante, que les deux morceaux de chair ont disparu, tandis qu'il est resté deux monstres, sortis du royaume de la viscosité, égaux par la couleur, la forme et la férocité. Ne parlez pas de ma colonne verté-brale, puisque c'est un glaive! Oui, oui ... je n'y faisais pas attention ... votre demande est juste. Vous désirez savoir, n'est-ce pas, comment il se trouve implanté verticalement dans mes reins? Moi-même je ne me le rappelle pas très clairement; cependant, si je me décide à prendre pour un souvenir ce qui n'est peut-être qu'un rêve, sachez que l'homme, quand il a su que j'avais fait vœu de vivre avec la maladie et l'immobilité jusqu'à ce que j'eusse vaincu le Créateur, marcha, derrière moi, sur la pointe des pieds, mais, non pas si doucement, que je ne l'entendisse. Je ne perçus plus rien, pendant un instant qui ne fut pas long. Ce poignard aigu s'enfonça jusqu'au manche, entre les deux épaules du taureau des fêtes, et son ossature frissonna, comme un tremblement de terre. La lame adhère si fortement au corps, que personne, jusqu'ici, n'a pu l'extraire. Les athlètes, les mécaniciens, les philosophes, les médecins ont essayé, tour à tour, les moyens les plus divers. Ils ne savaient pas que le mal qu'a fait l'homme ne peut plus se défaire! J'ai pardonné à la profondeur de leur ignorance native, et je les ai salués des paupières de mes yeux. Voyageur, quand tu passeras près de moi, ne m'adresse pas, je t'en supplie, le moindre mot de consolation: tu affaiblirais mon courage. Laisse-moi réchauffer ma ténacité à la flamme du martyre volontaire. Va-t'en ... que je ne t'inspire aucune pitié. La haine est plus bizarre que tu ne le penses; sa conduite est inexplicable, comme l'apparence brisée d'un bâton enfoncé dans l'eau. Tel que tu me vois, je puis encore faire des excursions jusqu'aux murailles du ciel, à la tête d'une légion d'assassins, et revenir prendre cette posture, pour méditer, de nouveau, sur les nobles projets de la vengeance. Adieu, je ne te retarderai pas davantage; et, pour t'instruire et te préserver, réfléchis au sort fatal qui m'a conduit à la révolte, quand peut-être j'étais né bon! Tu raconteras à ton fils ce que tu as vu; et, le prenant par la main, fais-lui admirer la beauté des étoiles et les merveilles de l'univers, le nid du rouge-gorge et les temples du Seigneur. Tu seras étonné de le voir si docile aux conseils de la paternité, et tu le récompensera par un sourire. Mais, quand il apprendra qu'il n'est pas observé, jette les yeux sur lui, et tu le verras cracher sa bave sur la vertu; il t'a trompé, celui qui est descendu de la race humaine, mais, il ne te trompera plus: tu sauras désormais ce qu'il deviendra. Oh! père infortuné, prépare, pour accompagner les pas de ta vieillesse, l'échafaud ineffaçable qui tranchera la tête d'un criminel précoce, et la douleur qui te montrera le chemin qui conduit à la tombe.[1]

---

1. Probably the most celebrated of the nightmarish visions conjured up by Isidore Ducasse is that of Maldoror immobilized for four centuries and half-grown into vegetation. Ducasse's Satan is a patient sufferer, bearing his ills with resignation. The incongrui-

ties developed with great virtuosity produce a masterpiece of *humour noir*. Its material
—primeval nature and zoological species—suggest a preoccupation of the author encour-
aged by the Darwinian speculation popular during his day. See Anna Balakian, *Surrealism:
The Road to the Abstract* (New York: Noonday Press, 1959). The literary echoes—Milton,
Dante, Walpole (the author of *Melmoth*), the Book of Job, etc.—remind us how bookish
a young man Isidore Ducasse must have been.

Poetry of Rimbaud

Une Saison en Enfer (Brussels: Alliance Typographique, 1873).
Les Illuminations in *La Vogue*, 1886.
Le Reliquaire (Genonceaux, 1891).
Poésies complètes (Vanier, 1895).
Œuvres Complètes (Gallimard, 1946). Texte établi et annoté par Rolland de Renéville et Jules Mouquet. Bibliothèque de la Pléiade.

Readings

Bernard, Suzanne. *Le Poème en prose*, pp. 151–211.
Chauvel, Jean. *L'Aventure terrestre de Jean Arthur Rimbaud* (Seghers, 1971).
Cohn, Robert Greer. *The Poetry of Rimbaud* (Princeton: Princeton University Press, 1973).
Etiemble, René. *Le mythe de Rimbaud* (Gallimard, 1952–1961), 4 vols. [vol. 3 in preparation].
Houston, John Porter. *The Design of Rimbaud's Poetry* (New Haven: Yale University Press, 1963).
Richer, Jean. *L'Alchimie du Verbe de Rimbaud* (Didier, 1972).
Ruff, Marcel. *Rimbaud* (Hatier, 1968).
St. Aubyn, F. C. *Arthur Rimbaud* (Boston: Twayne, 1975).
Starkie, Enid. *Arthur Rimbaud* (New York: New Directions, 1961).

Arthur Rimbaud

1854–1891

It is about the time of Ducasse's death that Arthur Rimbaud arrived in Paris. Born and brought up in a country town near the Belgian border, he burst upon the capital at the age of seventeen and, after a few years of astonishing the literary world with his genius and bad character, took his leave of poetry forever. Despite the short span of his career, Rimbaud is reckoned to be one of the greatest French poets and one of the major precursors of the moderns in poetic theory. At the age of thirty-seven, he died in a hospital in Marseilles.

Rimbaud's father was a captain in the army, as easygoing in temperament as Rimbaud's mother was uncompromising and severe. They got along very badly and, when Rimbaud was six, they separated forever. Vitalie Rimbaud had remained with her father in Charleville because of the difficulty of following her husband from garrison town to garrison town, with small children. Now with her father dead and her husband gone for good, she faced the task of bringing up four children alone. This she did with the greatest devotion and discipline. On Sundays, setting off for church they made an edifying spectacle: first the two little girls Vitalie and Isabelle with their white gloves, then the two boys with their round white collars and their blue umbrellas, finally Madame Rimbaud in solemn, unrelieved black. On the surface the children were docile; but Arthur at least, chafing at the inflexible rules and constant surveillance, kept down his rebellion only by withdrawal into reading and daydreaming. Arthur and his brother were sent to a good school where, although Arthur was a year younger, he soon outdistanced Charles.

He was in fact the best in his class. He was particularly good at Latin verses and at the age of fifteen found a friend and mentor in one of his teachers, Georges Izambard. This young man encouraged Arthur to read widely and to pursue his own writing. It was surely due to Izambard that Rimbaud wrote a great many poems while a pupil in the lycée of Charleville and carried off the highest academic honors. In May of 1870, he sent some of his poetry to Théodore de Banville, a member of the selection committee for *Le Parnasse Contemporain.* "Ophélie," which was among them, shows that before becoming an original artist Rimbaud leaned heavily upon the masters of the day. Before becoming a *voleur de feu* young Rimbaud was simply a *voleur de vers!* But his exploitations were felicitous and a poem like "Ophélie" shows extraordinary technical mastery for a schoolboy. The suave melody of this poem, which is still popular, has an old-fashioned charm reminiscent of English pre-Raphaelite poetry and anticipates a poet more like Albert Samain than the later Rimbaud. The year 1870 was an eventful one for the young scholar. Because of the war Izambard had left Charleville and Rimbaud, bored and restless, took a train to Paris. Since he had neither ticket nor money he was arrested. Izambard got him out of jail and took him back to his mother, who received him so badly that he ran away again. This time Madame Rimbaud called in the police to return the prodigal. But in February of the following year, he sold his watch to buy a ticket for Paris. The capital was in the throes of the defeat: Rimbaud, without money or friends, ate out of garbage pails and slept where he could find shelter. At odd moments he continued to write. The "Cœur supplicié," dating from this time yet totally unlike "Ophélie," is thought to indicate a traumatic sexual experience suffered in Paris. When Izambard found the poem simply disgusting, Rimbaud turned away from his former friend.

Arthur Rimbaud returned to Charleville to become the town's bad boy. He refused to go back to school, refused to wash or to comb his hair. He spent his time in the bars scrounging drinks and tobacco for his pipe. There he encountered one Charles Bretagne who got him interested in occult philosophy. No longer in school and having nothing else to do, Rimbaud steeped himself in illuministic lore. The result may be seen in the concept of the poet as a seer that he formulated in the letter that he wrote to Izambard in May of 1871 and included the "Cœur supplicié" and in another letter written at the same time to another friend. Only the poet, Rimbaud declares, is privileged to look upon the real face of the universe. But to do so, the poet must break through all conventional limitations, must expand his mind through a "long, immense et raisonné dérèglement de tous les sens."[1] He must be ready to sacrifice not only

his health and his reason but even his identity, for the poet is but a vehicle
—"Je est un autre." [2] Rimbaud's own faith in his mission faded into dis-
appointment and despair. But the poetic credo that he enunciated in these
so-called "lettres du voyant" has inspired poets ever since who have held
their art to be a sacred science.

"Le Bateau ivre," Rimbaud's longest and most famous poem, was
written while the poet was still pondering the implications of his newly
formulated doctrine. A welter of images from his readings, it describes
the course of the drunken boat until, on the verge of an ascent into the
heavens, it drops back into the waters of the earth. The poem is witness
to the spiritual exaltation and confidence that Rimbaud was feeling as a
result of his theory of poetry as divination. In this mood, he returned to
Paris upon an invitation obtained from Paul Verlaine. The latter's message
dated September 1871, "Venez, chère grande âme," was the "Open
Sesame" for the lad from Charleville.

The society of Parisian letters greeted him less warmly and even the
most Bohemian elements found Rimbaud hard to accept. He was dirty
and rude and, reacting to feelings that he inspired, deliberately made
matters worse. Verlaine had opened the home of his parents-in-law to
him and introduced him everywhere. Rimbaud disgraced himself and
his sponsor, so alone together they went off on one of the most famous
sprees in the history of literature. Verlaine was just naturally depraved;
Rimbaud apparently considered sensual excesses a means to the "dérègle-
ment de tous les sens" essential to art. For a while, carried aloft by an
absinthe dream, Rimbaud knew ecstasies that might justify in his mind
the abuses that he inflicted upon himself. But the heights that he first
reached with Verlaine could not be sustained. He soon found his partner
exasperating and tormented him cruelly. Their quarrels and scenes in
Paris, London, and Brussels culminated in Verlaine's attempt to shoot
Rimbaud.

Rimbaud had come to Paris with high confidence in himself and in the
mystical value of art. His association with Verlaine intensified it and
incited great activity in verse. Then the disgust that he began to feel for
his personal life became complicated with doubts concerning his work.
Finally, faith in himself and in art faded out almost completely. The
record, at least in part, is in *Une Saison en Enfer* and the *Illuminations*.

He finished *Une Saison en Enfer* back in Charleville in August of 1873.
In October he was in Brussels to collect the author's copies from the
publisher. Shortly thereafter began his wandering. He went back to

England where he had been the previous winter with Verlaine. Then he went to Germany, reading as usual in the libraries, studying language, and seeking congenial employment whereby he could continue to satisfy his wanderlust. To get to the Far East he joined the Dutch army, went to Java, deserted, and returned as a sailor on an English ship. Then, after further wandering in Europe, he ended up in Alexandria in 1878. Between trips Rimbaud always returned home. He was back there for his twenty-fifth birthday, regaining his strength for another trip to the Mediterranean.

He went first to Cyprus, where he took a job for a time as a foreman of a construction crew. Then knocking about the Red Sea ports, he settled in Aden, working in the store of a coffee exporter. Later in 1880, Rimbaud was sent by his employer to open a post in Harar. This Ethiopian town, for centuries closed to foreigners, had its first French resident in Rimbaud. He was to live there for much of the time that he remained in the East; first as agent for the exporter, then as an independent trader. Possessed of great drive and energy, Rimbaud entertained a thousand fancies for bettering his lot. He read books on exploring, on hydraulics, mechanics, and everything that might push him toward a lucrative career in opening the country for the West. His plans amounted to little, but Rimbaud worked indefatigably on in the ports of the Somali coast; bringing in the coffee, hides, guns, and ivory that he had obtained for cheap European goods. His life was hard, and with peasant stubbornness he pushed himself to the physical limit in order to make and to save a little money. Whatever success he had, though, he owed to his grudging; for his grandiose scheme of running guns to the king of Shoa ended badly and his exploration brought him only the fame of an article in the proceedings of the Société géographique. The years went by: Rimbaud, although discouraged about ever making something of himself, sank into the routine of his life in Harar. He apparently got along well with the Ethiopians and his fellow Europeans. Deciding that if he stayed he needed a wife to run his house, he was on the point of returning to France in search of one when his health broke. An ache in his right knee first caught his attention, then swellings. The pain became intense and was accompanied by fever and nausea; nevertheless Rimbaud continued to walk and ride. Only after six weeks was he forced to give up and make plans to get to Aden. He was carried to the coast in a litter and put aboard a ship. At the hospital in Aden he was given treatment, but since his condition did not improve, he was shipped back to France. The journey which had been torture all the way from Harar ended in Marseilles, where his right leg was amputated. After his convalescence he returned to his mother's home, but soon signs appeared that the disease was spreading. Rimbaud felt that the northern climate was retarding his cure and insisted on getting back to the Mediterranean. His sister Isabelle accompanied him to Marseilles where the doctors decided that he had carcinoma. After weeks of suffering, Rimbaud died. Isabelle reported that the onetime blasphemous rebel became a deathbed convert.

While Rimbaud was in the East and literature was far behind him, the fame of his poems was spreading through the Symbolist circles of Paris. In 1891, just as the symptoms of the malady that would prove fatal first appeared, the editor of *La France moderne* wrote to ask him to assume leadership of "l'école décadente et symboliste." The new school did not, of course, know him personally or very much of his work. The *Saison en Enfer*, except for a few author's copies distributed among friends, had remained at the printer's. In 1883, several of the earlier poems had appeared in magazines—notably "Voyelles" and "Bateau ivre." The next year Verlaine published them in his *Poètes maudits*, accompanied by a brief introduction to the author. On this basis, by 1886, when the *Illuminations* came out, Rimbaud had acquired for the young poets the features of the romantic escapist *par excellence*. For want of additional real poems by Rimbaud, they began to circulate false ones in keeping with their conception of the "Symbolist" Rimbaud, author of the Vowel sonnet. They recognized the similarity between this poem and the "Correspondances" of Baudelaire and hailed in its author the continuer of Baudelairian metaphysics. Verlaine protested that Rimbaud was no Symbolist, and it is true that if there are philosophical affinities with the new school, the poetics and the politics are quite different. The violent imagery of Rimbaud is, for example, worlds apart from the delicate tints of the Symbolists, and Rimbaud preached revolution not escape. Several more poems actually by Rimbaud were presented by periodicals and anthologies in the latter 1880s, and in 1891, as the author lay dying in Marseilles, the collection entitled *Le Reliquaire* appeared.

The falsification implied in Rimbaud "symboliste" is no greater, however, than the falsification in Rimbaud "mystique à l'état sauvage," the image created by Paul Claudel and publicized from 1912 on. Claudel's interpretation had the merit of taking Rimbaud out of the hothouse of Symbolism and putting him in the countryside of his native province, out of abstraction and into concrete reality. Yet it aided and abetted the whitewashing that Isabelle Rimbaud had been guilty of in presenting her brother to posterity. Only the overzealous can make much of Rimbaud's Catholic disposition; just as only the overzealous on the other side can make him, on the basis of his politics in 1870, a Communist. Rimbaud's interest in the occult sciences has also been a subject of much exaggeration. Very wide reading in the field has been attributed to him and very precise occult interpretation has been made of his work—all on very little real evidence. Following Claudel, an increasing number of readers burned candles before the Rimbaud that they imagined—Claudel's associates at the *Nouvelle Revue Française*, the group of the Abbaye, and others. Then after World War I, Rimbaud "symboliste" became Rimbaud "surréaliste." André Breton acclaimed in Rimbaud the "génie de la puberté" and recognized as an ancestor this poet who had crossed the frontier of convention and reason to explore what lay beyond, who had aspired beyond art to change life itself. All the "false" Rimbauds were exposed by René Etiemble in a great thesis, but they are false only in the sense that all artists must be interpreted according to the needs and wishes of different publics. The "real" Rimbaud, if we could know him, might not interest very many persons, and what he actually meant to say in a given work might limit its significance disastrously. Paul Valéry must have felt this to be true of his own work when he declared, "Mes vers ont le sens qu'on leur prête."[3]

Viewed in the dispassionate light of simple literary history, Rimbaud's work is still one of the most audacious and authentic in French literature. The young revolutionary set out to destroy the view of life established by convention and tradition in order to impose his own. He was convinced that the function of the poet—for him, a seer and a sorcerer—was to obtain a purer and fresher vision to impart to humanity. In the "lettres du voyant," he not only restates emphatically the Romantic dogma of the poet's superior vision, he prescribes the method for obtaining it—a voluntary switching the tracks of perception by any means deemed effective. The affinity to Baudelaire is here most apparent.

The *Illuminations* demonstrate Rimbaud's achievement. Reality is transformed into a wild and beautiful fairyland as images and rhythms surge forth out of what seems to be a primitive vision of the cosmos. The barbaric sensuality of "Le Bateau ivre" is intensified in these prose poems where sounds, smells, and colors fuse in hallucinatory evocations. From languorous and lilting to strident and thunderous, the measures are modulated upon the quickly shifting moods of the poet. They seem wholly spontaneous, but an examination of the alliterative patterns, the rhythms, internal rimes, and the combinations of phonic and syntactic symmetries suggest that Rimbaud was a conscious craftsman, who worked over the formulation of his visions. We possess no rough drafts of the *Illuminations*, but we have of other works. The manuscripts of *Une Saison en Enfer*, for example, demonstrate that the beauty of Rimbaud's poetry was the result of hard labor.

Une Saison en Enfer is generally read as a repudiation of the Promethean enterprise recorded in the *Illuminations*, Rimbaud's recognition that his accomplishment was only literary, that his poetry had not changed life as his adolescent ambition had led him to think possible. Begun on rather a bantering, even jovial note, the "story of his follies" that Rimbaud entitled *Une Saison en Enfer* gradually becomes more bitter; and, in the "Alchimie du verbe," he treats as fatuous and naive the articles of poetic faith that he had set down in the "lettres du voyant." The text has been minutely glossed for the light it throws on those letters and on Rimbaud's great experiment with poetry; certain of its cryptic phrases, however, have not even yet yielded up their full meaning. The interpretation of the work as a whole depends to a large extent upon the chronology of its composition in relation to the *Illuminations*. Once it was thought that *Une Saison en Enfer* was a sort of official good-bye to literature which Rimbaud further solemnized by a bonfire of his remaining manuscripts prior to setting out on his travels. Investigations such as those conducted by Bouillane de Lacoste show that this account of Rimbaud's abandonment of literature is too neat since some of the *Illuminations* at least were written after *Une Saison en Enfer* and that the dramatic burning of manuscripts as reported by his sister is an exaggeration.[4] All this suggests that Rimbaud's decision was less abrupt than supposed and that the object of repudiation in *Une Saison* is less certain.

Nevertheless, he did leave literature, a fact that defines the totality of his work as essentially adolescent in character; and, although we cannot be sure whether what he repudiates in *Une Saison* is a way of life or a view of life, it stands as a Faustian effort all the more meaningful because of its ambiguity. Without denying altogether the personal and confessional nature of the work, John Porter Houston stresses its mythic generality.[5] He sees the account of fall and redemption which is told progressively throughout the chapters as involving mankind as a whole rather than just the poet. Rimbaud's preoccupation with Christian themes is intermittent throughout his poetry; *Une Saison en Enfer* may well be taken as a symbolic summary of his position regarding the tenets of the faith in

1873. The theological virtues, salvation and damnation, grace and inno-
cence are among the themes treated, the history of the church is traced to
the present time, and the various levels of hell are described as the subject
sinks gradually into the pit. Considered from the angle stressed by Pro-
fessor Houston, *Une Saison en Enfer* appears less as an autobiographical
account framed by generalities than as a poetic commentary on religious
problems with the personal element merely incidental. Doubtless either
reading is justified.

Notes

1. Rimbaud, *Œuvres Complètes*, p. 254.
2. Ibid., pp. 252 and 254.
3. Paul Valéry, *Œuvres* (Gallimard, 1965), vol. 1, p. 1509.
4. See Bouillane de Lacoste, *Rimbaud et le Problème des Illuminations* (Mercure de France, 1949).
5. Houston, *The Design of Rimbaud's Poetry*.

LE BATEAU IVRE[1]

Comme je descendais des Fleuves impassibles,
Je ne me sentis plus guidé par les haleurs:
Des Peaux-Rouges criards les avaient pris pour cibles,
Les ayant cloués nus aux poteaux de couleurs.

J'étais insoucieux de tous les équipages,
Porteur de blés flamands ou de cotons anglais.
Quand avec mes haleurs ont fini ces tapages,
Les Fleuves m'ont laissé descendre où je voulais.

Dans les clapotements furieux des marées,
Moi, l'autre hiver, plus sourd que les cerveaux d'enfants,
Je courus! Et les Péninsules démarrées
N'ont pas subi tohu-bohus plus triomphants.

La tempête a béni mes éveils maritimes.
Plus léger qu'un bouchon j'ai dansé sur les flots
Qu'on appelle rouleurs éternels de victimes,
Dix nuits, sans regretter l'œil niais des falots!

Plus douce qu'aux enfants la chair des pommes sures,
L'eau verte pénétra ma coque de sapin
Et des taches de vins bleus et des vomissures
Me lava, dispersant gouvernail et grappin.

Et dès lors, je me suis baigné dans le Poème
De la Mer, infusé d'astres, et lactescent,[2]
Dévorant les azurs verts; où[3] flottaison blême
Et ravie, un noyé pensif parfois descend;

Où, teignant tout à coup les bleuités, délires
Et rhythmes lents sous les rutilements du jour,
Plus fortes que l'alcool, plus vastes que nos lyres,
Fermentent les rousseurs amères de l'amour![4]

Je sais les cieux crevant en éclairs, et les trombes
Et les ressacs et les courants: je sais le soir,
L'Aube exaltée ainsi qu'un peuple de colombes,
Et j'ai vu quelquefois ce que l'homme a cru voir!

J'ai vu le soleil bas, taché d'horreurs mystiques,

Illuminant de longs figements violets,
Pareils à des acteurs de drames très-antiques
Les flots roulant au loin leurs frissons de volets!

J'ai rêvé la nuit verte aux neiges éblouies,
Baiser montant aux yeux des mers avec lenteurs,
La circulation des sèves inouïes,
Et l'éveil jaune et bleu des phosphores chanteurs![5]

J'ai suivi, des mois pleins, pareille aux vacheries[6]
Hystériques, la houle à l'assaut des récifs,
Sans songer que les pieds lumineux des Maries
Pussent forcer le mufle aux Océans poussifs!

J'ai heurté, savez-vous,[7] d'incroyables Florides
Mêlant aux fleurs des yeux de panthères à peaux
D'hommes![8] Des arcs-en-ciel tendus comme des brides
Sous l'horizon des mers, à de glauques troupeaux!

J'ai vu fermenter les marais énormes, nasses
Où pourrit dans les joncs tout un Léviathan!
Des écroulements d'eaux au milieu des bonaces,
Et les lointains vers les gouffres cataractant!

Glaciers, soleils d'argent, flots nacreux, cieux de braises!
Echouages hideux au fond des golfes bruns
Où les serpents géants dévorés des punaises
Choient, des arbres tordus, avec de noirs parfums!

J'aurais voulu montrer aux enfants ces dorades
Du flot bleu, ces poissons d'or, ces poissons chantants.
—Des écumes de fleurs ont bercé mes dérades[9]
Et d'ineffables vents m'ont ailé par instants.

Parfois, martyr lassé des pôles et des zones,
La mer dont le sanglot faisait mon roulis doux
Montait vers moi ses fleurs d'ombre aux ventouses jaunes
Et je restais, ainsi qu'une femme à genoux …

Presque île, ballottant sur mes bords les querelles
Et les fientes d'oiseaux clabaudeurs aux yeux blonds.
Et je voguais, lorsqu'à travers mes liens frêles
Des noyés descendaient dormir, à reculons! …

Or moi, bateau perdu sous les cheveux des anses,
Jeté par l'ouragan dans l'éther sans oiseau
Moi dont les Monitors et les voiliers des Hanses
N'auraient pas repêché la carcasse ivre d'eau;

Libre, fumant, monté de brumes violettes,
Moi qui trouais le ciel rougeoyant comme un mur
Qui porte, confiture exquise aux bons poëtes,
Des lichens de soleil et des morves d'azur;

Qui courais, taché de lunules électriques,
Planche folle, escorté des hippocampes noirs,
Quand les juillets[10] faisaient crouler à coups de triques
Les cieux ultramarins aux ardents entonnoirs;[11]

Moi qui tremblais, sentant geindre à cinquante lieues
Le rut des Béhémots[12] et les Maelstroms épais,
Fileur éternel des immobilités bleues,
Je regrette l'Europe aux anciens parapets!

J'ai vu des archipels sidéraux! et des îles
Dont les cieux délirants sont ouverts au vogueur:
—Est-ce en ces nuits sans fonds que tu dors et t'exiles,
Million d'oiseaux d'or, ô future Vigueur?—

Mais, vrai, j'ai trop pleuré! Les Aubes sont navrantes.
Toute lune est atroce et tout soleil amer:
L'âcre amour m'a gonflé de torpeurs enivrantes.
O que ma quille éclate! O que j'aille à la mer!

Si je désire une eau d'Europe, c'est la flache[13]
Noire et froide où vers le crépuscule embaumé
Un enfant accroupi plein de tristesses, lâche
Un bateau frêle comme un papillon de mai.

Je ne puis plus, baigné de vos langueurs, ô lames,
Enlever leur sillage aux porteurs de cotons,
Ni traverser l'orgueil des drapeaux et des flammes,
Ni nager sous les yeux horribles des pontons.

---

1. Rimbaud wrote this poem shortly before leaving for Paris in the fall of 1871. One
may imagine that it was composed in the joy of saying good-bye to Charleville and of

savoring in advance the reception that awaited him in the capital. One suspects that it reflects an esthetic solution to the personal problems that had beset him in the spring. There can be no doubt that at the time of writing he was exulting in the full awareness of his talents and in the self-confidence that his recent formulations of poetic theory had brought him. In "Le Bateau Ivre" Rimbaud utilized the techniques that he had expounded in one of his letters to Paul Demeny, the first of the so-called "lettres du voyant." He meant his poem to be a show piece, and of course it was.

Nothing of the wolf of Alfred de Vigny nor of Leconte de Lisle's eagle in this poem about a boat. The Romantic technique had served a morality, the Parnassian a philosophy: in neither case was the symbol more than an abstract demonstration. On the contrary, this boat which is also the poet or mankind has a real personality and a real adventure. The analogy is not established by a series of parallels leading to a concluding statement but is woven tightly into the fabric of the poem so that it is impossible to isolate images of the boat as just a boat from those suggesting what the boat may stand for. Total fusion of this sort, this basic ambiguity has a strong modern appeal. We may choose to see in the poem a continuation of the "Cœur supplicié," that strange and violent poem which some critics think was inspired by a traumatic sexual experience that the poet suffered during his escapade in Paris at the time of the Commune. The course of the boat, beginning in the intoxicating joy of freedom and ending in disaster may relate to this emotional experience or even the early enthusiasm followed by disillusionment over the Commune. We may see it representing the superhuman career that Rimbaud had undertaken in poetry—through a systematic abuse of his faculties a venture into unchartered waters and the faltering of his courage. Or we may see it, as does Bernard Weinberg (*The Limits of Symbolism*), as a statement of the various stages in any man's life. Jean Richer has made an elaborate gloss of the poem in terms of Tarot cards (*L'Alchimie du Verbe de Rimbaud*, pp. 169–95). However we may see it, it remains a boat, but a boat that has a spirit like a man's.

The boat's reality for us is due in great part to the strong physical quality in the poem. First there is the enormous sense appeal: fresh sights, sounds, and smells replace the faded images of poetic rhetoric as Rimbaud describes his vision of primitive nature. Like Mallarmé, he is bent on giving "un sens plus pur aux mots de la tribu." He takes words from technical manuals, digs rare ones out of the dictionary, and invents still others to sharpen our awarenesses and bring us into direct contact with reality. We are startled by neologisms such as *bleuités* and in general his abstract nouns in the plural—the *lenteurs* and *azurs verts*, which give a pervasive sensual effect. Spell-casting rhythms based greatly on repetition enhance the physical appeal and the emotional impact created by the tropes, making the poem a veritable orgiastic experience.

If it is difficult to choose the most delirious of the praise that this poem has evoked among critics, it is easy to point out its most sober appraisal. For René Etiemble, the symbol of the boat is a banal figure and the whole poem a compilation of borrowings from the Parnassian poets whom it was intended to please: "un brillant exercice de style sur un cliché parnassien." He calls Rimbaud a "virtuose du pastiche." (*Le mythe de Rimbaud*, vol. 2, pp. 78 and 81) Although Etiemble's remarks cannot be taken very seriously, the bookish inspiration of the poem is undeniable. At seventeen, Rimbaud had never seen the sea. He had, however, read Jules Verne and Hugo (*Les Travailleurs de la Mer*) and Baudelaire (*L'Invitation au Voyage*). The list of sources is long and so evident that they impose constant comparison. There is no better way, incidentally, to measure how greatly Rimbaud surpassed his models.

2. One of the unusual words that the Symbolists took over and abused.

3. The antecedent is poem.

4. The sea is represented as a great still whose metal dazzles in the sunlight.

5. Michelet may be the source of the sea imagery here.

6. From stampeding herd of wild buffaloes, an image found perhaps in Poe, Rimbaud moves to herd of fighting bulls in the Camargue. The little town of Les Saintes-Maries-de-la-Mer may account for the reference in the third line, for that is where the Marys landed after being tossed about at sea like the Bateau Ivre.

7. Rimbaud's insertion of this familiar and provincial expression is frequently remarked upon by commentators.

8. An unusual rhythm pattern complicates the image. The verse including the run-on *D'hommes* is actually a three-part unit.

9. *Dérader* =leaving the rade=drifting out to sea.

10. Synecdoche? Summer heat and storms.

11. Hypallage? Rain falls *from* the skies.

12. Like leviathan, a biblical word.

13. A variation in the north for *flaque* (puddle).

VOYELLES[14]

A noir, E blanc, I rouge, U vert, O bleu: voyelles,
Je dirai quelque jour vos naissances latentes:[15]
A, noir corset velu des mouches éclatantes
Qui bombinent[16] autour des puanteurs cruelles,

Golfes d'ombre; E, candeurs[17] des vapeurs et des tentes,
Lances des glaciers fiers, rois[18] blancs, frissons d'ombelles;[19]
I, pourpres, sang craché, rire des lèvres belles
Dans la colère ou les ivresses pénitentes;

U, cycles, vibrements[20] divins des mers virides,[21]
Paix des pâtis[22] semés d'animaux, paix des rides,
Que l'alchimie imprime aux grands fronts studieux;

O, suprême Clairon plein des strideurs[23] étranges,
Silences traversés des Mondes et des Anges:
—O l'Oméga, rayon violet de Ses Yeux!

14. No other work by Rimbaud has evoked more discussion than the Sonnet of the Vowels, written in 1871 and published in 1883. The question of hearing in color, which the poem raises, is the first point of contention. Scientific evidence on the subject has been gathered from as far back as the eighteenth century, and Voltaire and Goethe have been called upon to testify. Literary evidence has been obtained chiefly from the Romantics, from Nodier, Gautier, Balzac, and Baudelaire. The "Correspondances" of Baudelaire has been looked to as a particularly important source, seeming to offer a philosophic basis for the phenomenon of synesthesia. Madame E. Noulet points out, however, that the Swedenborgian concept of unity in nature that Baudelaire expresses in his poem suggests an attitude not at all conforming to Rimbaud's state of mind at the time of the poem. In 1871, Rimbaud was in complete revolt against life. Moreover, in the poem itself, rather than from the many to the one, Rimbaud's direction seems toward dispersion and multiplicity. (E. Noulet, *Le Premier Visage de Rimbaud*, Brussels: Palais des Académies, 1953, p. 155.) Without making too much of these differences, we feel they are sufficient nonetheless to keep us from seeing in "Voyelles" only an endorsement of the thought in Baudelaire's poem.

In the 1930s, *Les Nouvelles Littéraires* provoked a lively discussion in the press over whether the inspiration for the Sonnet of the Vowels might not be an ABC book that Rimbaud had known as a child. Actually the subject had come up before and such a book had been uncovered with the letters colored as in the poem. From this explanation of the colors, speculation developed over what had inspired the accompanying images: association between the form of the letters and the images, between words and images, were pursued with indefatigable and humorless zeal to the extent that the whole matter became quite absurd. Before interest in the ABC books died down critics were on a new track, led by the distinguished Francisant Miss Starkie. In her work on Rimbaud, which first appeared in 1938, she demonstrated that the colors of the sonnet follow the order of an experiment in alchemy. Moreover, the correspondence between colors and vowels is in keeping with the alchemist symbols, i.e., the letter *A* evokes the idea of decomposition and is black, etc. J. Gengoux, inspired by Enid Starkie's contentions, has elaborated the thesis of Rimbaud's debt to occult literature to the point of seeing all his work as structured on cabalistic lore. (Jacques Gengoux, *La Pensée Poétique de Rimbaud*, Nizet, 1950) In spite of the fact that there are allusions to alchemy in numerous other poems and that this poem may indeed be read as symbolizing the various stages of the *œuvre*, we suspect that Gengoux's position is too extreme. This seems to be also the opinion of Jean Richer, who, after his work on Nerval, had studied the sources of the occult in Rimbaud (*L'Alchimie du Verbe de Rimbaud*). Neither the question of the ABC's nor of the wizard books has been answered satisfactorily, but it seems best to read the poem first as just a poem. Thus we do not risk forgetting, as Verlaine put it, that "Voyelles" constitutes "tout simplement quatorze des plus beaux vers d'aucune langue." (See *Rimbaud raconté par Paul Verlaine*, Mercure de France, 1934, p. 108.)

15. hidden

16. A neologism with apparently the meaning of buzz.

17. whitenesses

18. A reading of *rais* for *rois* inspired Lucien Sausy to an interpretation of the poem based on the form of each vowel in various positions. Thus if the letter *E* is laid on its

back, the three vertical bars may be thought to be icicles or white spokes. See *Œuvres Complètes*, p. 657.

19. umbels: a cluster of flowers with stems in the formation of umbrella ribs.

20. A neologism created to avoid the word *vibration*, which would have badly affected the sound.

21. green

22. pastures

23. stridencies: a rare word which pleased the Symbolists.

DEPART[24]

Assez vu. La vision s'est rencontrée à tous les
airs.
Assez eu. Rumeurs des villes, le soir, et au soleil,
et toujours.
Assez connu. Les arrêts de la vie.—O Rumeurs et
Visions!
Départ dans l'affection et le bruit neufs!

24. Professor Houston reminds us that, in spite of its odd pattern, this is an authentic poem, with the three initial rime phrases each followed by an approximate alexandrine (*The Design of Rimbaud's Poetry*).

In the development of the prose poem in France, Arthur Rimbaud holds a key position because he made of it the instrument par excellence to accomplish the metaphysical ambition which has characterized poetry since Baudelaire. Baudelaire got closer to the mark in his verse; Rimbaud, moving from conventional verse into doggerel and eventually into prose, found here the greatest fulfillment of his poetic genius and, by his concept and example, has oriented French poetry since.

We know, even though we interpret the term quite strictly, that Rimbaud did not invent the genre. Limiting ourselves to the poets of the nineteenth century, we have in previous discussions, named his illustrious predecessors from Aloysius Bertrand on. It should be added that when Rimbaud was composing the *Illuminations*, the prose poem was also being cultivated by those poets whom he encountered in Paris, poets preferring to emulate Baudelaire's *Petits Poèmes en prose* rather than the Parnassian poems in formal alexandrines. But their plastic or tone poems were quite different from the extraordinary pieces that make up the *Illuminations*. Rimbaud's works were like glimpses of a marvelously transfigured world, chaotic and paroxysmal, in which the rules of ordinary perspective, the laws of causality, the distinctions of rational category are all ignored as the abstract blends with the concrete, colors and sounds mingle, and flowers appear that never grew on the face of the earth.

The *Illuminations*, which Rimbaud said meant colored plates, have no over-all theme nor do the poems possess common structure like those of Bertrand or Baudelaire. They take widely diverse forms and derive from a variety of inspiration. Discontinuity is the rule also of the inner progression of each poem marked by jolts, unexpected breaks, or false starts and stops. The syntactic confusion reinforces the strange yokings of words that create the startling, hallucinatory effects. One feels a strong hand, a dynamic force that destroys while it builds anew, sweeping away all the old poetics to create an art that would recreate the world as well, give if not the authentic at least a fresh view of the cosmos.

Instead of linear or progressive composition, one might describe Rimbaud's technique as a crystallization process or the operation of a magnetic field which attracts to itself a number of elements. The unity of the poem is therefore chiefly conceptual although there may be occasional features of a more formal pattern such as internal refrains or echoes. Perhaps crystallization, though, is the better word to characterize Rimbaud's composition, for it reinforces the idea of concentration, which is the remarkable feature of all the *Illuminations*, a sort of distillation or reduction of the world to a poem, strikingly evident here in "Villes," where are compressed pêle-mêle places from all over the world and widely separated moments in history. It may be that Rimbaud is describing an actual place, say a town in the Alps seen from the funicular. But in his evocation it is as if the doors of some operatic warehouse were thrown open and the settings for a hundred exotic productions were rolled out. I say rolled out not only because of the reference in the poem to invisible pulleys, etc., but because everything seems intensely animated. In Rimbaud's poems the verbs are very important.

VILLES

Ce sont des villes! C'est un peuple pour qui se sont
montés ces Alleghanys et ces Libans de rêve! Des cha-
lets de cristal et de bois qui se meuvent sur des rails
et des poulies invisibles. Les vieux cratères ceints
de colosses et de palmiers de cuivre rugissent mélodi-
eusement dans les feux. Des fêtes amoureuses sonnent
sur les canaux pendus derrière les chalets. La chasse
des carillons crie dans les gorges. Des corporations
de chanteurs géants accourent dans des vêtements et

des oriflammes éclatants comme la lumière des cimes.
Sur les plates-formes au milieu des gouffres les Rolands
sonnent leur bravoure. Sur les passerelles de l'abîme
et les toits des auberges l'ardeur du ciel pavoise les
mâts. L'écroulement des apothéoses rejoint les champs
des hauteurs où les centauresses séraphiques évoluent
parmi les avalanches. Au-dessus du niveau des plus
hautes crêtes, une mer troublée par la naissance éter-
nelle de Vénus chargée de flottes orphéoniques et de la
rumeur des perles et des conques précieuses;—la mer
s'assombrit parfois avec des éclats mortels. Sur les
versants, des moissons de fleurs grandes comme nos
armes et nos coupes, mugissent. Des cortèges de Mabs
en robes rousses, opalines, montent des ravines. Là-
haut, les pieds dans la cascade et les ronces, les
cerfs tettent Diane. Les Bacchantes des banlieues san-
glotent et la lune brûle et hurle. Vénus entre dans les
cavernes des forgerons et des ermites. Des groupes de
beffrois chantent les idées des peuples. Des châteaux
bâtis en os sort la musique inconnue. Toutes les légendes
évoluent et les élans se ruent dans les bourgs. Le para-
dis des orages s'effondre. Les sauvages dansent sans
cesse la fête de la nuit. Et, une heure, je suis descendu
dans le mouvement d'un boulevard de Bagdad où des compa-
gnies ont chanté la joie du travail nouveau, sous une
brise épaisse, circulant sans pouvoir éluder les fabuleux
fantômes des monts où l'on a dû se retrouver.

Quels bons bras, quelle belle heure me rendront cette ré-
gion d'où viennent mes sommeils et mes moindres mouvements?

Works

Œuvres (Mercure de France, 1923–1926). 2 vols.

Readings

Butler, John Davis. *Moréas, A Critique of His Poetry and Philosophy* (The Hague: Mouton, 1967).
Georgin, René. *Jean Moréas* (Nouvelle Revue Critique, 1930).
Jouanny, Robert A. *Jean Moréas écrivain français* (Minard, 1969).

Jean Moréas

1856–1910

Jean Moréas (pseud. of Kannis Papadiamantopoulos) was the chief of the Symbolist school for a time and formulator of the Symbolist esthetic platform. The young poets of the 1880s flocked around Mallarmé and Verlaine because they were masters, revered elders. Moréas was, however, their own age, and his force with them depended less on his accomplishment (although this was fully recognized) than on his energetic articulation of their goals and ideals for poetry.

Another factor in his success with the young was unquestionably his personal attraction. Handsome and colorful, this Athenian transplanted to Paris held forth in the cafés of the Latin Quarter before an adoring throng. In 1891, a dinner was given in his honor to celebrate the triumph of his volume *Le Pèlerin passionné*, implicitly the triumph of Symbolism. Shortly afterwards, he announced his break with Symbolism and the founding of a new school, L'Ecole Romane. But a new band of disciples soon formed about him to replace those whom he had abandoned.

Moréas was born in Athens the son of a judge whose family was one of the most distinguished in Greece. His introduction to French was very early. A French governess trained him in the language and encouraged his love of literature. From the age of ten, his great ambition was to become a French poet. Later he told an interviewer that in coming to France he left a library of 2000 volumes, poets of the Renaissance and classics. When he arrived in Paris in his late teens to study law, he spent most of his time in the literary company of the cafés. With his tall, fine figure, his jet black hair and beard, his accent, he created an impression. Soon he exchanged his full beard for a moustache and affected a monocle.

All his life Moréas would remain an habitué of cafés and a night owl, who, even in later years, often did not make his way back to his rooms at the Porte d'Orléans until dawn.

He made his official début in French letters in 1884 with *Les Syrtes*, a collection of poems marked by the influence of Baudelaire and Verlaine. Two years later *Les Cantilènes* appeared. It is Moréas's most Symbolist work, with its Germanic motifs, its language full of archaisms and neo-logisms, its twisted syntax. 1886 is also the year of his famous manifesto published in the *Figaro*. In it, as spokesman for the Symbolists, he set forth the platform of the new school. It instigated a lively reaction in the press, the most notable being the article that Anatole France wrote for *Le Temps*. The month following the manifesto, in October, the first issue of the magazine *Le Symboliste* appeared with Moréas as editor, Gustave Kahn director and Paul Adam secretary. Moréas replied to France in its pages, and on all fronts—the little magazines, the daily papers, the cafés—defended the Symbolist cause. The publication of *Le Pèlerin passionné* brought Moréas to the peak of his fame, and the dinner organized to honor him marked an important date in the history of Symbolism. The event was given wide publicity; Barrès and Régnier had signed the invitations; Mallarmé gave the toast. The work, which was the occasion for the celebration, is a strange mixture of the old and new, with imita-tions in subject and manner of the Middle Ages and the Renaissance cast in the most modern forms of *vers libre*.

Perhaps the journey into the past that this collection presents was already an indication of Moréas's dissatisfaction with the present and the values represented by Symbolism. At any rate, in explaining his apostasy and the founding of the Ecole Romane he complained of the obscurity and melancholy of Symbolism as well as of its attachment to foreign literature. What he was advocating for the new school was a reaffirmation of the Mediterranean tradition, the French tradition, which had been broken by Romanticism and its derivatives Symbolism and Naturalism. The Symbolists considered that they had been betrayed and protested bitterly. A new literary quarrel broke out, one which would eventually become more political than literary and one in which the influence of the Chauvinistic philosopher Charles Maurras, already Moréas's comrade in arms, would play a far more important rôle. Moréas, for his part, culti-vated only his muse and, gradually ridding himself of all recherché orna-ment and affectation, composed the poems that would constitute his masterpiece *Les Stances*. The poems of this collection, distinguished for the purity of their form and their Apollonian tranquillity, reveal Moréas in full maturity to be very close to the great Romantic poets of the early part of the century.

If Symbolism was only a phase in the poetic career of Moréas, it was very important, nonetheless, and his role in the movement was a major one. The manifesto that he composed has been treated as inconsistent and incomprehensible. This seems unjust. Although expressed in a rhetoric that is at times florid, the program that he proposes is a quite concise and lucid statement. The break with Romanticism and with Parnasse is succinctly affirmed in the phrase "ennemi de l'enseignement, la déclamation, la fausse sensibilité, la description objective." The philosophical basis for the Symbolist esthetic is Hegelian, reality being located in the idea behind the phenomenon. Therefore the phenomenon must be described only as a manifestation of the idea: "Ainsi, dans cet art, les tableaux de la nature, les actions des humains, tous les phénomènes concrets ne sauraient se manifester eux-mêmes; ce sont là des apparences sensibles destinées à représenter leurs affinités ésotériques avec des Idées primordiales." The idea itself is the ultimate subject of their art: "la poésie symboliste cherche à vêtir l'Idée d'une forme sensible qui, néanmoins, ne serait pas son but à elle-même, mais qui, tout en servant à exprimer l'Idée, demeurerait sujette." The idea behind the phenomenon is suggested by the analogies which Symbolism exposes in the world of things. From Baudelaire to Breton, French poets have based their art on the philosophy of idealism. The Symbolists elaborated the statements of the Romantics and the moderns—Breton, Claudel, Proust, Giraudoux—however differently in emphasis and implication, maintained idealism as a fundamental assumption.

Implementation of the Symbolist doctrine demands a return to pre-Classical liberties in style and rhythm, Moréas goes on to say with a grandiloquence that Anatole France will gently mock: "Pour la traduction exacte de sa synthèse, il faut au symbolisme un style archétype et complexe: d'impollués vocables, la période qui s'arcboute alternant avec la période aux défaillances ondulées, les pléonasmes significatifs; les mystérieuses ellipses, l'anacoluthe en suspens, tout trope hardi et multiforme ..." Along with "la bonne et luxuriante et fringante langue française d'avant les Vaugelas et les Boileau-Despréaux" he calls for "l'ancienne métrique avivée; un désordre savamment ordonné, la rime illucescente et martelée comme un bouclier d'or et d'arain, auprès de la rime aux fluidités absconses; l'alexandrin à arrêts multiples et mobiles; l'emploi de certains nombres premiers—sept, neuf, onze, treize—..." [1]

As a poet, Jean Moréas has scarcely survived today. His place in literary history is assured chiefly as a theorist and as a personality that conjures up a colorful prewar Paris. Yet the homage paid his verse during his lifetime was not entirely undeserved, as we may judge from the poems that follow.

Note

1. *Figaro*, 18 September 1886.

LE RHIN[1]

I

Aux galets le flot se brise
Sous la lune blanche et grise,
O la triste cantilène
Que la bise dans la plaine!
—Elfes couronnés de jonc,
Viendrez-vous danser en rond?

II

Hou! hou! le héron ricane
Pour faire peur à la cane.
Trap! trap! le sorcier galope
Sur le bouc et la varlope.
—Elfes couronnés de jonc,
Viendrez-vous danser en rond?

III

Au caveau rongé de mousse
L'empereur à barbe rousse,
Le front dans les mains, sommeille.
Le nain guette la corneille.
—Elfes couronnés de jonc
Viendrez-vous danser en rond?

IV

Mais déjà l'aurore émerge,
De rose teignant la berge,
Et s'envolent les chimères
Comme un essaim d'éphémères.
—Elfes couronnés de jonc,
Vous ne dansez plus en rond!

---

1. From *Les Cantilènes*, this ballad is an example of imitation from the German. Hugo, Aloysius Bertrand, and others had already exploited material from the folk legends popularized by the German Romantics. The Symbolists, influenced by Wagner's example, renewed the vogue.

Note here the seven-syllable lines, each stanza with two feminine couplets followed by one masculine as refrain.

UNE JEUNE FILLE PARLE[2]

Les fenouils m'ont dit: Il t'aime si
Follement qu'il est à ta merci;
Pour son revenir va t'apprêter.
—Les fenouils ne savent que flatter!
Dieu ait pitié de mon âme.

Les pâquerettes m'ont dit: Pourquoi
Avoir remis ta foi dans sa foi?
Son cœur est tanné comme un soudard.
—Pâquerettes, vous parlez trop tard!
Dieu ait pitié de mon âme.

Les sauges m'ont dit: Ne l'attends pas,
Il s'est endormi dans d'autres bras.
—O sauges, tristes sauges, je veux
Vous tresser toutes dans mes cheveux ...
Dieu ait pitié de mon âme.

2. From *Le Pèlerin passionné*, this poem harks back to the classical pastoral genre which has flourished throughout the ages. Minor Symbolists cultivated these pretty, sentimental themes.

FIER PRINTEMPS[3]

Fier printemps ravisseur, que tu m'as abusé,
Et de quel faux semblant tu as mon cœur brisé!
L'hirondelle à présent sur la mer s'est enfuie,
Le cri de l'échassier nous ramène la pluie;
Le prudent laboureur qui songe à ses guérets
De la cognée abat dans les tristes forêts
L'yeuse qui répand à terre son feuillage.
Automne malheureux, que j'aime ton visage!

3. From *Enone au clair visage*. The inspiration here, as in "Une Jeune Fille parle," is classical. Moréas's nature is, of course, purely conventional. Such discreet and fetching depiction of sentiment must have appealed to the genteel public of the end of the century.

Poetry of Albert Samain

Au Jardin de l'Infante (Mercure de France, 1893).
Aux Flancs du Vase (Mercure de France, 1898).
Le Chariot d'or (Mercure de France, 1901).
Polyphème (Mercure de France, 1906).

Readings

Bocquet, Léon. *Albert Samain, sa vie, son œuvre* (Mercure de France, 1905).
Bonneau, Georges. *Albert Samain poète symboliste* (Mercure de France, 1925).
Lowell, Amy. *Six French Poets* (New York: Macmillan, 1915), "Albert Samain," pp. 51–104.

Albert Samain

1858–1900

A minor poet but exquisite in his mood pieces and genre sketches, Albert Samain deserves a place in Symbolism for his adherence to basic Symbolist principles and for his attachment to Baudelaire and to Verlaine. True, he derives also from the Romantics and the Parnassians: like Régnier, who also emulated the lapidary art of Heredia, Samain shows the fin-de-siècle blending of these two dominant strains in French poetry, Parnassianism and Symbolism, that developed out of Romanticism during the second half of the nineteenth century. He is more than just a historical figure, however, for, if the languid and tender sentiment of his verses that made him popular in his times is not in the taste of today, there is still great merit in his poetic craftsmanship and, in his modest worship of beauty, an appeal for all times. The life of Samain was one of those forlorn existences that we associate with early Romanticism. Like Sainte-Beuve and Aloysius Bertrand, he was an impecunious celibate with a mother to support. Like Bertrand and Maurice de Guérin, he suffered from poor health and died young. Differing from his Romantic precursors, however, he went to work every day to earn his living. His office jobs took most of his time and energy: two slender volumes of verse, to which one could add a play, comprise all his major literary production. Life, if not temperament, made Albert Samain a minor poet.

He was born in Lille in 1858 of shopkeeper parentage. When he was fourteen, his father died, leaving a wife and three children. Albert, as the oldest, left school and went to work first in a bank and then in a brokerage office. At his job long hours and pretty much to himself when at leisure, he was a sad and lonely boy, finding fulfillment only in his daydreams.

He continued his studies on his own and longed to leave Lille for Paris and his job for a career in literature. His one friend and confidant, a Victor Lemoigne, did his best to draw Albert out of his shell and tried to open doors for him in Parisian journalism. His efforts came to nothing, chiefly because of Albert's timidity and passiveness. However, in 1880 he did succeed in having him transferred to the capital. Madame Samain soon joined her son in Paris. The daughter was now married, but there was a younger brother still at home. The home life that Albert knew in Lille was thus gradually reestablished. He changed jobs. In spite of the risks involved, he was determined to leave an employment that took all his time. Civil service looked like a means of escape and, after passing his tests, he left the brokerage firm for a job in the Hôtel de Ville. He had to face daily there a dull routine; yet the new job did not displease him, for the hours were shorter and his colleagues were men of a certain culture.

Through his co-workers at the Hôtel de Ville, Samain made contact with the literary world of the Montmartre cafés. He had written to several eminent men of letters previously and had sent them samples of his own verse. Banville, Richepin, and Octave Feuillet had received his advances just as homage due them and did little or nothing for Samain's career. But his contacts with the young militant poets of the day bore fruit. In December 1884, his poem "Tsilla" appeared on the front page of *Le Chat Noir*. Samain was troubled and confused. Having been brought up on Hugo and Musset, he could not fully share the enthusiasms of his comrades and benefactors of *Le Chat Noir*. He withdrew from their company and, although he went on writing, offered little for publication. The poems of *Au Jardin de l'Infante* composed at this time show Samain's attachment to the old and his honest effort to adapt to the new. Although much of the time alone with his reading and composing, he did not shun all associations. Paul Morisse and Raymond Bonheur became his fast friends. With Morisse, Samain visited Germany, with Bonheur, Samain went to England and to the Low Countries. On another occasion, Bonheur and Samain went down to Spain, stopping off at Orthez to see Jammes.

Early in the 1890s, Albert Samain began again to frequent literary groups, notably the one which was to found the *Mercure de France*. In the magazine some of his poems appeared, in 1893, the volume was brought out by the affiliated publishing house. Parnassians and Symbolists alike hailed *Au Jardin de l'Infante*; it received an Academy award and sold so well that a second printing was authorized. Success did not change Samain's character. Although he was often present at literary gatherings, he remained retiring and self-effacing. In private he was, as always, the patient drudge devoted to his mother and without illusions as to his material future. His greatest strength lay in his stubborn resistance to the encouragement and exhortations of his more sanguinary friends. Nothing could persuade him to exploit his successes; to blame was his bad health or his native temperament or a fatalistic philosophy born out of his reading of deterministic philosophers. He went to work, nevertheless, on the poems that would make up *Aux Flancs du Vase*. This volume appeared in 1898 and passed almost unnoticed. Samain had refused to go out all winter because of a disfiguring skin ailment. Then his mother died and the grief-stricken poet gave little heed to the publicity for his book. The death of his mother was doubtless the calamity of his life and hastened his own death. Friends took him off to spend the next winter in the south. Upon his return in the spring, he set to work on his little play *Polyphème*. But his health, undermined by tuberculosis, soon grew worse and he had to request a leave of absence from his job. He went to be cared for first by his sister in Lille, then by Raymond Bonheur who had a house in the country near Paris. There Albert Samain died in 1900.

Of the two collections of Samain's poetry published during his lifetime, it is the first that is the more Symbolistic. *Au Jardin de l'Infante* opens with a quotation from Edgar Allan Poe and is strongly marked by Baudelaire and by Verlaine. With Poe one may see a certain kinship in the gothic and satanic elements present in the early Samain. Whether the source is Poe or Baudelaire or even Hugo is moot, of course. Some of the sonnets, though, are obvious imitations of the *Fleurs du Mal*, and the Baudelairian themes of evil and concupiscence thread through the entire volume. More characteristic, however, is the sentimental theme reminiscent of Verlaine, with tender tête-à-têtes, walks in the autumnal twilight, landscapes drenched in the Watteau-like atmosphere of the *Fêtes Galantes*. There is little to remind one directly of that other master of Symbolism, Mallarmé. Yet if the Infante of the title and the introductory poem first reminds one of Hugo, she is actually more the sister of Hérodiade than of earlier feminine figures. Moreover, Samain's exquisite descriptions of vases and teacups suggest that his debt to Mallarmé was not entirely limited to an epigraph or two. Thematic material aside, *Au Jardin de l'Infante* reveals basic concepts of art and life that link Samain with Symbolism. First and most important is the concept of universal analogy which lies behind the coupling, in these poems, of disparate phenomena and behind the blending of the subjective with the objective in soulscapes. For example, the poet's hesitant, ambiguous feeling is translated into indistinct colors and forms in a nature scene, his tears flow with the tears of the fountain or his sighs blend with the sound of the flute. Similar fusions and minglings are involved in the sensory evocations which are very strong in this poetry. It is full of "accords de mots mystérieux, / Doux comme le baiser de la paupière aux yeux." [1] Moreover, Samain, faithful to the Symbolist principles set forth in the "Art Poétique" of Verlaine, declares, "J'adore l'indécis, les sons, les couleurs frêles, / Tout ce qui tremble, ondule, et frissonne, et chatoie ..." [2]

Colorist in the Symbolist manner, Samain is also a musician in the Symbolist manner in his use of assonance and alliteration and in the emphasis that he places on rhythmic structure. This is not to say that Samain was at all radical in matters of prosody. He was not tempted by free verse and rarely departed from the traditional alexandrine or octosyllabic line. The liberties that he permitted himself were limited to relocating (or suppressing) the caesura and to running over the line. His rimes were likewise generally quite conventional, although sometimes more exact in sound than in spelling and sometimes departing from normal succession. Drawn particularly to the sonnet, Samain varies, on occasion, the rime scheme established by the sixteenth- or seventeenth-century models and adds a fifteenth line for a dramatic effect of recapitulation. Little of the Symbolist permissiveness in lexicon and syntax can be found in Samain. He compensates for a rather limited vocabulary by an occasional archaism or neologism, sometimes by an expression borrowed from a foreign language. But he is neither very daring nor does he abuse poetic licence in deviations from ordinary grammatical usage.

Aux Flancs du Vase is, in décor, somewhat deserving of the epithet "symbolisme du centaure" that has been applied to Henri de Régnier. The setting is Greece, and in the background one senses the presence of the half-divinities of mythology. But they remain for the most part hidden. Instead of centaurs and fauns we see human beings, bucolic types like Daphnis and Chloe yet who had their grosser counterparts in Samain's France. Without the Arcadian luster here are the maidens and their swains, or the children and their parents that Samain could have encountered in his own village streets or country roads. The poems constitute little *genre tableaux* depicting a woman nursing her baby, a girl setting the table for supper, a butcher slaughtering an ox. The bejeweled sumptuousness and the sentimental posturing associated with Symbolism are absent in this volume. There is sentimentality, to be sure, but it is, one might say, a sentimentality à la Chardin, a homely and earthy sort, and the glitter of décor is here only the effect of lighting and the Apollonian perspective.

In comparing the first volume with the second, critics have applied to Samain the words of his own sonnet: "Tu bus à larges traits l'Artifice excitant. / Mais voici que déjà, las des vaines fanfares, / Tu songes au profond silence où l'on s'entend; / ... Va, ne t'attarde plus aux parades étranges. / Si la vie a rentré quelque blé dans tes granges, / Fais ton pain simplement dans la paix du Seigneur."[3] Yet if *Aux Flancs du Vase* represents the better and more original Samain, there was much that was very fine in the poetry that he had written previously. Even the poems that he had excluded from *Au Jardin de l'Infante* have superior merit and their inclusion in the volume of *inedita* published after Samain's death was surely justified. *Le Chariot d'or* contains many poems rejected by Samain perhaps because he feared that they might be too bombastic, too grandiloquent, too much in the Romantic manner no longer in favor. But judged as examples of heroic poetry, these verses are of first quality. This volume contains, moreover, the "Elégies," lovely poems which the poet possibly thought too indiscreet to publish himself. Samain culled his verse with excessive rigor; fortunately his friends who put together the volume entitled *Le Chariot d'or* recognized that without these gleanings, specimens of his different periods and different manners, our image of Albert Samain would be poorer. The same may be said of *Polyphème*, the little drama which, without recapitulating the stages of Samain's poetry, offers echoes and reminiscences. Needless to say, the poetry of the play is its important feature. Plot and character are just as slight as in Samain's several prose pieces, likewise published posthumously, in which poetic themes are treated in beautifully cadenced prose.

Notes

1. *Le Chariot d'or*, p. 44.
2. "Dilection," in *Au Jardin de l'Infante*.
3. "Fleurs suspectes, miroirs ténébreux, vices rares," in *Au Jardin de l'Infante*.

PROMENADE A L'ETANG[1]

Le calme des jardins profonds s'idéalise.
L'âme du soir s'annonce à la tour de l'église;
Ecoute, l'heure est bleue et le ciel s'angélise.[2]

A voir ce lac mystique où l'azur s'est fondu,
Dirait-on pas, ma sœur, qu'un grand cœur éperdu
En longs ruisseaux d'amour, là-haut, s'est répandu?[3]

L'ombre lente a noyé la vallée indistincte.
La cloche, au loin, note par note, s'est éteinte,
Emportant comme l'âme frêle d'une sainte.

L'heure est à nous; voici que, d'instant en instant,
Sur les bois violets au mystère invitant
Le grand manteau de la solitude s'étend.

L'étang moiré d'argent, sous la ramure brune,
Comme un cœur affligé que le jour importune,
Rêve à l'ascension suave de la lune ...

Je veux, enveloppé de tes yeux caressants,
Je veux cueillir, parmi les roseaux frémissants,
La grise fleur des crépuscules pâlissants.[4]

Je veux au bord de l'eau pensive, ô bien-aimée,
A ta lèvre d'amour et d'ombre parfumée
Boire un peu de ton âme, à tout soleil fermée.

Les ténèbres sont comme un lourd tapis soyeux,
Et nos deux cœurs, l'un près de l'autre, parlent mieux
Dans un enchantement d'amour silencieux.

Comme pour saluer les étoiles premières,
Nos voix de confidence, au calme des clairières,
Montent, pures dans l'ombre, ainsi que des prières.

Et je baise ta chair angélique aux paupières.[5]

---

1. There are at least four versions of this poem from *Au Jardin de l'Infante*. Although not interested in virtuosity and putting content above expression, Samain was a painstaking craftsman (see Bocquet, p. 190). The structure of the poem reveals a favorite

procedure of Samain's: single-rime stanzas of three lines each, followed by a final single line. Habitually exploiting feminine endings for their sweet and soft effect, in this poem where feminine stanzas alternate with masculine, Samain ends the poem with a feminine line.

2. Neologism is not very frequent in Samain, whose lexicon is much more limited and conventional than many poets of his day. This line contrasts with the awkwardly contrived line just before it.

3. Reminders of Baudelaire underline the mediocrity of Samain's achievement. The images like this one seem just tasteless.

4. Others, in spite of being terribly mannered, may charm.

5. It is interesting to plot the progression of the symbolic image throughout the poem: soul of evening → hour → blue of sky → blue sea → rivers → drown → sound dies → saint dies → hour is ours → pond → pensive water → drink one's soul → voices rise → like prayers → angelic flesh. It moves along through associations, back and forth from the real to the figurative.

LE REPAS PREPARE[6]

Ma fille, laisse là ton aiguille et ta laine;
Le maître va rentrer; sur la table de chêne
Avec la nappe neuve aux plis étincelants
Mets la faïence claire et les verres brillants.
Dans la coupe arrondie à l'anse en col de cygne
Pose les fruits choisis sur des feuilles de vigne,
Les pêches que recouvre un velours vierge encor,
Et les lourds raisins bleus mêlés aux raisins d'or.
Que le pain bien coupé remplisse les corbeilles,
Et puis ferme la porte et chasse les abeilles ...
Dehors le soleil brûle, et la muraille cuit.
Rapprochons les volets, faisons presque la nuit.
Afin qu'ainsi la salle, aux ténèbres plongée,
S'embaume toute aux fruits dont la table est chargée.
Maintenant, va puiser l'eau fraîche dans la cour;
Et veille que surtout la cruche, à ton retour,
Garde longtemps, glacée et lentement fondue,
Une vapeur légère à ses flancs suspendue.

6. From *Aux Flancs du Vase*. In a Virgilian setting transposed, a charming still life. It recalls genre painting and, in poetry, scenes painted by Sainte-Beuve. The sonorities of the words complement the sensuous quality of the images. Amy Lowell speaks of "a set of engravings by Boucher, or Fragonard, or Watteau. Not paintings, but engravings, each set in an oval, and faintly coloured." *Six French Poets* (Macmillan, 1915), p. 87. We might think that in this poem luminosities, texture, colors of blues and golds suggest rather more than faint colorations, but we understand her over-all characterization of Samain as a delicate painter of porcelains, what he himself speaks of as his fondness for "couleurs frêles." See p. 172.

Poetry of Gustave Kahn

Premiers Poèmes (Mercure de France, 1897). A collective volume including
   Les Palais Nomades, Chansons d'Amant, Domaine de Fée, and a preface
   on free verse.
La Pluie et le Beau Temps (Vanier, 1896).
Limbes de Lumière (Brussels: Deman, 1897).
Le Livre d'Images (Mercure de France, 1897).

Readings

J. C. Ireson. *L'Œuvre Poétique de Gustave Kahn* (Nizet, 1962).

Gustave Kahn

1859–1936

The name Gustave Kahn evokes first of all the story of free verse. Who-
ever among the Symbolists invented this form of poetic expression (and
the question to be answered requires very specific definition and photo-
finish evidence), Kahn was one of its most assiduous practitioners. Besides
producing volume after volume of verses more or less free, prose pieces,
and criticism, Kahn was also an editor, and this, next to his association
with free verse, makes him important as a Symbolist. In January of 1886,
he became director of *La Vogue*, the magazine whose weekly issues
brought to public attention the work of Rimbaud, Laforgue, Verlaine,
and Kahn himself. Several months later Kahn joined Moréas and Paul
Adam to found *Le Symboliste*. René Ghil had just founded *La Décadence*
in an effort to contest Moréas's leadership, and *Le Symboliste* was designed
as a counter-weapon. Neither review survived beyond three numbers. In
1888, Kahn was invited by Dujardin to direct the *Revue Indépendante*,
and in 1889 he launched *La Vogue* once again. In spite of their short lives,
these little reviews, for the style they set and the names they advanced,
had great importance. Kahn remained a key figure as long as they lasted.

He was born in Metz and received his higher education in Paris at the
Ecole des Chartes and the Ecole des Langues Orientales. While still a
student, he began frequenting the literary cafés and publishing in the
little reviews. But he was abruptly lifted out of the literary world to
spend four years in North Africa as a soldier. They were significant years
for him since, although when he returned to Paris late in 1884 he took up
his life where he had left it, memory of Africa would remain with him
throughout his days and lend his writing an exotic coloration. During

the latter 1880s, Gustave Kahn rose to become one of the pontiffs of the Paris literary world, as we have seen an important editor and proselytizer of free verse. In the cafés he held forth on literature and life, a dapper little man with a goatee and a cigar. In spite of his family's wealth, he was on a strict allowance which, with the help of his friends, was all used up after the first week of every month. He had an apartment near the Hippodrome filled with art and bric-à-brac, a blackboard, and a piano, on which he liked to play the lieder that he often imitated in his poems.

The bankruptcy of *La Revue Indépendante* in 1889 marked an end for Kahn's role as leader of a literary faction. The next year he married and left Paris for Brussels. The five years that he spent in Belgium were productive ones; away from the cafés of Paris he forged ahead with his own work. To his first collection of verse, *Les Palais Nomades*, which had appeared already in 1887, he now added in succession the volumes of *Chansons d'Amant, Domaine de Fée, La Pluie et le Beau Temps, Limbes de Lumière*, and a novel, *Le Roi fou*. When he returned to Paris, now a man with family responsibilities, although he continued to remain at his writing table, an increasing bulk of his work was in journalism. Through his reviews and literary columns, his name became one of the best known in French letters. As for creative works, in the list of his publications from 1900 to 1914 novels figure prominently. At the outbreak of World War I, he abandoned all literary work of any sort to contribute to the national effort. Where he was assigned—at the Ministry of Public Works—Kahn met Léon Blum, who would be his close friend for the rest of his life. After the war, when he returned to literature, it was chiefly as an art critic. He remained, however, a novelist and a poet, with several works of fiction and two collections of poems. In the works of Kahn's last period, the influence of the Old Testament is very strong. He had always been quite conscious of his ethnic origins, what with his name and the Semitic cast to his features, although he was in matters of religion in no sense an Orthodox Jew. He had lived during the Dreyfus period and the rise of National Socialism in Germany. His death in 1936 may have spared him the martyrdom that awaited many other distinguished European Jews during World War II.

Whereas Jean Moréas, in his manifesto of 1886, stressed the philosophic aspirations of Symbolism, Gustave Kahn was chiefly concerned with technical matters. With reserves and restrictions we might say that Moréas was more in line with Baudelaire and Rimbaud, while Kahn derives from Verlaine and his "Art poétique." When Kahn was invited to succeed

Teodor de Wyzewa on the *Revue Indépendante* he might have become chief of the Symbolists. The fact that he was mainly concerned with prosody may explain why he did not; it most assuredly defines his contribution to the movement. His new verse form, illustrated first in the *Palais Nomades*, structured the line on rhythmic measures instead of syllables. The idea may have come from the *Illuminations;* in a sense it answered Verlaine's call for reform; it may also derive from Mallarmé, who counted Kahn as one of his earliest disciples. In any event, free verse evolved rather than burst upon the scene and, as practiced by Kahn and others, bore little resemblance to the work of those who may have paved the way for it.

A technician rather than a philosopher, Kahn never pretended for his poetry more thought than what was evident, plus melody and image. His symbolism was chiefly of the conventional sort, without any implication of a correspondence in phenomena or a linking with a world behind the world. What obscurity that his poetry may be accused of cannot be laid to the door of esoteric purpose but rather of conviction as to how the subject should best be presented. Ellipsis, neologism, grammatical and syntactical innovation are some of the procedures characteristic of Kahn's poetic style. In these ways he follows Baudelaire in suggesting rather than explicitly describing, Verlaine in blending sensation and idea, and the Germans Heine and Wagner in stressing poetic polyphonies.

After the *Palais Nomades*, in Kahn's next two volumes of verse, his manner became increasingly assured, increasingly fixed, the result of his own maturity and the crystallization of his esthetic. By 1891, the date of *Chansons d'Amant*, free verse was quite established and Kahn would henceforth use no other kind. The theme of this new volume was love, as the title indicated. *Domaine de Fée* (1895) had the same theme, but the treatment of it was more strongly personal than in *Chansons d'Amant*. One might say that with this volume Kahn had reached in theme the personal expression that he had already found in style. It may be discerned in future volumes even though he explored other subjects, shifted emphasis, or altered technique according to the circumstance. *La Pluie et Le Beau Temps* (1896) turned away from the sentimental to the descriptive and the contemplative, evoking pictures of the world and recording impressions. In *Limbes de Lumière* (1897), the inspiration came not from the outside world but from books, notably from Shakespeare. From volume to volume Kahn's imagery remained exuberant, but his syntax became somewhat less eccentric. Of all his works, the most accessible is the next one, *Le Livre d' Images*, published later in 1897. The poems are light, whimsical pieces that echo legends and tales of the French provinces.

After *Le Livre d'Images*, Kahn left poetry to take up prose. The vein of whimsy that was more and more noticeable in his verse was exploited now in stories. Some are volume length, others are brief, all are marked by lyricism and humor without any claim to realism.

Yet however dissimilar their art, Kahn had something in common with the novelists of the Realistic tradition, that is, the interest they all took in social problems. Kahn did not express this interest in painting the proletariat; instead he addressed himself to it directly. For example in *Odes de la Raison*, which dates from 1902, he adopted for his verse a declamatory style designed to touch the masses. With this book he revived a verse form not popular since Romanticism and took up the humanitarian cause espoused by Hugo and his generation. Kahn was not an engaged poet or a pamphleteer. Yet he did not hide his views either, and his latter works especially show him to belong to the tradition of the Revolution: an optimist, a rationalist, a progressive, and a socialist.

During the first two decades of the twentieth century, Kahn's writing was chiefly journalistic, with only occasionally some fiction and some verse. In poetry, there was nothing of note until *La Pépinière du Luxembourg* (1923), a poetic drama that offered the unusual attraction of an imagined dialogue between Baudelaire and Banville. Full of allusion and parody, it is a piece of virtuosity. *Le Childebert* is a poetic novel dating from the same period. As we have noted, the work that occupied Kahn during the very last years of his life (aside from diverse poems collected after his death) was biblical and Jewish in inspiration. The poems of *Images Bibliques* (1929) have a place between the *Contes Juifs* and *Terre d'Israël*, often linking up in verse the biblical subjects already treated in the stories. Published at a time when André Breton was getting ready to issue the second manifesto of Surrealism, these poems seemed to belong to a remote past. Kahn had outlived many of the younger poets whom he had influenced. In technique, poetry had moved far beyond him, and in spirit, the concept of the ideal, humanistic or metaphysical, had become almost unrecognizable to a Symbolist who had come of age in the 1880s.

LES VOIX REDISAIENT[1]

Les voix redisaient: la chanson qui brise
En son cœur, son cœur enseveli
C'est le son des flûtes aux accords des brises
Et la marche nuptiale des pâles lys.

Et que des perrons d'idéal porphyre
Elle descendrait lente et front baissé
En lacis perlé d'idéals Ophirs
Et les mains soumises et lèvres blessées.

Qu'il faudra bercer la candeur surprise
A l'éveil si brusque au matin d'aimer—
O si court mirage des bonnes méprises
Et réveil si brusque et fini d'aimer.

1. From *Les Palais Nomades*. Sounds and images here make one think of the author as a Verlaine with Baudelaire's sense of opulence. What they add up to in meaning is not clear; contrary to his great forerunners, Kahn is deliberately obscure, aiming at evocation rather than communication and avoiding the overprecise even in sensory suggestion. The verse is free with a variety of beats in the lines but with end rimes and internal assonances. Yoking the abstract with the concrete and using words for their rarity and their phonic value alone mark the poem as a product of fin-de-siècle Symbolism.

CHANSON[2]

O bel avril épanoui
qu'importe ta chanson franche,
tes lilas blancs, tes aubépines et l'or fleuri
de ton soleil par les branches,
si loin de moi la bien-aimée
dans les brumes du Nord est restée!

O bel avril épanoui
La revoir est la fête sans merci,
O bel avril épanoui.
Elle vient à moi. Tes lilas,
tes floraisons de soleil d'or
alors me plairont—merci
ô bel avril épanoui.

2. From *Domaine de Fée*. On the theme of longing for the absent beloved, Kahn creates this little complaint with its repeated line reminiscent of popular and naive poetry. The metrical arrangement is predominantly a ballad-like beat—four to a line, with an occasional uneven one.

LE VIEUX MENDIANT[3]

La masse d'airain du temps pesa dès son enfance
sur son front; car des gardes emmenèrent son père
les pieds gênés d'entraves, les mains jointes de fer:
la justice en pesa la tête dans sa balance.

Sa mère, au souffle de la colère, s'égara
dans les bois touffus, où des yeux jamais las
veillent sur tout sentier, meublant la fondrière
de passants nus, leurs yeux de misère encore ouverts;
et l'enfant grandissait quand cette tête tomba.

Il fut le fils des assassins; lors une pierre
(la marmaille jouait) lui creva la paupière
et le mire ne guérissant qu'honnêtes gens,
l'autre œil se détruisit, dans son masque d'enfant
pareil dès lors à un mur blanc.

Puis il fut un jouet, et les forts gravèrent
leur rancœur et leur impatience en cicatrices
sur sa face, muette table de supplices,

et des rôdeurs, par pitié, le grisèrent
par gouaille, pour qu'il dansât
et, quand il pleura, le fouaillèrent.

Comme pour chacun de ses doigts
sans cesse était prête une épine,
que ses pieds sanglants avaient froid
et qu'on poussait dans les ravines
son corps pitoyable et sa face d'effroi,

chaque fois que vers les auvents
du village il allait quêtant
par le soleil ou le grand vent
son pain, à la complainte de son chant,

il suivit des vagabonds
dont la gourde lui donnait le songe;
il eut l'os que le mâtin ronge
et les servit sans mensonge.—
Aussi on le mit en prison.

Et lorsqu'il fut l'exemple de la mauvaise route
et des tourments de la pire conscience,
un marguillier, aux écoutes
des merveilles de la grâce en son inconscience,

le plaça pour que la main des dames
s'honorât du sou qui rachète les âmes
sous un parvis d'église en évidence:
leçon de choses pour toute l'enfance.

Le vieux mendiant est lézardé
comme la pierre des piliers;
ils subissent les mêmes outrages
du temps, des chiens et de l'orage.

Ils semblent attendre d'un même âge
parmi le nombreux passage
des gens recouverts de velours et de fourrures,
les êtres doux dont la parure
serait la douceur aumônière
et l'âme en généreuse prière.

Et le Temps pleut, lentement, lentement
sur leur attente et leur tourment.

3. From *Le Livre d'Images*. There is a ferocity in this narrative poem that one associates more with some Romantic poems than with Symbolism, probably because of the patent philosophical or moralizing aspect. As with Hugo's *Crapaud*, this poem constitutes a bitter rebuke to humanity for its cruelty.

PROVENCE[4]

C'est une face fine et légère;
pourtant quelle noblesse vit dans ses traits menus
et sa chair est claire,
non qu'elle évoque aucun aspect floral
elle est chair, et elle est claire
comme de la lumière astrale.

Le front est ample
et blanc comme un marbre de temple
où un fidèle a beaucoup prié;
les lèvres sont rouges pourpres,
non pourpres comme un hochet royal,
mais comme une baie au goût profond,
au goût profond comme un sens
et qui renaît dès qu'on la cueille ...

. . . .

4. From *Le Livre d'Images*, an evocation of Provence by means of a symbolic portrait. The inner rimes characteristic of Kahn's free verse form complicated patterns. Here the *è:r* sound, which ends the first line, is repeated throughout the stanza and combines with *al;* which occurs at the end of lines four and six. In the second stanza [ã] and [u] thread through the verses.

Poetry of Jules Laforgue

Œuvres Complètes de Jules Laforgue (Mercure de France, 1922–1930). 6 vols.

Readings

Chauvelot, Dr. R. *Jules Laforgue inconnu* (Debresse, 1973).

Debauve, J. L. *Laforgue en son temps* (Neuchâtel: Baconnière, 1972). Letters to his publisher.

Guichard, Léon. *Jules Laforgue et ses poésies* (Presses Universitaires, 1950).

Ramsey, Warren. *Jules Laforgue and the Ironic Inheritance* (Oxford: Clarendon Press, 1953).

Ramsey, Warren, ed. *Jules Laforgue: Essays on a Poet's Life and Work* (Carbondale: Southern Illinois University Press, 1969).

Reboul, Pierre. *Jules Laforgue* (Hatier, 1960).

Ruchon, François. *Jules Laforgue* (Geneva: Ciana, 1924).

Sakari, Ellen. *Prophète et Pierrot: Thèmes et attitudes ironiques dans l'œuvre de Jules Laforgue.* (Jyväskylä, Finland, 1974).

Jules Laforgue

1860–1887

Discussion of Jules Laforgue is apt to raise the question of who invented free verse or of whether Laforgue owed something to Tristan Corbière. It is likely also that allusion will be made to his life as following with painful exactness the pattern of the unhappy poet. But what is sure to be brought up is the prestige which Laforgue has enjoyed abroad, particularly in England and America, so great that by comparison one might think that he has generally been unappreciated at home. There is no doubt that it is his importance abroad that makes him unique, but the French have not been entirely unmindful of Laforgue's merits and have not begrudged him his rightful place in the Symbolist and modernist tradition.

He was born in Montevideo, Uruguay, where his father, originally from Tarbes, had been brought at the age of eight. In adulthood Charles-Benoît Laforgue ran a private school in Montevideo and married one of his pupils, the daughter of a French merchant in that city. She was not very close to Jules. As he says, "J'avais presque pas connu ma mère."[1] At home there were other children and, from the age of seven to fifteen he was away at school in Tarbes. When, in 1875, the whole family returned to France, he joined them in Paris, but his mother had only two more years to live. She died giving birth to her twelfth child.

Solitude would always be Jules Laforgue's complaint. At school in Tarbes he was a lonely, unhappy boy; in Paris at the Lycée Condorcet he does not seem to have changed. However, the three older children seem to have been rather close. Emile had been with Jules all the while he was in Tarbes; in Paris he went to Beaux-Arts and took up painting, Jules following at a distance with visits to museums and attendance at

Taine's lectures. Marie, Jules's confidante, worked at her music. But soon Emile went off to do his military service and M. Laforgue moved his family back to Tarbes. In 1881, Jules was living alone in a furnished room, homesick and sometimes hungry.

To earn a living, Laforgue had found a job with the art historian Charles Ephrussi. His pay was not much, but through his employer, Laforgue learned a good deal about art. Ephrussi and Paul Bourget were Laforgue's good angels: what Ephrussi did for his education in art, Bourget did for his education in literature. When Laforgue was not in museums he was in libraries, and every Sunday he carried to Bourget the verses and the prose pieces that he had composed during the week. Besides his two sponsors, Laforgue acquired two important friends. Gustave Kahn, one of the most active poets in the Symbolist campaign, was a companion of Laforgue's own age. So, too, was Charles Henry, who made a third in rambles around the Latin Quarter and in literary discussions, redolent of pipe smoke. Kahn introduced him to Mallarmé and Henry introduced him to a lady author who went under the name of Sandâ Mahâli. As plain Mme. Mültzer, she opened her parlor every Sunday to young musicians and poets. One would think that Laforgue was being rather abundantly served from the social and artistic resources of Paris and had no cause for complaint. Perhaps though, loneliness and want are more a state of mind than actual circumstances: someone else might not have made such a drama of eating a solitary meal out of a paper bag or not have been intimidated by the clerks in a delicatessen. Even with the sinecure of a readership to the Empress Augusta, Jules Laforgue found reason to be miserable.

Bourget and Ephrussi had got him the job. It was well paid and not very demanding. Jules could send money home to help support all the brothers and sisters that the death of his father had orphaned. For five years (1881–1886) Laforgue remained attached to the German empress, living in luxury and enjoying a rich social life divided between court functions and the concerts, theaters, and cafés that he went to with friends. Yet he had time to read and to write; it is in Germany that Laforgue composed the bulk of his published work.

Already in 1880, he had thought of bringing out a volume of verse inspired by his philosophical meditations and readings. Yet in looking over the poems that he was about to publish under the title *Sanglot de la Terre*, Laforgue had a change of heart. They seemed too pompous, not at all in keeping with the ideal of unemphatic expression and freer form toward which he had most recently been working. He explained, "J'ai abandonné ... mes poèmes philosophiques. Je trouve stupide de faire la grosse voix et de jouer de l'éloquence.[2] Nevertheless, it seems likely that some of the pieces intended for the *Sanglot de la Terre* were saved and reworked for the new collection *Les Complaintes*. To be sure their effusions of philosophy and sentiment would have had to be corrected by irony and understatement to turn them into *complaintes*, a genre characteristically humble and familiar. Their contours would have to be softened considerably to satisfy Bourget, who recommended that Laforgue drown his descriptions in dreams![3] By 1884, the *Complaintes* were finished and the following year they were published. The work as a whole is very uneven, revealing a young poet trying his hand at a variety of new forms. There are pretty pictures, lyrical or ironical outbursts, popular jingles, and parodies. The light and irreverent touch does not preclude a fundamental seriousness: Laforgue's profession of faith in the new philosophy of the unconscious as preached by the German philosopher Hartmann takes the form of a parody of the Lord's Prayer ("Complainte propitiatoire à l'Inconscient").

Part of the reason for discarding *Le Sanglot de la Terre* was possibly the feeling that the influences were too apparent. Laforgue's debt to the Romantic and Parnassian poets shines through both in subject and in technique. Baudelaire, Verlaine, and others are not entirely forgotten in the *Complaintes*, but the big question is how much is owed Tristan Corbière. Jules Laforgue answers, nothing. "Tout le monde me jette Corbière à la tête," he wrote in 1885 to Léon Trézenik, editor of *Lutèce*.[4] But he assures Trézenik that the *Complaintes* were all written before he had read *Les Amours Jaunes*. He recognizes some affinity between the two works, however, amid a great deal of dissimilarity: "Si j'ai l'âme de Corbière un peu, c'est dans sa nuance bretonne, et c'est naturel; quant à ses procédés, point n'en suis ... Corbière a du chic et j'ai de l'humour; Corbière papillotte et je ronronne; je vis d'une philosophie absolue et non de tics; je suis bon à tous et non insaisissable de fringance; je n'ai pas l'amour jaune, mais blanc et violet gros deuil. Enfin Corbière ne s'occupe ni de la strophe ni des rimes ... et jamais de rythmes, et je m'en suis préoccupé au point d'en apporter de nouvelles et de nouveaux ..." The question is far from settled despite Laforgue's reply; a close comparison of texts, which might decide the issue, remains to be done.

After the *Complaintes*, Laforgue went to work on another volume of verse, *L'Imitation de Notre-Dame la Lune*, which consists of forty-one brief poems evoking the Lady Moon and the pallid Pierrots that we had already glimpsed in the *Complaintes*. *Notre-Dame la Lune*, which was published in 1886, is generally considered an advance over the previous one. In handling his images and his rhythms, Jules Laforgue shows that he has achieved real mastery and no longer feels the necessity of being original at all costs.

From these sentimental fantasies the poet passed to the theme of love in writing his *Fleurs de Bonne Volonté*. They were never published as such but figure in the *Concile Féerique* and the *Derniers Vers*. Sentimental, melancholy, at times quite crude, these poems show characteristic moods of Laforgue during the last month of his stay in Berlin. They demonstrate also the final stages of his evolution in verse technique, free verse. Whether Laforgue can be called the inventor of the genre is a difficult and somewhat pointless question. The part Whitman played in Laforgue's evolution is a question that perhaps has more point but is just as difficult. The translations of the American that he did for *La Vogue*, the Symbolist periodical edited by Gustave Kahn, cannot be discounted as a possible influence. Laforgue could have been influenced, too, by Kahn, although his spontaneous improvisation bears little resemblance to the formal and systematized metrics that his friend favored. Both Kahn and a poetess of the time, Marie Krysinska, claimed priority. Finally, he could have been influenced by Rimbaud, who had appeared in *La Vogue*. Whatever, if anything, he owed to others in the matter, free verse was the logical culmination in Laforgue's development.

From the free verse of the *Derniers Vers*, Laforgue moved easily into the prose of the *Moralités Légendaires*. Pieces began to appear in *La Vogue* in 1886. The book came out in 1887, a collection of parodies of famous literary subjects such as Hamlet, Lohengrin, Salomé, the Faun, all treated comically without, however, being divested of their hieratic significance. In form, these prose pieces are more finished than the poems.

Jules Laforgue died in 1887 some time before the volume appeared. He had left the service of the empress and, after marrying an English girl whom he had met in Berlin, established himself in Paris with the hopes of living by his pen. At this point in his life, Laforgue's misery was no longer a pose. He was seriously ill and beset by financial problems. What he earned from his articles and columns fell far short of what he needed to run his household and pay his medical bills. The letters that he wrote right up to his death are pleas for loans and advances. His old friends Bourget and Ephrussi, along with Teodor de Wyzewa, came to his aid. It was to Wyzewa that Leah Lee Laforgue handed her husband's papers and manuscripts. The most important part of his work had already appeared, however, in some form or other. The *Concile Féerique* had appeared in *La Vogue* in 1886 and shortly afterwards was separately published as a little plaquette. Although *Les Derniers Vers* did not come out until 1890, the poems had already appeared in magazines. What has come out since his death is miscellaneous writing and correspondence. Material is still being uncovered and the *Œuvres Complètes* are still in process.

Gustave Kahn said that literature for Jules Laforgue was only the translation of a philosophy.[5] He was an avid reader of the philosophers and never denied the effect that they had upon his writing. His earliest works reflect a wide range of study, from Buddhism and Christianity to modern European systems of thought. *Le Sanglot de la Terre* reiterates the plight of man and the futility of life in terms that echo now the despair of *Ecclesiastes*, now oriental resignation, now the pessimism of Schopenhauer, now the principle of universal necessity as found in Spinoza. But the greatest influence was that of Eduard von Hartmann, whose *Philosophy of the Unconscious* Laforgue began to read in 1880. Here he encountered a thinker who, without denying that life was as dreary as the other philosophers had claimed it to be, seemed to offer a means of willing acceptance and reconciliation. Its first appeal to the young man weary of intellectual responsibility was the peace of self-abandonment. He wrote, "Aujourd'hui, tout préconise et tout se précipite à la culture exclusive de la raison, de la logique, de la conscience. La culture bénie de l'Avenir est la déculture, la mise en jachère. Nous allons à la dessication: squelettes de cuir, à lunettes, rationalistes, anatomiques. Retournons, mes frères, vers les grandes eaux de l'Inconscient. ..."[6] What folly, he concluded, to place any confidence in the individual reason or will. Man can neither understand nor control the universe into which he has been brought. But if the part of wisdom is to renounce and accept, one may do so with irony and detachment. The adjustment that Laforgue arrived at was to belittle the self and the universe, to assume the posture of the dilettante. Like the Romantic dandies and the fin-de siècle esthetes, he would smoke "au nez des dieux de fines cigarettes."[7]

Laforgue's position regarding matters of art and literature does indeed seem quite patently to have been determined by his philosophy. In his art criticism he defended beauty of the moment against the champions of formal and universal beauty such as Taine, whose lectures at Beaux–Arts Laforgue did not forget. Hartmann had convinced him that just as the unconscious creates in an everlasting becoming, beauty exists only in the particular, the individual, and the concrete. Laforgue is here already in the modern tradition. Through Impressionism, Esprit Nouveau, and Surrealism, the concept of ephemeral beauty will grow in importance to become one of the fundamentals of twentieth-century art. In addition to relativism, the irony and detachment that Laforgue adopted as philosophical principles are invoked as artistic devices. In literature as in life, Laforgue valued above all else whatever sustained emotional control. He had begun by pouring out his heart in the conventional verses of *Le Sanglot de la Terre*. With the *Complaintes*, however, he dominated his feelings and put on an exhibition of technical virtuosity and bravado.

In the *Complaintes*, Laforgue's stanzas vary in length, alexandrines alternate with shorter lines, the caesura moves all over the line, the rimes are nonchalant. Whereas the verse in this collection is still syllabic, it is extremely liberated. Syntax and vocabulary as well as metrics show how completely Laforgue has shifted his interest to matters of technique, how bent he is on being original. His sentences lack connectives, are frequently dislocated, depend heavily on adjectives and adverbs. He is less iconoclastic in matters of syntax than Mallarmé, however; it is with words that Laforgue is most original. He revives archaic expressions, borrows foreign words, supplies defective forms, makes up words entirely. A characteristic innovation is the monstrosity that resembles the portemanteau words of Lewis Carroll, a form of epenthesis, created by the addition to a word of a piece of another. Because of a graphic likeness, the foreign body is tolerated, so to speak, and the effect is a humorous enhancement of the host word.

> Mais, fausse sœur, fausse humaine, fausse mortelle,
> Nous t'écartèlerons de honte sangsuelle.[8]

Such verbal playfulness, which begins with the *Complaintes*, constitutes a defense against sentiments and ideas. It gives Laforgue's work its characteristic manner.

Ironic whimsy, which harks back to Musset and anticipates the twentieth-century fantasists, sets Laforgue apart from most of his contemporaries. Symbolists, in the main, strictly avoid "l'esprit et la pointe assassine." This brings us to the problem of Laforgue's association with Symbolism as such. We know that before leaving for Germany he frequented the cafés where the new poets gathered and that even while away he kept in touch with what was going on in Paris. Like the others, he read Mallarmé, Corbière, Rimbaud. His special friends Kahn and Charles Henry were in the thick of the Symbolist revolution. At its height in the mid-eighties he brought out the *Complaintes*. He contributed prominently in the reviews. In 1887, the success of the *Moralités Légendaires* made him widely known and thereby pushed still further the identification with the avant-garde group of the day. It was the *Revue Indépendante* that brought out the volume. There can be no question about his physical association with the Symbolists. Spiritual affinity can, however, be challenged. One should remember, however, from the outset, that if he differed from others on points such as the one we began with, all the poets called Symbolists differed one from the other on many points of theory or practice and, in each, theory was liable to differ from practice. What did they have in common? François Ruchon could serve as point of departure for a discussion which we can only begin here: "L'œuvre de Laforgue coïncide en tous points avec les tendances principales du Symbolisme. On y retrouve le souci du symbole (*Moralités Légendaires*), le sens du mystère, de l'angoisse métaphysique, le pessimisme, le recours au rêve comme moyen de salut. Comme ses contemporains, Laforgue éprouva le besoin de rompre l'ancienne harmonie du vers, il innova en prosodie, s'accorda toutes les licences, et il alla jusqu'au vers libre ..."[9] Léon Guichard feels that Ruchon exaggerates, pointing out that Laforgue is little interested in symbols as such and that the other items mentioned could be passed around equally well among the Romantics and the Parnassians. Such arguments demonstrate best that labels are only approximate and at best suggestive. Some historians prefer calling Laforgue a *Décadent* rather than a *Symboliste*, indeed the chief *Décadent*. Lagarde et Michard classify him thus and, citing one of his poems in free verse, mention the mixture of preciousness and trivial realism as typically *Décadent*.[10] Before them Pierre Martino, on the basis of dates and tendencies, considers himself obliged to call him a *Décadent* instead of a *Symboliste*. He defines *décadence* as an earlier form of *symbolisme*, as a revolutionary spirit that began in politics and philosophy with some of the little reviews. The word may come from Verlaine, who describes in a sonnet the decadence of Rome with its listlessness and cynicism. Jules Laforgue himself used the word to express his admiration for the spirit of the new generation. To be sure, *Décadent* may be no more totally accurate for Laforgue than *Symboliste*, since, for one thing, he had no use for Naturalism, at least in poetry: "Quand il s'agit de poésie," he wrote his sister, "soyons distingués comme des œillets."[11] Martino declares, "Les Décadents ne sont point du tout hostiles au naturalisme que mépriseront bientôt les symbolistes."[12] The fact remains that for the critics from Remy de Gourmont on, it is generally as a *Symboliste* or as a *Décadent* that Laforgue takes his place in literature.

Doubtless his association with Symbolism has been a factor in his reputation as a poet. His earliest successes, based chiefly on publications scattered in reviews, were with the ingroup, who hailed him as a leader and an ally. When his fame spread it was through the support of critics like Kahn and Gourmont, closely identified with Symbolism. On the other hand, at least a part of the hostility that he has met in academic critics may be due to such an identification.[13] Many dislike his mood, his manner, find his verbal pranks tiresome and his versification shocking. Jules Laforgue's work is for them a *Déliquescences d'Adoré Floupette* which the author took seriously. Of course all academic critics have not reacted in the same fashion: if Brunetière does not seem to favor Laforgue or Symbolism in general, René Lalou seems hostile only to Laforgue. And professors like Durry and Michaud show that even academic critics can fall under Laforgue's spell. The quarrel about Laforgue cannot really be defined as just between partisans of poetry and the professors. In the early part of the twentieth century, Alain-Fournier argued on his behalf with Jacques Rivière, who won out. In the 1920s, another editor of the *Nouvelle Revue Française*, Marcel Arland, took Laforgue severely to task for limited range and absence of profound originality. It has been said that Laforgue's popularity thereby suffered considerably. Possibly so. But the condemnation of a powerful editor—any more than that of Apollinaire, Max Jacob, and the Surrealists—could not destroy him. That his spiritual heirs survived and prospered is sufficient proof that the French public retained a taste for wistful whimsy and verbal legerdemain. After the Cubists and the Fantaisistes, there were writers like Cocteau, Carco, and Giraudoux to enrage the professors, the editors, and the carping colleagues.

Although Laforgue has not been so scorned or neglected in France as some have supposed, the enthusiasm of Americans has been so great that one has been tempted to see Laforgue as a sort of Poe, inversely—Poe, whose poetry is less esteemed at home than in France; Laforgue, whose poetry is less esteemed in France than in the United States. T. S. Eliot is, of course, Laforgue's great champion in English. He encountered him in

Arthur Symons, *The Symbolist Movement in Literature* (1899). At Harvard in Eliot's day there was something of a cult of the French poets. Then after Eliot, there is Ezra Pound along with the other Imagists who found Laforgue's whimsy and understatement much more to their taste than the bumptious Rimbaud. Malcolm Cowley and Hart Crane were subsequent converts. The latest of the American poets to worship at the shrine is William Jay Smith. There will doubtless be others. With the recent vogue for fin-de-siècle art, whether it be painting or wallpaper, it is surprising that the *Moralités Légendaires* have not been reissued. A public attracted by Beardsley should take to Laforgue.

Notes

1. "Avertissement," in *Œuvres Complètes*, vol. 2, p. 7.
2. *Œuvres Complètes*, vol. 2, p. 226.
3. *Œuvres Complètes*, vol. 5, p. 21.
4. Ibid., pp. 136–37.
5. *Symbolistes et Décadents* (Vanier, 1902), p. 181.
6. See Ruchon, *Jules Laforgue*, p. 45.
7. "La Cigarette"
8. "Complainte des Voix"
9. Ruchon, p. 223.
10. *XIXᵉ Siècle*, p. 541.
11. *Œuvres Complètes*, vol. 5, p. 21. He adds that he does not object to Naturalism in the novel.
12. *Parnasse et Symbolisme* (Colin, 1938), p. 144.
13. See Ruchon, p. 235.

LA CHANSON DU PETIT HYPERTROPHIQUE[1]

C'est d'un' maladie d' cœur
Qu'est mort', m'a dit l' docteur,
    Tir-lan-laire!
    Ma pauv' mère;[2]
Et que j'irai là-bas,
Fair' dodo z'avec elle.
J'entends mon cœur qui bat,
C'est maman qui m'appelle!

On rit d' moi dans les rues,
De mes min's incongrues
    La-i-tou!
    D'enfant saoul;
Ah! Dieu! C'est qu'à chaqu' pas
J'étouff', moi, je chancelle!
J'entends mon cœur qui bat,
C'est maman qui m'appelle.

Aussi j' vais par les champs
Sangloter aux couchants,
    La-ri-rette!
    C'est bien bête.
Mais le soleil, j'sais pas,
M'semble un cœur qui ruisselle!
J'entends mon cœur qui bat,
C'est maman qui m'appelle!

Ah! si la p'tite Gen'viève[3]
Voulait d' mon cœur qui s' crêve.
    Pi-lou-i!
    Ah, oui!
J' suis jaune et triste, hélas!
Elle est ros', gaie et belle!
J'entends mon cœur qui bat,
C'est maman qui m'appelle!

Non, tout le monde est méchant,
Hors le cœur des couchants,

Tir-lan-laire!
Et ma'mère,
Et j' veux aller là-bas
Fair' dodo z'avec elle ...
Mon cœur bat, bat, bat ...[4]
Dis, Maman, tu m'appelles?

---

1. From *Le Sanglot de la Terre*. Anticipating a future manner, this poem seems out of place in the *Sanglot*. With its short lines of six, three, or five syllables, its frequent elisions, and spontaneous rimes, it has the air of a popular refrain quite unlike the *Gedankenlyrik* that make up the bulk of this collection.

2. Laforgue grieved deeply over the death of his parents, particularly of his mother whom he said he scarcely knew. He himself had heart trouble.

3. Is this Marguerite, the love of his fifteenth year, glimpsed daily at her window? This girl with blond braids and a dimple scorned the young poet, who avenged himself by throwing a stone against the windowpane.

4. Since there are verses of six syllables, another *bat* would seem called for.

COMPLAINTES DES PIANOS QU'ON ENTEND DANS LES QUARTIERS AISES [5]

Menez l'âme que les Lettres ont bien nourrie,
Les pianos, les pianos, dans les quartiers aisés!
Premiers soirs, sans pardessus, chaste flânerie,
Aux complaintes des nerfs incompris ou brisés.[6]

Ces enfants, à quoi rêvent-elles,
Dans les ennuis des ritournelles?

—"Préaux des soirs,
Christs des dortoirs![7]

"Tu t'en vas et tu nous laisses,
Tu nous laiss's et tu t'en vas,
Défaire et refaire ses tresses,
Broder d'éternels canevas."

Jolie ou vague? triste ou sage? encore pure?
O jours, tout m'est égal? ou, monde, moi je veux?
Et si vierge, du moins, de la bonne blessure,
Sachant quels gras couchants ont les plus blancs aveux?

> Mon Dieu, à quoi donc rêvent-elles?
> A des Roland, à des dentelles?

> —"Cœurs en prison,[8]
> Lentes saisons!

"Tu t'en vas et tu nous quittes,[9]
Tu nous quitt's et tu t'en vas!
Couvents gris, chœurs de Sulamites,
Sur nos seins nuls croisons nos bras."

Fatales clés de l'être un beau jour apparues;
Psitt! aux hérédités en ponctuels ferments,
Dans le bal incessant de nos étranges rues;
Ah! pensionnats, théâtres, journaux, romans!

> Allez, stériles ritournelles,
> La vie est vraie et criminelle.

> —"Rideaux tirés,
> Peut-on entrer?

"Tu t'en vas et tu nous laisses,
Tu nous laiss's et tu t'en vas,
La source des frais rosiers baisse,
Vraiment! Et lui qui ne vient pas ..."

Il viendra! Vous serez les pauvres cœurs en faute,
Fiancés au remords comme aux essais sans fond,
Et les suffisants cœurs cossus, n'ayant d'autre hôte
Qu'un train-train pavoisé d'estime et de chiffons.

> Mourir? peut-être brodent-elles
> Pour un oncle à dot, des bretelles?

> —"Jamais! Jamais!
> Si tu savais!

"Tu t'en vas et tu nous quittes,
Tu nous quitt's et tu t'en vas,

Mais tu nous reviendras bien vite
Guérir mon beau mal, n'est-ce pas?"

Et c'est vrai! l'Idéal les fait divaguer toutes,
Vigne bohème, même en ces quartiers aisés
La vie est là; le pur flacon des vives gouttes
Sera, *comme il convient*, d'eau propre baptisé.

Aussi, bientôt, se joueront-elles
De plus exactes ritournelles.

"—Seul oreiller!
Mur familier!

"Tu t'en vas et tu nous laisses,
Tu nous laiss's et tu t'en vas.
Que ne suis-je morte à la messe!
O mois, ô linges, ô repas!"

5. From *Les Complaintes*. Ezra Pound selected this poem for the *Little Review* (February 1918). Malcolm Cowley demonstrates how his own "Nocturne" derives from this poem. See Warren Ramsey, ed., *Jules Laforgue: Essays on a Poet's Life and Work*, p. 10.

6. Warren Ramsey says that in the four-line introduction, "a literary young man is shown strolling down the rue Madame in the springtime, and in the sound of the practicing coming from the windows he hears the plaint of miserable imprisoned souls." *The Ironic Inheritance*, p. 124.

7. Is this the voice of the pianos? Allusion to dormitories and school yards reminds us that he was alone, away from his family, at school in Tarbes. In Berlin he watched with considerable interest the young ladies of the English school.

8. Cowley says that the effect here is "brilliantly reproduced in J. Alfred Prufrock's 'I grow old . . . I grow old . . . I shall wear the bottoms of my trousers rolled.'" See note 5.

9. This is an exact line of the popular song of the day on which Laforgue modeled the rhythm of this poem.

PIERROTS[10]

C'est, sur un cou qui, raide, émerge
D'une fraise empesée *idem*,

Une face imberbe au cold-cream,
Un air d'hydrocéphale asperge.

Les yeux sont noyés de l'opium
De l'indulgence universelle,
La bouche clownesque ensorcèle
Comme un singulier géranium.

Bouche qui va du trou sans bonde
Glacialement désopilé,
Au transcendental en-allé
Du souris vain de la Joconde.

Campant leur cône enfariné
Sur le noir serre-tête en soie,
Ils font rire leur patte d'oie
Et froncent en trèfle leur nez.

Ils ont comme chaton de bague
Le scarabée égyptien,
A leur boutonnière fait bien
Le pissenlit des terrains vagues.

Ils vont, se sustentant d'azur,
Et parfois aussi de légumes,
De riz plus blanc que leur costume,
De mandarines et d'œufs durs.

Ils sont de la secte du Blême,
Ils n'ont rien à voir avec Dieu,
Et sifflent: "Tout est pour le mieux[11]
"Dans la meilleur' des mi-carême!"

---

10. From *L'Imitation de Notre-Dame la Lune*. Pierrot appears first in France with the Commedia dell' Arte. Already notable in the eighteenth century (Watteau, for example), he becomes increasingly popular in the nineteenth. Duburau, the famous mime, established the custom of white face and black skullcap. The Romantics flocked to the Théâtre des Funambules, and their successors were no less enthusiastic throughout the whole century. Laforgue, who went often to the circus to watch the clowns, found in the derisive and pathetic figure of Pierrot a character to represent himself.

11. Elsewhere he says, "Tout est pour le mieux dans le pire des mondes possibles!"

DIMANCHES [12]

Hamlet: Have you a daughter?
Polonius: I have, my lord.
Hamlet: Let her not walk in the sun: conception
is a blessing; but not as your daughter may
conceive.

Le ciel pleut sans but, sans que rien l'émeuve,
Il pleut, il pleut, bergère! sur le fleuve ..

Le fleuve a son repos dominical;
Pas un chaland, en amont, en aval.

Les Vêpres carillonnent sur la ville.
Les berges sont désertes, sans idylles.

Passe un pensionnat (ô pauvres chairs!)
Plusieurs ont déjà leurs manchons d'hiver.

Une qui n'a ni manchon, ni fourrures
Fait, tout en gris, une pauvre figure.

Et la voilà qui s'échappe des rangs,
Et court? ô mon Dieu, qu'est-ce qu'il lui prend?

Et elle va se jeter dans le fleuve.
Pas un batelier, pas un chien Terr'-Neuve.

Le crépuscule vient; le petit port
Allume ses feux. (Ah! connu, l'décor!).

La pluie continue à mouiller le fleuve,
Le ciel pleut sans but, sans que rien l'émeuve.

---

12. From *Des Fleurs de Bonne Volonté*. Using a technique particularly prominent in the
Moralités Légendaires of putting a well-known literary figure in quaintly modern dress,
Laforgue imagines Ophelia a schoolgirl suicide. The poem narrates a newspaper item
against a background of a dreary rainy Sunday in a city like Berlin. Laforgue knew the
melancholy and tedium of that day of rest for a man living in a room. "Ever-spleen
day" is a theme from the *Sanglot de la Terre* to the *Derniers Vers*. So is autumn, with its
dismal gray days.

NOTRE PETITE COMPAGNE[13]

Si mon air vous dit quelque chose,
Vous auriez tort de vous gêner;
Je ne la fais pas à la pose;
Je suis la Femme, on me connaît.

Bandeaux plats ou crinière folle,
Dites? quel Front vous rendrait fou?
J'ai l'art de toutes les écoles,
J'ai des âmes pour tous les goûts.

Cueillez la fleur de mes visages,
Buvez ma bouche et non ma voix,
Et n'en cherchez pas davantage ...
Nul n'y vit clair; pas même moi.

Nos armes ne sont pas égales,
Pour que je vous tende la main,
Vous n'êtes que de naïfs mâles,
Je suis l'Eternel Féminin!

Mon But se perd dans les Etoiles!
C'est moi qui suis la Grande Isis!
Nul ne m'a retroussé mon voile.
Ne songez qu'à mes oasis ...

Si mon Air vous dit quelque chose,
Vous auriez tort de vous gêner;
Je ne la fais pas à la pose:
Je suis La Femme! on me connaît.

---

13. From *Des Fleurs de Bonne Volonté*. The poem, a masterpiece of irony, brings together in one statement the divergent attitudes Laforgue entertained on the subject of women and love. An unfulfilled lover and a victim of basically ambivalent reactions of idealization and vilification, Laforgue vented his disgust, but also betrayed his adoration of the female. He had nothing of the sensualist, however, being embarrassed by his own body and preferring in women the unvoluptuous sort. He was looking for "a friend, but one with hips," as someone said.

Poetry of René Ghil

Œuvres Complètes (Messein, 1938). 3 vols.

Readings

Montal, Robert. *René Ghil, Du Symbolisme à la Poésie cosmique* (Brussels: Lahor, 1962).

René Ghil

1862–1925

Symbolism is in many respects the opposite of Realism. The latter, allied with positivism and science, seems to express the spirit of the latter half of the nineteenth century, whereas Symbolism, allied with idealism and the spiritualistic, represents the reaction and the spirit which will succeed positivism. Among the French poets, René Ghil is best remembered for having reconciled the two enemies, of bringing science into the camp of Symbolism.

Ghil (actually Ghilbert) was born in Tourcoing (Nord) and educated at Condorcet along with Ephraim Mikhaël, Pierre Quillard, Stuart Merrill, and André Fontainas. He made his literary début in 1885 with *Légende d'Ames et de Sangs*. The influence of Mallarmé is extremely pronounced in the early Ghil, whose poems are products of craftsmanship far more than of sentiment. Never a lyrical poet, Ghil soon showed himself to be first of all a theoretician. In 1886, he brought out a little volume entitled *Traité du verbe*, in which, backed by an "Avant-Dire" by Mallarmé, Ghil explained a new poetic theory. Rimbaud had established a linking between vowel sounds and colors. Ghil found that what was true of vowels was also true of consonants and extended the linking beyond colors to include musical instruments. A consonant placed before a certain vowel suggested a certain color, the sound of a certain musical instrument, and finally suggested a certain sentiment. The 1887 edition of the *Traité du verbe* incorporated some modifications and refinements of the first edition; the 1888 edition pushed the correspondences into the sciences: the poet's work, it asserted, reflects the same laws that govern chemistry, biology, sociology. The idea of "les correspondances" intrigued the public; Ghil drew upon himself praise and ridicule equally, but at least he was the center of attraction; and for some years following the initial essay, scientific poetry, "instrumentation verbale," inspired lively discussion. However, his peers for the most part soon abandoned him.

The theorist René Ghil was also a polemicist. Acquainted with the literary world of Paris since school days, active in its campaigns and its squabbles, Ghil had early locked horns with Moréas over the leadership of the Symbolists. In 1886, both Moréas and Ghil were loudly proclaiming their theories and each claiming paternity of Symbolist doctrines. In 1887, in his fight for leadership, Ghil assumed direction of a new review, *Ecrits pour l'Art*. It began propitiously with Mallarmé's preface for the *Traité du verbe* and with contributions by Merrill, Verhaeren, and Régnier. Ghil had, furthermore, obtained from Merrill the dedication of Merrill's first book with something like a statement of discipleship. Although the discipleship was not very real, Merrill did remain faithful to Ghil longer than Vielé-Griffin or Régnier who, alienated by Ghil's theories of a scientific poetry, left the magazine before the year was half over. Eventually, too, the great elders Mallarmé and Verlaine, who had first encouraged Ghil, withdrew their support. Of course, neither he nor Moréas could be taken seriously enough to be generally acceptable as a leader. Henceforth, frustrated in his attempts to form a school of "instrumentation verbale," René Ghil would pursue his vocation alone.

He set about putting into practice the theories that he had formulated in the several editions of the *Traité du verbe*. The result was his chief work, simply entitled the *Œuvre*, which would be spread over twenty volumes and forty years, constantly reworked, reorganized, never finished. Conceived of as a cosmic epic, it begins with the origins of the earth, follows the evolution of plant and animal life, reaches finally man, whose history it traces into the present age with all its sociological and technological problems. Finally it looks to the future, to worldwide wars and to matters involving the Orient and the Occident. In subject and, to an extent, in technique it anticipates the great twentieth-century epics of Claudel and Saint-John Perse.

Technically the *Œuvre* offers a great variety of procedures, each dependent upon the subject treated and the stage in the author's artistic evolution. But one may still speak of general characteristics. As a pupil of Mallarmé, René Ghil favored an expression not governed by the laws of habitual communication. His syntax is unconventional and his vocabulary marked by rarity, neologism, obscurity. He seems quite capricious regarding punctuation and capitalization. Since his aim is to suggest and conjure up through sounds and pictures, meaning of words on the level of ordinary discourse must frequently be sacrificed. And the rhythm system that he uses tends to destroy logical word clusters. This rhythm system is very free or loose, designed to modulate the poet's thought and the subject expressed. Harmonic effects are enhanced by assonance and alliteration. In imagery, the *Œuvre* offers a vast repertory of metaphors, remarkable enough to interest Breton and the Surrealists. Only a computer could tell us to what extent Ghil practiced his theory of correspondences, but from samples studied, it seems highly doubtful that he applied it with scientific exactitude or comprehensiveness.

Anticipating twentieth-century trends in technique and preoccupation, René Ghil does not seem to have been much of a Symbolist. He faced with excitement the machine and the urban collectivities, allying himself with Verhaeren, his friend and follower, and the Unanimists, who reacted against the artificial, hothouse culture of the Symbolists. In the preface to his very first volume, he had praised Zola, the Realist and the bard of modern society. If he admired Mallarmé, it was because he saw a master of technique allied with a visionary whose scope, on a metaphysical plane, was as great as Zola's on the sociological. His own resembled that of a Hugo or an Auguste Comte more than that of the run of his contemporaries. Yet René Ghil subscribed to, often claimed to have first formulated, the essential principles of Symbolism from the symbol and all its implications to free verse. If, as Valéry said, "Symbolism amounted to poetry's taking back from music some things that belonged to it,"[1] then there is no question of Ghil's credentials. Musicality was always an objective with him, at times taking precedence over meaning. Furthermore, the preoccupation with synthesis identifies Ghil with the generations that had made a cult of Wagner and his *Gesamtkunstwerk*. The Faustian ambition to combine the arts, to create a literary work that would symbolize all life, all the world, was René Ghil's chimera as it had been Mallarmé's.

After his unsuccessful bid for leadership and retiring to concentrate upon his work, René Ghil lived out his life as a typical French bourgeois. He was married, had a flat near the Etoile and a country residence, the legacy of his parents, where he spent the summer months of each year. His only occupation seems to have been his *Œuvre* to which he devoted himself with absolute conviction and determination. This sedentary life was marked, however, by one escapist dream, by what one might call a love affair with South East Asia. Ghil had always been attracted to the Far East, and at the World Exposition of 1889, he had the opportunity of seeing a troupe of Javanese dancers and listening to the musicians who accompanied them. At the Exposition of 1900, he met a Malayan dancer and for a month went every night to watch her perform and to chat with her afterwards. He learned Malayan and wrote the *Pantoun des Pantoun* to record the brief encounter.

Note

1. Paul Valéry, *Œuvres*, vol. 1, p. 1272.

POUR L'ENFANT ANCIENNE[1]

Tue en l'étonnement de nos yeux mutuels
Qui délivrèrent là l'or de latentes gloires,
Que, veuve dans le Temple aux signes rituels,
L'onde d'éternité réprouve nos mémoires.

Tel instant qui naissait des heurts éventuels
Tout palmes de doigts longs aux nuits ondulatoires
Vrais en le dôme espoir des vols perpétuels
Nous ouvrit les passés de nos pures histoires

Une moire de vains soupirs pleure sous les
Trop seuls saluts riants par nos vœux exhalés,
Aussi haut qu'un néant de plumes vers les gnoses.

Advenus rêves des vitraux pleins de demains
Doux et nuls à pleurer, et d'un midi de roses,
Nous venons l'un à l'autre en élevant les mains.

(1886)

---

1. This early sonnet is almost a pastiche of Mallarmé. The vocabulary in the first place with *tue, vols, plumes, pures, pleure, gloires, trop, roses*. Then the complicated, ambiguous syntax and the abstruse metaphor. The effect is of extreme Mallarméan concentration. One is sure that like Mallarmé, René Ghil avoids describing the thing in favor of describing the impression of the thing. Here, against a background of solemnity, of formal ritual, there is a fluttering of sighs, feathers, petals, and hands.

LA HACHE DE PIERRE[2]

... Mais par les horizons engloutissants des lourds
continents d'Ages morts,
                       plus épais que l'Espace
et le Temps qu'ils avaient pénétrés, les sangs sourds
unissent et divisent aux veines de Race
les hommes sous les sorts.

Les temps s'attroupent, des
cornes luisantes et pointues du Bétail
dompté,—qui tout autour des toits s'en vont guidés,
après les nuits sans lune où le vent du poitrail
se ride d'inquiétude auprès des Feux, par le
croissant nouveau de la douce Vache ...

Après les nuits sans lunes où l'âme des Morts, parle ...

... La hache
chasse dans les roseaux noueux et les prairies
de plants épais, et taille à grandes voix meurtries
aux têtes à la mort, de la proie!—la hache
teinte du temps des vieux sangs noirs (le sang des morts
donne la mort!) la hache—et l'épieu rouge hors
de l'entraille que, transissant d'un sourd tumulte
le ventre aux sourdes vies des Forêts, insulte
coléreusement

l'Homme-de-quatre-mains ras-
étendu d'aguets aux rameaux, et dont exulte
la haine, delà les terres et samûdras!

. . .

(Dire des Sangs: le Toit des hommes.)

---

2. This section of the Œuvre represents Ghil in his epic manner, grandiloquent and lofty. The epithet sustains the desired Homeric or biblical tone, while the curious alignment of the verses permits crescendos, crashing climaxes, and diminuendos that are enhanced by the imagery.

FRAGMENT[3]

La petite Javanaise parle:

. . .

Yiau ...

c'était Fête—hier, dans Batavia. Tout en haut
de la mer, et ses soleils qui sont dans ma tête
ainsi qu'un resplendissement de regrets! ah
tout en haut de mes Yeux en détresse, il monta
des voiles et des mâts, et des ailes plissées
au dos de rêve de dragons, d'ediong'-tshina:[4]
et, trouant l'horizon des lourdes traversées!
en roulis de sommeil qui sont pleins du départ
les vapeurs s'en allaient vers l'ouest—où va trop tard
la lumière d'aurore entr'ouvrant mes pensées ...

Le murmure du vent roulé—soumarouwoun'g—
du vent roulé parmi les plantes, parle doux.
Mais la nuit, le vent-mêlé-de-pluie à grands trous
d'eaux, a tapé dans les plantes: ah! ma roumah[5]
a tressailli dans son immense et sourd oumoun'g
ainsi qu'une âme d'homme qui ne peut reprendre
haleine! et dans mes mains ouvertes l'air était
chaud, et sourd ...

 Et mes doigt eussent voulu s'étendre!
et, ngoun'ggout'-toun'ggout'! et gémir à doux hoquet
le retroussis aigu de mes lèvres arides ...

Et mes yeux, qui de tous les soirs d'ouest se sont tus
ont revu les vapeurs au loin de soleils vides:
les vapeurs d'Iroupa[6] qui ne m'emportent plus!

Le murmure du vent roulé—soumarouwoun'g—
du vent roulé parmi les plantes, tarde et dort.

Mon repos est pareil au lent germe dian'toun'g
d'ou naît la grappe des pissang'[7] à lunes d'or.

. . .

(Le Pantoun des Pantoun)
(Poème Javanais)

3. Possibly this fragment shows Ghil at his worst, certainly at his most touching. The Madame Butterfly sentimentality, the silly imitation of the "petite Javanaise," the outlandish words that are sprinkled throughout make it a rather dreadful period piece. At least Pierre Loti had some firsthand experience. All Ghil ever had was a month's acquaintance with a World's Fair performer and a dictionary. Enough to fancy himself an expert in Malayan and to pursue his dream amid the incense and the oriental bric-à-brac of his Paris apartment.

4. Jonque chinoise
5. Maison indigène
6. Europe
7. Banane

Poetry of Stuart Merrill

Les Gammes (Vanier, 1887).
Les Fastes (Vanier, 1891).
Les Petits Poèmes d'automne (Vanier, 1895).
Poèmes (1887–1897) (Mercure de France, 1897).
Les Quatre Saisons (Mercure de France, 1900).
Une Voix dans la foule (Mercure de France, 1909).

Readings

Henry, Marjorie Louise. *Stuart Merrill, La Contribution d'un Américain au Symbolisme français* (Champion, 1927).

Stuart Merrill

1863–1915

Like Vielé-Griffin, this poet was an American educated in France. His ties with his native country were, however, stronger because of frequent trips back and prolonged residence in the United States. Moreover, Stuart Merrill used his native tongue more than Vielé-Griffin; although his French was better than his English, he wrote in both languages and offered translations and articles for American publication. He was probably more receptive to Anglo-American influence than Vielé-Griffin, but as he wrote to him in 1887, "Je ne suis pas le seul Américain qui essaye d'introduire dans l'alexandrin français un peu de la musique enchanteresse des vers anglais." Besides enriching French prosody by Anglo-American techniques, on moral or philosophic grounds Merrill proposed William Morris and Walt Whitman as great models for young Frenchmen.

Merrill's mediation between French and English literature is, however, a minor aspect of his accomplishment. Throughout his career, which coincides with the Symbolist movement, he exemplifies, particularly in the early poems, its characteristic procedures. In his later work, his essentially lyric genius discards some of the Symbolist trappings to appear simple and clear, yet he never discards the Symbolist ideal. "Le poète doit être celui qui rappelle aux hommes l'Idée éternelle de la Beauté dissimulée sous les formes transitoires de la vie imparfaite." (*Credo*, 1892) In spirit, too, his optimism eventually leads him away from the masters of Symbolism, Verlaine and Mallarmé, yet he is not without the company of other poets of his generation like Verhaeren and Vielé-Griffin who, their enthusiastic involvement in the daily world notwithstanding, remained Symbolist poets.

Stuart Merrill was born in Hempstead, Long Island, in 1863. His family was distinguished and well-to-do. At the age of three, he was taken to Paris where his father had accepted a diplomatic post. There Merrill spent his childhood and youth. The discipline in the home along the lines of New England puritanism was no less strict than that of the French lycée in those days: the boy had a most rigorous upbringing. At Fontanes (later Condorcet, where Mallarmé taught) he impressed his teachers as an "esprit distingué et sérieux," an "esprit solide et docile."[1] Literature occupied a place of honor at Fontanes. Merrill and his comrades, some of whom like René Ghil and Ephraim Mikhaël were to be his lifelong companions in literature, were ardent devotees of the Muse. In 1883, they published a little review, *Le Fou*, which opened on some verse by Merrill. The following year Merrill passed the baccalauréat. Armed now with a thorough education in the classics and burning with zeal for literature and politics, young Merrill was ready to enter the fray. Alas, the battle of Symbolism was fought without his presence, for from 1884 to 1892 he was in New York City.

Forced to return to the States because of his father's health, Stuart Merrill registered at the Columbia law school in the fall of 1884. Law did not interest him, but he persisted in his studies and had even begun to practice when an illness furnished him the excuse to quit. The social ideals that he had formulated while still at school in Paris led him, in New York, to seek an active participation in civic reform. He wrote articles for newspapers and even founded a political club. The results of his efforts were disappointing to the young poet whose eyes were as starry as they were blue. He consoled himself by going to hear Wagner at the opera and by keeping in close contact with his friends in Paris. He associated with some writers in New York, particularly with William Dean Howells, but he was not tempted to write in English. The poems and prose pieces that he composed were in French and were sent off to Europe to appear in the Symbolist reviews.

Les Gammes is the title of his first volume of poems. It appeared in 1887, a great year for Symbolism, the year that volumes by Kahn, Mallarmé, Mockel, Régnier, Verhaeren, Vielé-Griffin also appeared. Merrill had sent the manuscript to his friend René Ghil to take charge of the proofs and make on-the-spot decisions with his publisher Léon Vanier. Ghil was recompensed by a dedication and the right to advertise the poems as having been composed according to his own principles of "instrumentation verbale." This is true only in a very general sense, for Merrill never followed the scientific formula set down in the *Traité du verbe*. On the other hand, musicality is the first quality of these poems—the first but not the only because Merrill believed that a poem transmitted meanings rather than pure melody. Meanings must not be confused with messages, however, for in spite of his political zeal, Merrill did not believe in "engaging" his art. The derivative nature of these early poems is evident. Verlaine, Baudelaire, Mallarmé, Poe all contributed in one way or another —Verlaine for melody, Mallarmé for the concept of ideal beauty, Baudelaire and Poe for the melancholy tone, the strong rhythmic quality of the verses. The prosody of this first collection harks back to Parnassianism with even lines, formal rimes, conventional syntax and vocabulary. Its chief merit lies in its musicality, which is also its chief weakness in that it is often exaggerated. Contrived musical effects and artificiality of sentiments flawed the work to the point that Merrill wished to forget his first volume, although critics received it well and for some Merrill would always remain the poet of *Les Gammes*.

Les Fastes, Merrill's second volume, appeared early in 1891. His father had died in the summer of 1888. The following year Mrs. Merrill took her children back to Europe. Stuart could renew his literary friendships in Paris only briefly for the family was constantly travelling. In London he met Walter Pater and Oscar Wilde whom he was later to defend with courage. Merrill's work during these years was both in English and French. Besides contributing poems to French periodicals he wrote articles for the *New York Evening Post* and translated a collection of prose poems (*Pastels in Prose*, Harpers, 1890). The poems that made up *Les Fastes* had for the most part already appeared in magazines. The legends of Wagner and of the Middle Ages furnish the main themes of the volume and its sumptuous décor; visual effects share importance with music in evocations reminiscent of Moreau paintings. In the alliterations, assonances, and sound combinations Merrill achieves something akin to Wagnerian polyphony; his music is complemented by the opulent colors and luminosities that he creates in these verses. The prosody of this collection is increasingly experimental. Uneven lines abound, and, compared to his first volume, a far greater variety of rhythmic effects helps to lighten the weight of the imagery and complicated orchestration. In spite of the remarkable achievement in *Les Fastes*, one has the impression that what Merrill does here is more a tour de force than personal expression. He is essentially a simple lyricist, and his accomplishment with symbols and décor is more the result of discipline than natural expression. He would gradually liberate himself from the forms and formulas of his day to let his heart sing out more naturally.

In the fall of 1890, Merrill returned to New York where he decorated an apartment and installed himself with the idea of being near his mother. The pull of Paris was too great, however; the following year he went back never again to return to the States.

Symbolism was in all its glory. Merrill went often to the cafés of the Latin Quarter where poets met, and he also entertained lavishly in his own apartment. At the age of thirty, he stood as a sort of Prince Charming among the rich patrons of the arts. Handsome and debonaire, he seemed the epitome of cosmopolitan grace. In poetry his own personality prevailed against the fashion of the day, and Merrill announced his emancipation from Mallarmé, Laforgue, Rimbaud, "trois noms qui ont trop pesé sur notre jeunesse."[2] He announced his return to the authentic French language and its masters, Nerval, Villiers de l'Isle-Adam, and Verlaine. His position is rendered a bit vague by the phrasing of these proclamations, but what is clear is his preference for a simple, direct poetic expression without, however, abandoning philosophic idealism as the basis for poetry. Moreover, he was in favor of turning poetry away from sound and pictures for their sake alone but, following Poe, Gautier, Baudelaire, and the pre-Raphaelites, did not want to make it social or utilitarian.

Yet as a person, rather than as a poet, he continued to be interested in social issues. During the early 1890s, Merrill manifested increasing sympathy for socialism, particularly as exemplified by William Morris. Once he was arrested for demonstrating on behalf of the anarchists. Jean-Paul Sartre is not the first French writer to "engage" himself quite actively in political matters, nor is the young generation of the 1960s the first to revolt against the "establishment" as represented by the army, school, government, etc. The outsider hero of the nineties was Paul Verlaine: Merrill adored him as a personality and, of course, as a poet. His next volume of poems continued the tradition of *Romances sans paroles*. The *Petits Poèmes d'automne* (1895) have the delicacy of sentiment and expression notable in Verlaine's collection, where all is nuance. Its subject is partly drawn from Merrill's intimate sentimental history, a side of his life discreetly veiled by his biographers.

The *Poèmes 1887–1897* indicate a return to the earlier Symbolist manner. Perhaps the explanation is the fact that some of the poems really date from the eighties and Merrill wished the new poems to conform; perhaps it was just nostalgia, since Merrill never found the opulent manner com-

pletely unattractive. Versatility was, in any case, one of Merrill's ambi-
tions. This is substantiated by his ventures into fiction, essay, drama,
which often piled up manuscripts seldom finished, seldom printed. His
verse, on the other hand, usually saw the light of day. Collection after
collection was published with regularity. *Les Quatre Saisons* appeared
in 1900, a volume that marks the full realization of Merrill's genius.
Dedicated to Francis Jammes, these poems sing of nature, the beauty of
rural France, in a very personal, natural, and spontaneous manner.
Although far less derivative than his early poetry, far less bookish, they
are not without indebtedness to the work of other poets, especially the
Sylvie of Gérard de Nerval. Seen through this little masterpiece, the
countryside of the Parisian region must have been for Merrill doubly
charming. He had, since 1898, possessed a retreat at Marlotte, near the
Fontainebleau forest. Artists and other writers lived nearby, whom
Merrill often joined for conversation and lighthearted pastimes. For
a period there was a sort of colony of craftsmen established after Morris's
Merton Abbey, with barns turned into studios. Merrill made plans to
become a printer there, but travel and other commitments kept the plans
from realization.

Then in 1908, Merrill got married and said good-bye to his Bohemian
life and his sentimental adventures which, we gather, were for the most
part, disappointing. With his young wife he established a residence in
Versailles. In 1909, *Une Voix dans la Foule*, his last volume of poems,
came out. These are poems on the themes of love, life, and death treated
with delicate nuance. Nature is often the setting. Although not perfectly
constant throughout, a Whitmanesque optimism dominates in the volume
as Merrill, like his great compatriot, lifts his eyes to encompass the whole
human adventure. In form, the verses mark a return to the conventional,
suggesting that by the end of his poetic career Merrill had achieved a
full circle.

The years that immediately preceded World War I were darkened for
Merrill by his declining health. He kept in contact with the literary world,
however, through correspondence and contributions to journals in Paris
and also in Brussels where he frequently sojourned. He still travelled in
spite of his bad health, spending the winter of 1913 and 1914 in Bavaria.
The outbreak of hostilities was a terrible blow for the idealist and inter-
nationalist that he was; it doubtless precipitated his death in 1915. The
war shattered all the fine hopes Merrill entertained for humanity and
its future. Utopianism had always been a basic element in his thinking,

a result partly of temperament and partly of idealistic conviction. Note that in his "Symbolism," idealism in the philosophic and moral sense persisted even though he abandoned other aspects of the doctrine. Morality in its loftiest sense was for Merrill, as for the English Romantics, always involved in the beautiful. He held it against the *Trophées* of Heredia that in spite of their formal perfection, they did not qualify "par leur signification de la noblesse d'une âme."[3] Art, religion, ethical behavior were all viewed by Merrill as ultimately in the service of human ameliorism. The war now made him feel that he had been deceived, that his splendid vision was but a delusion.

If Merrill believed that the artist was more than a craftsman, it is because he believed strongly in inspiration. The poet is privileged to glimpse the ideal, which he then records in his verses to transmit to humanity. In spite of the artist's privilege, his role is modest, essentially that of a medium, a seer as Rimbaud had said, a translator as Proust would call him. His work, although confined to the rendering of his vision, is notwithstanding arduous. In his concept of the poet's function, Merrill does not deviate from what all the Symbolists professed, a concept enunciated by the Romantics and reiterated most recently by the Surrealists. In matters of technique, which Merrill always considered secondary, he moved, as we have seen, gradually from the traditional alexandrine to the liberated alexandrine, free verse, the prose poem, and back to the traditional line. A maximum of musicality seems to have always been his major concern, an ambition which led him at times into overdoing repetition, echo, alliteration, end and internal rime. Musicality and mood probably best define Merrill and his contribution to French verse. Some would see here a result of his knowledge of English and make Merrill, for this reason, as well as for spreading the fame of Whitman and Morris, an important link between Anglo-American and French poetry. However, since such matters are extremely difficult to assess, one should hesitate to take a very positive stand. In spite of the comparative thesis in the only book written on Stuart Merrill (Henry, *Stuart Merrill, La Contribution d'un Américain au Symbolisme français*), specific influence on French poetry by Whitman, Morris, or Merrill's role are probably not very great.

Notes

1. See Henry, *Stuart Merrill*, pp. 18–19.
2. *Ermitage*, June 1893.
3. *Ermitage*, April 1893. Cited by Henry, p. 94. Merrill published his artistic credo in this magazine which for a time he served as poetry editor.

NOCTURNE[1]

La blême lune allume en la mare qui luit,
Miroir des gloires d'or, un émoi d'incendie.
Tout dort. Seul, à mi-mort, un rossignol de nuit
Module en mal d'amour sa molle mélodie.

Plus ne vibrent les vents en le mystère vert
Des ramures. La lune a tu leurs voix nocturnes:
Mais à travers le deuil du feuillage entr'ouvert
Pleuvent les bleus baisers des astres taciturnes.

La vieille volupté de rêver à la mort
A l'entour de la mare endort l'âme des choses.
A peine la forêt parfois fait-elle effort
Sous le frisson furtif de ses métamorphoses.

Chaque feuille s'efface en des brouillards subtils.
Du zénith de l'azur ruisselle la rosée
Dont le cristal s'incruste en perles aux pistils
Des nénufars flottant sur l'eau fleurdelysée.

Rien n'émane du noir, ni vol, ni vent, ni voix,
Sauf lorsqu'au loin des bois, par soudaines saccades,
Un ruisseau turbulent roule sur les gravois:
L'écho s'émeut alors de l'éclat des cascades.

(Les Gammes)

---

1. In this poem from Merrill's first collection, the mood is distinctly Verlainian and the setting one of those "paysages de l'âme" common to the "poèmes saturniens." The musical effects are somewhat overdone, typical of Merrill particularly in his early manner.

CELLE QUI PRIE[2]

Ses doigts gemmés de rubacelle
Et lourds du geste des effrois
Ont sacré d'un signe de croix
Le samit de sa tunicelle.

Sous ses torsades où ruisselle
La rançon d'amour de maints rois,
Sa prunelle vers les orfrois
Darde une viride étincelle.

Et c'est par l'oratoire d'or
Les alléluias en essor
De l'orgue et du violoncelle:

Et, sur un missel à fermail
Qu'empourpre le soir d'un vitrail,
Ses doigts gemmés de rubacelle.

(Les Fastes)

2. The Burne-Jones quality is apparent in this portrait in octosyllabic verse.

SOLITUDE[3]

On dit que des rois morts ont foulé ce sentier
Qui mène au banc de pierre où nous aimons nous asseoir,
Alors que sur la solitude tombe la paix du soir
Et que nos cœurs sont pleins de chants muets, comme des psautiers.

De ce rocher on vit, sous les fanfares de la conquête,
La plaine se hérisser soudain d'épis de fer,
Et des multitudes, revenues des étés et des hivers,
Rouler comme un fleuve rouge vers la grande ville en fête.

Mais ni la chevauchée ensoleillée sous les bannières,
Ni le doux tonnerré des tambours dans le printemps,
Ni le cri des clairons dressés en corolles d'or,

Ne valent ce silence où notre fatigue s'endort,
Et la caresse des ombres qu'entremêlent les vents
Et la minute éternelle de notre baiser, cette prière!

(Les Quatre Saisons)

---

3. Reminiscent of the Romantic manner, this poem seems also indebted to Parnassianism in its grandiose imagery.

Poetry of Vielé-Griffin

Œuvres de Francis Vielé-Griffin (Mercure de France, 1924–1930). 4 vols.

Readings

Cours, Jean de. *Francis Vielé-Griffin* (Champion, 1930)

Kuhn, Reinhard. *The Return to Reality, a Study of Francis Vielé-Griffin* (Minard, 1962).

Morier, Henri. *Vielé-Griffin, Le Rythme du Vers Libre Symboliste* (Geneva: Presses Académiques, 1944).

Paysac, Henry de. *Francis Vielé-Griffin, poète symboliste et citoyen américain* (Nizet, 1976).

Francis Vielé-Griffin

1863–1937

Son of an American general who was also a distinguished civil engineer and landscape architect, Egbert Ludovicus Viele, Jr., was born in Norfolk and spent his early childhood on country estates near New York City. At the age of seven, he was taken by his mother to Paris. Much has been made of Vielé-Griffin's foreign origin. It has seemed the source of certain qualities of his poetry and personality, of certain aims and aspirations that he entertained for poetic reform. Critics have spoken of a musicality in his verse that bears an Anglo-American stamp; of his spiritual affinity to Whitman and to the Lake poets in England, of a touch of American puritanism in his attitude, of his cavalier attitude toward traditional French prosody. Since he left the United States as a young boy, never returned, and wrote exclusively in French, one suspects that the foreign element in his work is negligible.

He was educated at the Collège Stanislas, where he had as classmate Henri de Régnier. The two became very good friends and remained so for almost thirty years. Together they went on to the university to study law and together they began writing for the little reviews. For the *Lutèce*, Vielé-Griffin wrote essays and stories as well as poems. In 1885, he was going to Mallarmé's Tuesdays and meeting the poets with whom he would be associated during the years to come. His first volume of verse, *Cueille d'Avril*, dates from 1886, full of Baudelairian spleen expressed in the mixture of learned and simple language that the Symbolists were affecting at the time. Verlaine commented favorably upon the volume.

The *Lutèce* and the *Vogue* failed before the end of 1886, creating a gap that Vielé-Griffin and his companions decided to fill with a new journal to be called *Ecrits pour l'Art*. René Ghil, Régnier, and Stuart Merrill were among the backers. For two years Vielé-Griffin took an active part in getting the publication out and published in its pages a number of his poems. He left it after it had become the mouthpiece for René Ghil. There was no problem of an outlet for his work. Gustave Kahn's *Revue Indépendante* accepted, in addition to his poems, translations of Whitman and Swinburne. *Art et Critique* accepted critical articles. The second *Vogue, La Wallonie, La Jeune Belgique* all welcomed his collaboration. But by 1890 he was ready to assume editorial responsibility again, and so, with Paul Adam and Henri de Régnier, he founded the *Entretiens Politiques et Littéraires*. The three years that he spent with the periodical were stormy ones. As champion of free verse and defender of Jules Laforgue, Vielé-Griffin did doughty combat in its pages. He tangled with Isabelle Rimbaud over a biographical sketch that he published of her brother. A slight directed at Catulle Mendès ended in a duel. Neophyte authors such as Gide and Claudel were introduced in the *Entretiens*. Vielé-Griffin published some of his own writing as well, and at the same time appeared in other journals of the day. The *Entretiens* was a success, but by 1893 Vielé-Griffin was tired of the responsibility and withdrew. Shortly afterwards, he married and went to live in the country.

While Vielé-Griffin was occupied with magazine publication, he was at the same time writing a great deal of verse. His second volume came out in 1887, *Les Cygnes*, poems generally still conventional as to metrics although the book contains a statement professing freedom from the strictures of the alexandrine and of Parnassian rime. The mood, however, is not the conventional pessimism that marked *Cueille d'Avril* but an optimism rare in Symbolist poetry—a love of life, an exultation in the ideal perceived and the real accepted. His next effort was *Ancaeus*, a poetic drama classical in form and subject. Only with the poems that make up *Joies* does Vielé-Griffin begin to practice the free verse that he had preached. In an issue of his *Entretiens* he sums up his views on the subject. They are not radical. For him the twelve-syllable line is generally long enough. Rhythm should complement the idea. Rime and alliteration are important elements. Regarding the mute *e*, Vielé-Griffin's conservatism has been interpreted as humility or ignorance of French. The latter explanation seems hardly reasonable in view of his schooling and long residence in the country.

The second *Cygnes* appeared in 1892, less ebullient than the volume called *Joies* and far more esoteric. The poems here reveal Mallarmé's influence in their density and in the ideal that they postulate. Perhaps it was Mallarmé who turned his attention to the Scandinavian folk epic, the *Edda*, the inspiration of *Swanhilde*, a poetic drama composed by Vielé-Griffin in the early nineties. In 1893 appeared *la Chevauchée d'Yeldis*, a volume which, besides the poem which gives the collection its title, contains some minor songlike poems typical of Vielé-Griffin on the theme of nature, animals, and Christian sentiment. This work hailed by his contemporaries as a masterpiece closes for Vielé-Griffin a period of great fruitfulness. It is at this time also that he abandoned the *Entretiens*. He was thirty years old.

The oscillation between optimism and pessimism which helps classify Vielé-Griffin's early works characterizes as well those of his middle period. It would seem that the problems of reality and the ideal or the dream, of life and death, remained throughout his career his greatest stimulus for writing, and that while optimism is a hallmark, much of his poetry is dark in mood. *La Clarté de Vie* (1897) is in the main as light as *Joies* but *Phocas le Jardinier* and *La Partenza* seem expressions of discouragement and despair. One remedy is suggested by the Nietzschean *Wieland le Forgeron* (1900), another by *L'Amour sacré* (1903); the two combined and reconciled seemed to restore the poet's morale. But only temporarily. If the years following *L'Amour sacré* were relatively barren, it is because Vielé-Griffin was very low in spirit and was hesitant to communicate his mood to the public. Like a woman who refuses to go out when she is not looking her best, this poet wanted to publish only when he could present a flattering image of life. He was just as reluctant to participate in journalistic ventures, but here he let himself be persuaded. He helped Gide with *L'Ermitage*, contributed anonymously but abundantly to *L'Occident*, worked for Paul Fort's *Vers et Prose*, for *Antée*, for *La Phalange*. He wrote reminiscences, editorials, literary criticism, and, on occasion, a column such as one on the stock market. During the years immediately preceding World War I he began again to publish creative works. *Sapho*, *La Lumière de Grèce*, *Voix d'Ionie* date from these years. By the time of the war, Vielé-Griffin had become one of the contemporary masters: his works were studied by eminent critics and every Wednesday his apartment on the Quai de Passy was the meeting place for young writers.

With the outbreak of war, Vielé-Griffin retired to the country. There he wrote occasional verse and worked on his *Souvenirs d'Enfance et de Première Jeunesse*. During the 1920s, he brought out two more volumes and did some translations of Whitman and Rossetti. *Le Livre des Reines*

(1929), three poetic dramas, is the last work published during his lifetime.

Vielé-Griffin is remembered first of all as a *vers-librist*. Henri Morier has devoted an entire volume to the analysis of his prosody.[1] His masters were Baudelaire, from whom he acquired the notion of correspondences exploited throughout his poetry; Verlaine, whose "Art poétique" served him as a blueprint and master plan; Laforgue, who before him had used the folk song and had worked in free verse. At one point in his career Vielé-Griffin came strongly under Mallarmé's influence. There was, of course, much in the masters that he rejected, such as Baudelaire's eroticism, Verlaine's naïveté, Laforgue's irony, Mallarmé's abstruseness.

In no sense an isolated poet, Vielé-Griffin, his story is the story of the Symbolist movement. As an editor and editorialist he was in the thick of the fray, friend or foe of every other poet who wrote at the time. And on the young who would take his place, such as Gide and Claudel, he left his mark. Critics have reproached him for lacking a philosophical system to support his poetry, for being a foreigner, for too great facility. Yet they concede that he gave Symbolism a breath of air and, at least at times, a glow of health and happiness.

Note

1. Vielé-Griffin, *Le Rythme du Vers Libre Symboliste*.

CARMEN PERPETUUM

Prélude

L'Aurore impériale et sa pourpre[1] ont passé;
Voici le chant des bois et la rumeur des plaines
Et le printemps, mêlant ses sons et ses haleines,
Grise d'amour mon âme éprise du passé.

L'herbe est joyeuse et, vers le fleuve qui dévie
Majestueux et lent aux horizons perdus,
S'élèvent des murmures doux, comme entendus
Par delà l'autre hiver, et par delà ma vie ...

Ainsi qu'en ce matin d'avril prestigieux,
Humant la volupté des Choses surhumaines,
Je foule, inconscient, le sentier où tu mènes
Mon être vers un but inconnu de tous deux;

Ainsi j'ai bu l'amour à tes lèvres diverses,
Dès l'aurore première et dès l'éternité;
Et, jusqu'en cet avril où rit ta nudité,
J'ai tendu le cratère aux baisers que tu verses;

Nos aveux oubliés me sont comme un remords,
Et j'ai suivi l'écho mystérieux des rires;
Et dans mes yeux émerveillés où tu te mires
S'est reflété l'éclat perdu des soleils morts.[2]

I

J'errais en un Pays sans nom, parmi des fleurs,
Sans rêve et sans passé, joyeux de joie étrange;
Enfantin et riant des sons et des couleurs,
Dans ma virilité virginale d'archange.

Lascive et blonde en l'herbe verte aux reflets bleus
Tu dormais à mes pieds dans l'attente fatale;
Et la rose, complice, effeuillant un pétale,
Epanouit ta lèvre en un souris moelleux ...

Tu gisais à mes pieds, rieuse et rougissante,
En ta passivité d'amante, tu gisais,

Et tu compris, d'abord, le Mot que je disais;
Et le baiser fut long et l'étreinte puissante.[3]

(Poèmes et Poésies: Cueille d'Avril)

1. Example of synecdoche reminding us of the frequent use Symbolists made of devices of metonymy that lift the object out of the concrete into the abstract. Note stanza four, *rit ta nudité*, etc. Vielé-Griffin's poetic effects seem unpleasantly contrived. Improper yokings such as *Par delà l'autre hiver, et par delà ma vie* …, *Lascive et blonde, rieuse et rougissante* are typical. They suggest that the poet either wished coyly to shock or was hard put to find rimes. Epithets are therefore sometimes silly or odd: *tes lèvres diverses; un souris moelleux.* Meaning is obscured by precious periphrases.

2. Threadbare figure of Baudelairian derivation.

3. The line is rendered comical by the Hugo-like cadence. It pulls the curtain for us on a scene typical of Symbolist painting at its worst. The full "Carmen Perpetuum" has, however, eight more parts.

CHANSON[4]

J'ai pris de la pluie dans mes mains tendues
—De la pluie chaude comme des larmes—
Je l'ai bue comme un philtre, défendu
A cause d'un charme;
Afin que mon âme en ton âme dorme.

J'ai pris du blé dans la grange obscure
—Du blé qui choit comme la grêle aux dalles—
Et je l'ai semé sur le labour dur
A cause du givre matinal;
Afin que tu goûtes à la moisson sûre.

J'ai pris des herbes et des feuilles rousses,
—Des feuilles et des herbes longtemps mortes—
J'en ai fait une flamme haute et douce
A cause de l'essence des sèves fortes;
Afin que ton attente d'aube fût douce.

Et j'ai pris la pudeur de tes joues et ta bouche
Et tes gais cheveux et tes yeux de rire,
Et je m'en suis fait une aurore farouche
Et des rayons de joie et des cordes de lyre
—Et le jour est sonore comme un chant de ruche!

(Poèmes et Poésies: Joies)

4. One would say that Vielé-Griffin is here at his best in these repeated lines evoking summer dawn in a rural setting and the delight of being in love.

MON REVE DE CE SOIR ...[5]

Mon rêve de ce soir est d'un cristal
Où tu versais le vin de ton rire
Diaphane comme une source qui bouillonne
Et qu'on boit à pleines lèvres de désir;
Mon désir de ce soir est d'un heurt de métal
Clair et vibrant à l'unisson de mon désir,
Vainqueur et joyeux—comme une armure sonore—[6]
Mâle et rieur et clair—que l'on s'y mire.

Mon amour de ce soir est de toi, toujours telle,
Fuyante comme un rayon au mur
En ta gaîté de feuillée;
Puis, lasse, qui te pends en guirlande mortelle,
Et bonne, comme une flamme en la veillée,
Et sapide au cœur comme un limon sûr;
Mon amour est de toi, toujours telle.

(Poèmes et Poésies: Joies)

5. Simple love lyric in keeping with its Verlainian title. Uneven lines, stanzas of different lengths show Vielé-Griffin as a *vers-librist*.

6. Interesting auditory imagery of clinking glass, resounding metal, etc., that complements evocation of liquids and luminosities.

Poetry of Henri de Régnier

The various volumes of Régnier's poetry have been published by the *Mercure de France*.

Readings

Berton, Henry. *Henri de Régnier* (Grasset, 1910).

Buenzod, Emmanuel. *Henri de Régnier* (Avignon: Aubanel, 1966).

Gourmont, Jean de. *Henri de Régnier et son œuvre* (Mercure de France, 1908).

Honnert, Robert. *Henri de Régnier, son œuvre* (Nouvelle Revue Critique, 1923).

Maurin, Mario. *Henri de Régnier, le labyrinthe et le double* (Montréal: l'Université de Montréal, 1972). Treats Régnier's novels.

Henri de Régnier

1864–1936

The aristocratic Henri de Régnier, with his monocle and drooping blond mustaches, was considered, around 1900, as the greatest French poet alive. His reputation has since dramatically declined, but only because sweet melancholy and grace no longer interest the public. Marcel Proust spoke for his generation when he exclaimed, "Le jardin d'Henri de Régnier, Dieu sait si je l'aime."[1] Régnier's garden evokes the formal gardens of Versailles and the parks of old châteaux, with mossy stone steps, balustrades, statuary, and fountains. Peacocks parade through their gravelled paths. Such settings are not unfitting for a gentleman poet who traced his family tree back to the sixteenth century. Doubtless that is what one of his panegyrists, Jean de Gourmont, had in mind when he says that "mille voix parlent par sa bouche, qui s'étaient tues, au cours des siècles: il est la parole d'une race. Tout ce que ses ancêtres éprouvèrent, toutes les joies et les tristesses dont ils furent effleurés, sans trop comprendre, c'est lui, le poète, qui les ressent, qui va leur donner l'expression musicale du vers."[2]

Régnier was born in Honfleur, where his father held a post in the customs service, and spent his early childhood there. In 1871, his father was transferred to Paris and Henri went to school at Stanislas. There he began to frequent the library reading rooms and to write verse. Some were published in *Lutèce*, where Vielé-Griffin was likewise making his début. After graduation, he went on to study law, took a foreign service examination, but soon gave up all thoughts of a diplomatic career in favor of poetry. His life would be nonetheless social for that, for Régnier's career in poetry meant active participation in the *mêlée symboliste*, contributing to the little reviews, mingling with his fellow poets, attending soirées, making calls on the great masters of the day. We can imagine him in evening attire as often as if he had stayed in diplomacy. He remained until he died the Parisian man of letters.

The year 1885 marks Régnier's formal entrance into literature with a volume of verse entitled *Les Lendemains*. Intended to immortalize fugitive moments, they are poems of a twenty-year-old, sentimental and melancholy, with scenes of nature in moonlight or under autumn skies, the "decadent" poems of the times. The next year *Apaisement* appeared, more poems of love marked by the same romantic spleen that afflicted Régnier's generation. The landscapes are "soulscapes," symbolic representation of the young man's mood and sensibility. The title indicates that he has found ease for his heartaches, abandoned his adolescent chimeras.

Before publishing his first verse, Régnier was, of course, an enthusiastic reader of the Romantic poets and the Parnassians, but the only poet whom he knew personally was Sully Prudhomme. The success of his verse began to open other doors to him. He went to the rue de Rome to see Mallarmé and for ten years returned there every Tuesday. Stuart Merrill says that he was a sort of choir leader for the habitués.[3] He went to the Cour Saint-François where Verlaine had his hovel. He joined the other young poets who sat before Leconte de Lisle, Léon Dierx, and Villiers de l'Isle-Adam. His poetry bore traces of his frequentations. In the twenty-five sonnets that make up *Sites* (1887) and in the *Episodes* that follow them, Régnier's emphasis was less on subjective lyricism than on décor. His soulscapes had become quite Symbolist and Wagnerian with their princesses and swans, their precious stones and onyx palaces. Out of the fashionable material of the time he constructed his refuge, his own transfigured and idealized universe, sites and episodes for his inner life. In the short time that separated these works from his first, Régnier had achieved great skill as a versifier. The sumptuous effects of sonority and visual evocation demonstrate the young poet's mastery of his art.

Not before *Poèmes anciens et romanesques* (1890) did Régnier try his hand at free verse and even here the line is often just a broken-up alexandrine. He begins also to use terza rima, which he will often use when he wishes to attain effects of hieratic solemnity. *Tel qu'en songe* (1892) continues to mingle free verse with alexandrine and octosyllabic verse. This is the volume honored by a review from the young Marcel Proust. It gave Proust an opportunity to promote what would later be called "poésie pure." No eloquence, no rhetoric in these poems, he said, just "un infini bruissant et bleuâtre, reflétant l'éternité du ciel."[4] The banishment of extraneous material from poetry, particularly moralizing, was, of course, implicit in the Symbolist doctrine. In this article on Régnier, Proust ponders over another matter important to Symbolists, that of intuition versus intelligence in poetry. Proust would never stop meditating upon these questions, his attitude remaining always the Symbolist point of view.

Les Jeux rustiques et divins are poems still strongly Symbolistic by their mystery, musicality, and melancholy. They could also be called supreme examples of what Clouard rather maliciously refers to as the "Symbolisme des Centaures,"[5] since Greek mythology, noticeable since *Episodes*, is very prominent here. The famous poem "Le Vase" figures in the collection, a pagan evocation of centaurs, dryads, and fauns, reminiscent of Mallarmé's "L'Après-midi d'un Faune." Mallarmé was, however, not the only strong influence on Régnier. Heredia, the Parnassian poet whose *Trophées* were published in 1893, impressed Régnier greatly. In his social rounds, Régnier had not neglected the Arsenal Library were Heredia held the post of administrator. Régnier would, incidentally, become Heredia's son-in-law, marrying in 1896 his daughter Maria, known in literature as Gérard d'Houville. Heredia's influence can still further be seen in *Médailles d'Argile*, even though they are dedicated to André Chénier. The year of this collection marks Régnier's début as a novelist. He had previously published short stories, but in 1900 *La Double Maîtresse* assured Régnier's success as a novelist. By the turn of the century, Régnier had won a place of distinction in the Paris of arts and letters that he had frequented for fifteen years. He was invited to lecture on French poetry in the United States. He spoke about Mallarmé, Villiers, Verlaine, and about Parnasse and Symbolism. Ten years later, after additional acclaim as a poet and a novelist, he was made a member of the French Academy.

Régnier publicly paid tribute to both Heredia and Mallarmé in *La Cité des Eaux* (1902), a volume that originated in a series of sonnets on Versailles written to accompany some drawings by Helleu. Always the poet of stately old parks and dwellings, he had here an ideal subject in the splendors of Lenôtre and Hardouin-Mansart which, in Régnier's day, presented a spectacle of neglect and decay. Touched and inspired by a number of other poets, some quite different from one another, Régnier still knew how to combine his influences gracefully and at the same time present a very distinct image of himself. It is perhaps in these Versailles poems that the image is most clearly seen, that of a noble melancholy poet, a poet of sentimental rather than metaphysical themes, that he expresses with melodious wistfulness through evocations of nature and ruins. His subsequent collections present no deviation from the main lines of his poetry already established. The verse is generally classic, although here and there one notes examples of freer forms, and instead of "soulscapes" and "centaur symbolism," a less indirect type of lyricism. Emmanuel Buenzod notes this evolution from the general and the abstract to subjective expression, commenting that with most poets it is just the reverse. (*Henri de Régnier*, p. 86) The lines in such an argument are apt to become entangled. It is, of course, true that direct outpourings are typical of young poets; yet this must be weighed against the impression of originality and authenticity that poets attain in maturity, now free from borrowed finery and perhaps from emotions only simulated.

Yet sincerity and mastery of an individual expression are not enough to assure greatness. Perhaps a lack of muscle was at fault, perhaps neither the emotions nor the expression rough enough: before Régnier stopped writing, the younger generation stopped reading what seemed to it an everlasting singsong—repetitious, easy, and inconsequential. In pre-World War I France a new raucous, dissonant esthetic was forming, and Régnier, along with other favorites of Marcel Proust, belonged definitely to the past.

Notes

1. *Correspondance générale*, vol. 2, pp. 232–33.
2. *Henri de Régnier et son œuvre* (Mercure de France, 1908), p. 30.
3. See Gourmont, *Henri de Régnier*, p. 15.
4. Proust, *Chroniques* (Gallimard, 1927), p. 175.
5. *Histoire de la littérature française* (Albin Michel, 1947), vol. 1, p. 241.

IL EST UN PORT ...[1]

Il est un port
Avec des eaux d'huiles, de moires et d'or
Et des quais de marbre le long des bassins calmes,
Si calmes
Qu'on voit sur le fond qui s'ensable
Passer des poissons d'ombre et d'or
Parmi les algues,
Et la proue à jamais y mire dans l'eau stable
La Tête qui l'orne et s'endort
Au bruit du vent qui pousse sur les dalles
Du quai de marbre
Des poussières de sable d'or.

Il est un port.
Le silence y somnole entre des quais de songe,
Le passé en algues s'allonge
Aux oscillations lentes des poissons d'or;
Le souvenir s'ensable d'oubli et l'ombre
Du soir est toute tiède du jour mort.
Qu'il soit un port
Où l'orgueil à la proue y dorme en l'eau qui dort!

---

1. From the collection *Tel qu'en songe*. A vision in a dream, this port where the still and stagnant waters are disturbed only by the play of light and shadows and by the movement of the goldfish among the algae. It is evening after a warm summer day and a slight breeze scatters the golden sand over the marble docks. Note that the second stanza moves patently to the symbolic level: silence sleeps, the past stretches out like filaments of algae, the memory clogs up with sand.

Régnier uses a relatively limited, classic vocabulary. Whether lofty, sensual, or playful, the image is evoked by a small selection of words mainly precise in nature. The effect of opulence and the complexity is created by what is evoked rather than by the author's lexicon in itself.

ODELETTE[2]

Un petit roseau m'a suffi
Pour faire frémir l'herbe haute
Et tout le pré
Et les doux saules
Et le ruisseau qui chante aussi;
Un petit roseau m'a suffi
A faire chanter la forêt.

Ceux qui passent l'ont entendu
Au fond du soir, en leurs pensées,
Dans le silence et dans le vent,
Clair ou perdu,
Proche ou lointain ...
Ceux qui passent en leurs pensées
En écoutant, au fond d'eux-mêmes,[3]
L'entendront encore et l'entendent
Toujours qui chante.

Il m'a suffi
De ce petit roseau cueilli
A la fontaine où vint l'Amour
Mirer, un jour,
Sa face grave
Et qui pleurait,
Pour faire pleurer ceux qui passent
Et trembler l'herbe et frémir l'eau;
Et j'ai, du souffle d'un roseau,
Fait chanter toute la forêt.

---

2. One of the most charming and best known of Régnier's poems, it belongs to *Les Jeux rustiques et divins*.

3. Note that in place of end rime there is assonance. Although in free verse, the poem has a rather fixed rhythm pattern. The alternance of long and short lines is typical of Régnier who achieves thereby effects of prolongation and cutting short, a rhythm based only on musical instinct.

MARSYAS PARLE:[4]

Tant pis! si j'ai vaincu le Dieu. Il l'a voulu!
Salut, terre où longtemps Marsyas a vécu,
Et vous, bois paternels, et vous ô jeunes eaux,
Près de qui je cueillais la tige du roseau
Où mon haleine tremble, pleure, s'enfle ou court,
Forte ou paisible, aiguë ou rauque, tour à tour,
Telle un sanglot de source ou le bruit du feuillage!
Vous ne reverrez plus se pencher mon visage
Sur votre onde limpide ou se lever mes yeux
Vers la cime au ciel pur de l'arbre harmonieux:
Car le Dieu redoutable a puni le Satyre.
Ma peau velue et douce, au fer qui la déchire,
Va saigner; Marsyas mourra, mais c'est en vain
Que l'Envieux céleste et le Rival divin
Essaiera sur ma flûte inutile à ses doigts
De retrouver mon souffle et d'apprendre ma voix;
Et maintenant liez mon corps et, nu, qu'il sorte
De sa peau écorchée et vide, car, qu'importe
Que Marsyas soit mort, puisqu'il sera vivant
Si le pin rouge et vert chante encor dans le vent![5]

(La Cité des Eaux)

---

4. Marsyas, in Greek mythology, is a Phrygian satyr who stands for a sort of earth spirit, a Dionysius ever the foe of Apollo. Athena had discarded the double flute and laid a curse on anyone who would play it. Marsyas discovered the instrument, learned to play it, challenged Apollo with his lyre to a musical contest. Apollo won, but only by trickery. He avenged himself on the presumptuous satyr by hanging him to a tree and flaying him alive. The river Marsyas was formed either from the satyr's blood or from the tears of his friends.

5. The influence of Hugo's "Le Satyre" is apparent in the inspiration of this poem.

Poetry of Paul Claudel

Œuvre poétique (Gallimard, 1957). Bibliothèque de la Pléïade.

Readings

Angers, Pierre. *Commentaire à l'Art Poétique de Paul Claudel* (Mercure de France, 1949).

Blanc, André. *Les critiques de notre temps et Claudel* (Garnier, 1970).

———. *Présence littéraire: Claudel* (Bordas, 1973).

Cattaui, Georges. *Claudel* (Desclée de Brouwer, 1968).

Plourde, Michel. *Paul Claudel: une musique du silence* (Montréal: l'Université de Montréal, 1970).

Vachon, André. *Le Temps et l'espace dans l'œuvre de Paul Claudel* (Seuil, 1965).

Waters, Harold A. *Paul Claudel* (Boston: Twayne, 1970).

Paul Claudel

1868–1955

It has been said that Symbolism could never have been if the church had not lost its hold during the latter part of the nineteenth century. The thought is that the lyrical and mystic impulse could find no longer its natural outlet and had turned to poetry, making of an art something of a religion. The example of Paul Claudel may disprove such a contention: at least he returned to the church, yet in so doing, did not renounce any of the Symbolist claims for poetry. He merely set poetry within the framework of his faith.

Poetry and religion were inextricably linked for Claudel almost from the first, since it was his discovery of Rimbaud that led him back to the church and also into poetry. In 1886, at the age of eighteen, he read the *Illuminations* and the *Saison en Enfer* in the periodical *La Vogue* Rimbaud appeared to him not only a genius, but a man touched by grace. On Christmas Day he himself was "touched" during mass at Notre Dame, and the following year, he started to attend the Tuesdays in the rue de Rome. The esthetic that he would later formalize in his *Art poétique* reaffirms Rimbaud's pronouncements and all the things that young Claudel heard in the poetic circles of the late 1880s—the poet is a seer; poetry is the revelation of cosmic verities; the key to poetry and to the world is the metaphor. Situating poetry in revelation rather than in prosody, Claudel felt as free of rime as any of the *vers librists* and the prose poets. His characteristic line is the *verset*, modeled on the natural rhythms of breath and pulse, repeating, he claimed, the harmonies of the inner and outer universe. This is the line that Claudel used not only for his poems but for his plays as well. As a playwright, he followed the Symbolist formula for the theater, with its emphasis on poetry, its avoidance of realism in favor of symbolic or allegorical presentation. After Maeter-linck, Claudel is the only Symbolist to succeed on the stage.

This writer who combined Symbolist drama with liturgy and inte-grated poetry and religion was born in 1868 in a small town some sixty miles northwest of Paris. His father was a tax collector, moving often from one little town to another. Paul lived in several localities before going to Paris, where his mother took the children so that Camille, the older daughter, could study sculpture. The family was not a very blissful one, neither parents nor children getting along well together. Paul had as bad a disposition as the others, mellowing only in old age. In Paris he went to school at Louis-le-Grand; he was an avid reader and already a poet before his discovery of Rimbaud. His first significant works are, however, plays—in 1888 *Une Mort prématurée, Tête d'or* and *La Ville* in 1889. They reflect his own spiritual adventure, his years of unhappy materialism, then his conversion.

In 1890, Claudel passed his foreign service examination and began his training in consular work. He still read widely, although most particu-larly in the Greek classics and in works of religion. He wrote his first *Jeune Fille Violaine* before leaving for his first post in 1893. One year in New York, another in Boston, did not make Claudel fond of the United States, and he denounced, as many before him had done, its materialism and its evil ways. His sojourn in American cities furnished material for *L'Echange*, a play that in form owed much to Aeschylus, whom he was reading at the time. He also made a translation of *Agamemnon* while in the States.

In 1895, after a trip back to France, he left for China, where he would remain for the next four years. That year he wrote *Vers d'Exil*, another work based on his recent American tour of duty, and, now turning to the Orient for inspiration, began the miscellany entitled *Connaissance de l'Est.* While in China he read Saint Thomas Aquinas and corresponded with André Gide and Francis Jammes. Religion became steadily more important to him; in *Le Repos du septième jour*, in the new versions of *La Ville* and the *Jeune Fille Violaine* there is evidence of the direction his thinking was taking. On his return to France in 1900, he was ready to give up his art and the world to become a priest. He entered a Benedictine monastery, but after several weeks he came out again, painfully aware that he did not have the vocation.

From this emotional crisis he was directly swept into another. En route back to China he met the young woman who was the prototype of Isé in *Partage de Midi*. She left her husband and her children for Claudel; their affair lasted four years. Some critics have seen in *Les Cinq Grandes Odes*, which date from this time, the drama of Claudel's liaison. When it ended Claudel went back to France and, during the year that he remained there, married the daughter of an architect in Lyon. He took his bride back with him to China. The marriage was a happy one, blessed by five children. As a husband and a father, a diplomat and a writer successful in both careers, as a firm Christian believer, Claudel would henceforth enjoy an emotional tranquillity that he had often been denied.

The Christian verities are the main subject of his work for the rest of his life. The trilogy of plays, *L'Otage*, *Le Pain dur*, *Le Père humilié*, cover the years from 1908 to 1916, the *Soulier de Satin*, 1919–1924. The latter play constitutes a sort of summa of Claudel's life and thinking, the resolution of all conflicts in a Christian order. With Darius Milhaud, who had already put to music several of Claudel's plays, he wrote the *Livre de Christophe Colombe* in the late 1920s and shortly before leaving his post in Brussels, the oratorio *Jeanne d'Arc au Bûcher*. *L'Histoire de Tobie et de Sara* (1938) was first conceived as a work with music too, but it was finally executed as an autonomous piece. Besides these plays and oratorios Claudel wrote, of course, much verse and prose of miscellaneous inspiration. But his major work from the 1930s on was his commentaries of the scriptures that fill many volumes.

After China, Claudel's tours of diplomatic duty took him to places nearer home—to Prague (1910–1911), Frankfort and Hamburg (1912–1914), Rome (1915–1916). He then was sent to Rio de Janeiro (1917–1918) where Milhaud served him as secretary, then back in Europe to Copenhagen (1919–1921). As ambassador he went to Tokyo (1921–1927), then to Washington (1927–1933), to Brussels (1933–1935). He retired to the château of Brangues in Isère and there, for the rest of his life, surrounded by his children and grandchildren, he lived as a venerable patriarch. His writings on the Bible were frequently interrupted by trips to Paris where, particularly in the years following the war, his plays scored major triumphs.

Although everything that Claudel wrote might be classed as poetry, particularly by his own definition, and although some of the best may be found in his plays, nevertheless a considerable body of his work is in various nondramatic forms similar to the conventional poetic genres

from the ode to the prose poem. Some of his first poems follow tradi-
tional prosody such as the sonnet in the style of Mallarmé ("Celui-là
seul saura sourire," 1897). While he was using free verse in his theater he
was writing the *Vers d'Exil* in formal quatrains. *Connaissance de l'Est* has
pieces that are hard to label since they are jottings of sights and thoughts
in China. But their esthetic quality, Claudel's musical and evocative
language, makes them all poems in a sense, these descriptions of exotic
cities, temples, and countrysides which alternate with musings on life
and the destiny of man. Many of the pieces are fine prose poems, deserving
of a high place in the tradition that runs through Symbolism back to
Romanticism, and to Aloysius Bertrand and to Maurice de Guérin. The
Cinq Grandes Odes assures Claudel a position among the great dithyram-
bic poets of his age. Opening with a salutation to the nine muses, they
continue with the sustained appeals to the creator and songs of gratitude.
In the fourth ode, the poet rebels against his muse who nevertheless
draws him further and further away from worldliness. The final ode
records the triumph of spirituality and ends in a paean to the church
wherein the poet has found his place and the reason for his being and
his art. Through the various themes one major one shines through, the
love theme, which makes *Les Cinq Grandes Odes*, like *Partage de Midi*, a
record of Claudel's own experience. The themes are exalted by the
sustained loftiness of style, the grandeur of the apostrophes, and the
majestic cadences of the versets.

La Cantate à trois voix is likewise in the *vers claudeliens* that we associate
mostly with the plays. It is itself something of a play, being a conversa-
tion among three women during the night of the summer solstice. Whether
speaking to one another or breaking away in an independent canticle,
the theme is love and its transformation from the momentary into the
eternal. The utterances are made melodic by their cadences and their
assonances. A lush imagery reminiscent of the Song of Songs expresses
transcendence and sublime resolution. The specifically Catholic nature
of the collection entitled *Corona Benignitatis Anni Dei* (1915) reminds us
that Claudel's pen was to become increasingly used in the service of the
church. The poems are chiefly prayers inspired by dates in the Catholic
calendar, evocations of saints, mementoes, hymns, or paraphrases of
Testament stories. They have the gentle tone of the French priest address-
ing his flock on Sunday morning, a homely familiarity that is sustained
by the easy flow of the riming couplets. *La Messe là-bas, Feuilles de saints,
Visages radieux* continue in the vein of *Corona* for the most part, although

some lay themes are treated. The collection of war poems is marred by a militant nationalism that reminds us that narrowness and intolerance often are met in the Claudel type of person. One prefers to turn to the *Psaumes*, that are free translations, or to the considerable miscellaneous verse, but even more attractive is the poetry of oriental inspiration. I believe that Claudel had only a smattering of Chinese or Japanese, but he was very curious about the art and calligraphy of both civilizations; doubtless he was more greatly inspired for not being an orientalist. For his poems "after the Chinese" I imagine that he had someone explain the poem to him and thereupon composed his "translations." For his *dodoitzu* he acknowledges the translations of Georges Bonneau. The *Cent Phrases pour éventails* are precious little poems which take their departure from the calligraphy that accompanies each one. For readers who find Claudel in his grand manner tedious or overwhelming, there are these little pieces that are quite delightful.

Celui-là seul saura sourire, s'il a plu[1]
A la Muse elle-même, institutrice et Mère,
De former, lui ouvrant la Lettre et la Grammaire,
Sa lèvre au vers exact et au Mot absolu.

La sécurité de l'office qui l'élut
Rit que rien d'éternel comme rien d'éphémère
N'échappe à la mesure adéquate et sommaire
De la voix qui finit où le verbe conclut.

Gardien pur d'un or fixe où l'aboi vague insulte!
Si, hommage rustique et témoignage occulte,
Ma main cherche quoi prendre au sol pour s'en armer,

Je choisis de casser la branche militaire
Dont la feuille à ton front honore, Mallarmé,
Amère, le triomphe, et verte, le mystère.

(Premiers Vers)

---

1. Written in China in 1897, this poem figured in an album composed by Mallarmé's disciples. The album was presented at a banquet in honor of the recently elected "Prince des Poètes." Besides being a homage to Mallarmé, the poem is also a pastiche that must have been executed tongue in cheek. The tortured syntax, the vocabulary, the abstract and hieratic character recall, as if to burlesque them, such poems as "Sainte" or "A la nue accablante tu."

TRISTESSE DE L'EAU[2]

Il est une conception dans la joie, je le veux, il est une vision dans le rire. Mais ce mélange de béatitude et d'amertume que comport l'acte de la création, pour que tu le comprennes, ami, à cette heure où s'ouvre une sombre saison, je t'expliquerai la tristesse de l'eau.[3]

Du ciel choit ou de la paupière déborde une larme identique.

Ne pense point de ta mélancolie accuser la nuée, ni ce voile de l'averse obscure. Ferme les yeux, écoute! la pluie tombe.

Ni la monotonie de ce bruit assidu ne suffit à l'explication.

C'est l'ennui d'un deuil qui porte en lui-même sa cause, c'est l'embesognement de l'amour, c'est la peine dans le travail. Les cieux pleurent sur la terre qu'ils fécondent. Et ce n'est point surtout l'automne et la chute future du fruit dont elles nourrissent la graine qui tire ces larmes de la nue hivernale. La douleur est l'été et dans la fleur de la vie l'épanouissement de la mort.

Au moment que s'achève cette heure qui précède Midi, comme je descends dans ce vallon qu'emplit la rumeur de fontaines diverses, je m'arrête ravi par le chagrin. Que ces eaux sont copieuses! et si les larmes comme le sang ont en nous une source perpétuelle, l'oreille à ce chœur liquide de voix abondantes ou grêles, qu'il est rafraîchissant d'y assortir toutes les nuances de sa peine! Il n'est passion qui ne puisse vous emprunter ses larmes, fontaines! et bien qu'à la mienne suffise l'éclat de cette goutte unique qui de très haut dans la vasque s'abat sur l'image de la lune, je n'aurai pas en vain pour maints après-midis appris à connaître ta retraite, val chagrin.

Me voici dans la plaine. Au seuil de cette cabane où, dans l'obscurité intérieure, luit le cierge allumé pour quelque fête rustique, un homme assis tient dans sa main une cymbale poussiéreuse. Il pleut immensément; et j'entends seul, au milieu de la solitude mouillée, un cri d'oie.

(Connaissance de l'Est)

2. A word painting in imitation of classic Chinese and Japanese artists whose subject is often landscape in the rain. The mingling of the subjective and objective worlds, a feature of Claudel and Symbolists, is also characteristic of the oriental poets and painters.

3. Henri Peyre notes the didactic quality of the pieces in this volume, Claudel's most "Mallarméan." Professor Peyre adds that in some other works Claudel unfortunately lets didacticism and oratory take over. See "Le classicisme de Paul Claudel" in *Les critiques de notre temps et Claudel* (Garnier, 1970), p. 137. We should say that in the poet Claudel one can often hear a preacher addressing his flock.

LA MUSE QUI EST LA GRACE[4]

. . . .

Strophe I

—O Muse, il sera temps de dormir un autre jour!
Mais puisque cette grande nuit tout entière est à nous,
    Et que je suis un peu ivre en sorte qu'un autre mot
parfois
    Vient à la place du vrai, à la façon que tu aimes,[5]
    Laisse-moi avoir explication avec toi,
    Laisse-moi te refouler dans cette strophe, avant que tu
ne reviennes sur moi comme une vague avec un cri félin!
    Va-t'en de moi un peu! laisse-moi faire ce que je veux
un peu!
    Car, quoi que je fasse et si que je le fasse de mon mieux,
    Bientôt je vois un œil se lever sur moi en silence
comme vers quelqu'un qui feint.
    Laisse-moi être nécessaire! laisse-moi remplir fortement
une place reconnue et approuvée,
    Comme un constructeur de chemins de fer, on sait
qu'il ne sert pas à rien, comme un fondateur de syndicats!
    Qu'un jeune homme avec son menton orné d'un
flocon jaunâtre
    Fasse des vers, on sourit seulement.
    J'attendais que l'âge me délivrât des fureurs de cet
esprit bachique.
    Mais, loin que j'immole le bouc, à ce rire qui gagne
des couches plus profondes
    Il me faut trouver que je ne fais plus sa part.
    Du moins laisse-moi faire de ce papier ce que je veux
et le remplir avec un art studieux,
    Ma tâche, comme ceux-là qui en ont une.

. . . .

(Cinq Grandes Odes)

---

4. From the fourth ode, a dialogue between poet and muse, who gradually becomes
divine grace. The poet resists for a time the exhortations to leave the secular life but must
finally give in.

5. Echo of the *Art Poétique* of Verlaine, the Symbolist repudiation of an esthetic of the *mot juste*. The failure to hit right on mark may be poetically effective because: it surprises and therefore has great impact; it creates an ambiguity conducive to multiple interpretation and creative activity on the part of the reader.

PETITS POEMES D'APRES LE CHINOIS

"La Rivière gelée"

Le mouvement de mille montagnes immobiles
pas un oiseau!
    Le chemin sous la double ornière qui passe
pas un passant!
    Et le pêcheur tout seul au milieu de la rivière gelée
    Qui tente sous le courant invisible un poisson inexistant!

Lieou Toung Yen

"Le Son de la cloche"

Quand le son de la cloche a eu le temps de s'éteindre,
il y a une autre cloche en moi qui ne fait que commencer.

Li Ka Yo

Poetry of Paul Valéry

Œuvres (Gallimard), vol. 1, 1957; vol. 2, 1960. Bibliothèque de la Pléiade.

Readings

Alain. *La Jeune Parque* (Gallimard, 1936).

Bellemin-Noël, Jean, ed. *Les critiques de notre temps et Valéry* (Garnier, 1971).

Grubbs, Henry A. *Paul Valéry* (Boston: Twayne, 1968).

Lawler, James R. *The Poet as Analyst: Essays on Paul Valéry* (Berkeley: University of California Press, 1974).

Noulet, E. *Paul Valéry, Etudes* (Brussels: Renaissance du Livre, 1951).

Scarfe, Francis. *The Art of Paul Valéry* (London: Heinemann, 1954), chap. 5, pp. 171–242 ("La Jeune Parque").

Sørensen, H. *La Poésie de Paul Valéry, Etude stylistique de la Jeune Parque.* (Copenhagen: Universitetsforlaget I, Aarhus, 1944).

Walzer, Pierre-Olivier. *La Poésie de Valéry* (Geneva: Cailler, 1953; Slatkine rpt., 1966).

Paul Valéry

1871–1945

If we call Paul Valéry the last of the Symbolists, as does Charles Chadwick in a recent monograph,[1] we must quickly add that there is nothing absolute or even very literal in such a remark. Many twentieth-century poets have traits in common with Symbolists; as for Symbolist principles, while there is much that they refute there is also much that they accept, and Taylor and Lucie-Smith are, of course, right in presenting French poetry since Gérard de Nerval as an unbroken line.[2] On the other hand, in many respects Valéry harks back to poets before Nerval, and his affinity with Symbolists is only partial and specific. If he defined Symbolism as simply a group of poets who wished to "reprendre à la musique leur bien"[3] and thereby echoed Verlaine's famous "de la musique avant toute chose," he did not conceive of poetry as just the sweet song of poor Lélian, but more what Mallarmé meant when he said that Wagner had "usurped the duty of the poet."[4] Valéry belongs to Symbolism chiefly as a disciple of Mallarmé in a hermetic and intellectual tradition that reaches far back in time.

Valéry was born in Sète, on the Mediterranean, of a French father of Corsican blood and an Italian mother. As a boy, looking out over the sea in his hometown, he dreamed of becoming a ship captain. But he was too deficient in mathematics to qualify for the Naval Academy, so after attending the lycée in Montpellier, where his family had moved, he went on to the university there as a student of law. However, literature interested him more than jurisprudence. In 1890, he met first Pierre Louÿs and then André Gide, who, during walks in the old Botanical Garden of Montpellier, spoke to him about the literary life in Paris.

Symbolism was the fashion of the day, and the young provincial who had been writing verse with increasing zeal for the previous five years was eager to make contact with the capital. He sent two of his poems to Mallarmé, who praised them, and during the next two years Valéry placed a number of his compositions in avant-garde magazines. Then, in the course of a night of violent lightning and thunder in the fall of 1892, while visiting relatives in Genoa, the very promising young poet had a psychological experience which reoriented his life. Biographers refer to it as the "nuit de Gênes." For reasons not entirely clear (a sentimental misadventure, professional discouragement, objection on principle and for practical reasons to writing as a career—doubtless all are factors), Valéry came out of his crisis with the decision not to go on with poetry but to dedicate himself solely to the pursuit of knowledge. He went to Paris and, in a bare hotel room, spent his days studying and meditating on problems of mathematics and psychology. There were, however, distractions. If Valéry had renounced poetry, he had not renounced the company of poets. Gide, Louÿs, Régnier came to see him in his room, and he went to the rue de Rome on Tuesdays when Mallarmé received. Nor had he, during what is referred to as the period of great silence, renounced all writing. In 1894, he began *La Soirée avec M. Teste*, the strange account of a man who strove to live by the intellect alone, and, in 1895, the *Introduction à la Méthode de Léonard da Vinci*, which, without having much to do with Da Vinci, posited an ideal of intellectual and creative ability for Paul Valéry. He had already made his first entries in the notebooks where for fifty years he would set down his reflections. *Teste* and *Da Vinci* were commissioned works; there were numerous others of a minor nature, requested by periodicals on a variety of subjects. But Valéry published no more verse.

The question of gainful employment for Valéry was settled provisionally by an appointment in the War Department. The job did not please him, however, and in 1900, the year of his marriage, he gave it up for a very attractive position as private secretary to an administrator of the Havas newspaper agency. For the next twenty years, Valéry spent three or four hours a day in his service, an employment which assured him a livelihood yet left him adequate leisure for his own work. During the early years of the century, Valéry was occupied by his young family (he had a son and a daughter) and by his friends (he counted among his personal friends the notables of arts and letters) and by the social and cultural events of the capital. Paul Valéry was a Parisian and, although he felt at times that his invitations in society were burdensome, he never refused them.

In 1912, at the urging of André Gide, Valéry assembled some of his old poetry for publication. It needed a little touching up, he decided, and in so doing he found himself once more composing verse. The "Jeune Parque" began as an exercise. When all of its five hundred verses had been written and the work presented to the literati of Paris, the acclaim was unanimous. Valéry went back to his writing table.

In the postwar period he published poetry and essays, gave speeches, while others wrote articles about him, gave lectures on his work and readings of his verse. As usual, Valéry attended plays, recitals, and dinner parties. The pattern of his life was fixed. He complained about his social chores, about his health, and worried about money. But he could not complain about lack of recognition. In France and abroad he was received everywhere as one of the greatest men of letters. Foreign heads of state decorated him and invited him to lecture; in his own country he was made a member of the Academy and appointed to a chair of poetry at the Collège de France. During the Second World War, in spite of discouragement and privation, Valéry carried on his duties much as before. At the liberation, he took part in literary manifestations, the most important of which being his lecture on Voltaire in the great amphitheater of the Sorbonne. Valéry died in 1945 and was given a state funeral. On his tomb in the cemetery of Sète are these lines from his famous poem: "O récompense après une pensée / Qu'un long regard sur le calme des dieux!"

Although Paul Valéry differs from Henri Bergson in many respects, he resembles the philosopher of the *Données immédiates de la Conscience* in being more intéressed in how the mind arrives at its goal than in the goal itself. All his study of mathematics, philosophy, psychology, art, architecture, literature, and the dance was for the purpose of understanding the mind at work. To be sure, he often felt that his quest was futile and that to renounce accomplishment or action for knowledge was a wrong choice. The question of doing versus knowing was for Valéry a lifelong preoccupation: it is the major theme in his writing, it was a major factor in his long silence, it is really the key to his psychology as an artist and as a man. But if writing had any justification in his eyes, it was primarily as an intellectual "method," a means of experimenting with verbal symbols, of observing how the mind makes forms and structures and in so doing modifies itself. "La Jeune Parque" is a description of consciousness. The sensual elements, Valéry declared, were but additions designed to keep the poem from being too abstract. Such an operation as Valéry conceived the poem to be must be accomplished in total lucidity.

Did he not say that he would prefer writing something weak in full consciousness to a masterpiece created in a trance? Hence the rigor, the precision, which Valéry demands of the verbal craftsman. It is reported that for "La Jeune Parque" Valéry prepared 250 typed drafts. Not inspiration or emotion creates the poem, but cool skill. It is for the reader, not for the poet, to feel.

It may seem that Valéry is too categorical in his utterances, that his own poetry is more confessional, more self-expressive, than he would make out. One can easily find inconsistencies, overstatements, and partial truths in Valéry's views on poetry or on any other subject. Pushing his thought too far makes it seem to turn on itself; expressing it in a flash often distorts it. But his lucubrations fascinate and his aphorisms dazzle. If he talked as he wrote, one understands his reputation for brilliant conversation. Valéry's reputation as a thinker has impinged upon his reputation as a poet. This is regrettable, for his poetry deserves to stand entirely alone. But because the creative artist is so closely tied to the critic in Valéry and because he has made himself a spokesman for definite points of view, whether it be to insist on craftsmanship in art or to refute Pascal or to disparage the historical sciences, Paul Valéry is not considered only as a poet. Since he was a poet in spite of himself, this is, of course, exactly what he would have wished.

Notes

1. Charles Chadwick, *Symbolism* (London: Methuen, 1971), p. 51.
2. Simon Watson Taylor and Edward Lucie-Smith, *French Poetry today* (New York: Schocken, 1971), p. 17.
3. *Œuvres*, vol. 1, p. 1272.
4. Mallarmé, *Œuvres Complètes*, p. 541.

LA JEUNE PARQUE[1]

Qui pleure là, sinon le vent[2] simple, à cette heure
Seule, avec diamants extrêmes? ...[3] Mais qui pleure,
Si proche de moi-même au moment de pleurer?

Cette main, sur mes traits qu'elle rêve effleurer,
Distraitement docile à quelque fin profonde,
Attend de ma faiblesse une larme qui fonde,
Et que de mes destins[4] lentement divisé,
Le plus pur[5] en silence éclaire un cœur brisé.
La houle me murmure une ombre de reproche,
Ou retire ici-bas, dans ses gorges de roche,[6]
Comme chose déçue et bue amèrement,[7]
Une rumeur de plainte et de resserrement...[8]
Que fais-tu, hérissée, et cette main glacée,[9]
Et quel frémissement d'une feuille effacée[10]
Persiste parmi vous, îles de mon sein nu?...[11]
Je scintille, liée à ce ciel inconnu...
L'immense grappe brille à ma soif de désastres.[12]

Tout-puissants étrangers, inévitables astres
Qui daignez faire luire au lointain temporel
Je ne sais quoi de pur et de surnaturel;
Vous qui dans les mortels plongez jusques aux larmes[13]
Ces souverains éclats, ces invincibles armes,
Et les élancements de votre éternité,
Je suis seule avec vous, tremblante, ayant quitté
Ma couche; et sur l'écueil mordu par la merveille,[14]
J'interroge mon cœur quelle douleur l'éveille,
Quel crime par moi-même ou sur moi consommé?...
...Ou si le mal me suit d'un songe refermé,
Quand (au velours du souffle envolé l'or des lampes)[15]
J'ai de mes bras épais environné mes tempes,
Et longtemps de mon âme attendu les éclairs?
Toute? Mais toute à moi, maîtresse de mes chairs,
Durcissant d'un frisson leur étrange étendue,
Et dans mes doux liens, à mon sang suspendue,
Je me voyais me voir, sinueuse, et dorais[16]
De regards en regards, mes profondes forêts.

J'y suivais un serpent qui venait de me mordre.[17]

QUEL repli de désirs, sa traîne! ... Quel désordre
De trésors s'arrachant à mon avidité,
Et quelle sombre soif de la limpidité![18]

O ruse! ... A la lueur de la douleur laissée
Je me sentis connue encor plus que blessée ...[19]
Au plus traître de l'âme, une pointe me naît;
Le poison, mon poison, m'éclaire et se connaît:
Il colore une vierge à soi-même enlacée,
Jalouse ... Mais de qui, jalouse et menacée?
Et quel silence parle à mon seul possesseur?

Dieux! Dans ma lourde plaie une secrète sœur
Brûle! ... qui se préfère à l'extrême attentive ...

"VA! je n'ai plus besoin de ta race naïve,
Cher serpent ...[20]

....

MAIS je tremblais de perdre une douleur divine!
Je baisais sur ma main cette morsure fine,
Et je ne savais plus de mon antique corps
Insensible, qu'un feu qui brûlait sur mes bords:

Adieu, pensai-je MOI, mortelle sœur, mensonge ...[21]

....

                                    Et moi, vive, debout,[22]
Dure, et de mon néant secrètement armée.[23]
Mais comme par l'amour une joue enflammée,
Et la narine jointe au vent de l'oranger,
Je ne rends plus au jour qu'un regard étranger ...[24]
Oh! combien peut grandir dans ma nuit curieuse
De mon cœur séparé la part mystérieuse,
Et de sombres essais s'approfondir mon art! ...[25]
Loin des purs environs, je suis captive, et par
L'évanouissement d'aromes abattue,
Je sens sous les rayons, frissonner ma statue,[26]
Des caprices de l'or, son marbre parcouru.

....

Que dans le ciel placés, mes yeux tracent mon temple![27]
Et que sur moi repose un autel sans exemple!

. . . .

MYSTÉRIEUSE MOI, pourtant, tu vis encore![28]
Tu vas te reconnaître au lever de l'aurore
Amèrement la même ...

                         Un miroir de la mer[29]
Se lève ... Et sur la lèvre, un sourire d'hier
Qu'annonce avec ennui l'effacement des signes,[30]
Glace dans l'orient déjà les pâles lignes
De lumière et de pierre, et la pleine prison
Où flottera l'anneau de l'unique horizon ...
Regarde: un bras très pur est vu, qui se dénude.
Je te revois, mon bras ... Tu portes l'aube ...[31]

                         O rude
Réveil d'une victime inachevée ... et seuil
Si doux ... si clair, que flatte, affleurement d'écueil,
L'onde basse, et que lave une houle amortie! ...
L'ombre qui m'abandonne, impérissable hostie,
Me découvre vermeille[32] à de nouveaux désirs,
Sur le terrible autel de tous mes souvenirs.

Là, l'écume s'efforce à se faire visible;
Et là, titubera sur la barque sensible
A chaque épaule d'onde, un pêcheur éternel.
Tout va donc accomplir son acte solennel
De toujours reparaître incomparable et chaste,
Et de restituer la tombe[33] enthousiaste
Au gracieux état du rire universel.[34]

SALUT! Divinités[35] par la rose et le sel,
Et les premiers jouets de la jeune lumière,
Iles! ... Ruches bientôt, quand la flamme première
Fera que votre roche, îles que je prédis,
Ressente en rougissant de puissants paradis;
Cimes qu'un feu féconde à peine intimidées,
Bois qui bourdonnerez de bêtes et d'idées,[36]
D'hymnes d'hommes comblés des dons du juste éther,
Iles! ... dans la rumeur des ceintures de mer,

Mères[37] vierges toujours, même portant ces marques,
Vous m'êtes à genoux[38] de merveilleuses Parques :
Rien n'ègale dans l'air les fleurs que vous placez,
Mais dans la profondeur, que vos pieds sont glacés !

. . . .

O N'AURAIT-IL fallu, folle, que j'accomplisse[39]
Ma merveilleuse fin de choisir pour supplice
Ce lucide dédain des nuances du sort ?
Trouveras-tu jamais plus transparente mort
Ni de pente plus pure où je rampe à ma perte
Que sur ce long regard de victime entr'ouverte,
Pâle, qui se résigne et saigne sans regret ?
Que lui fait tout le sang qui n'est plus son secret ?
Dans quelle blanche paix cette pourpre la laisse,
A l'extrême de l'être, et belle de faiblesse !
Elle calme le temps qui la vient abolir,
Le moment souverain ne la peut plus pâlir,
Tant la chair vide baise une sombre fontaine ! ...
Elle se fait toujours plus seule et plus lointaine ...
Et moi, d'un tel destin, le cœur toujours plus près,
Mon cortège, en esprit, se berçait de cyprès ...
      Vers un aromatique avenir de fumée,
Je me sentais conduite, offerte et consumée,
Toute, toute promise aux nuages heureux !
Même, je m'apparus cet arbre vaporeux,
De qui la majesté légèrement perdue
S'abandonne à l'amour de toute l'étendue.
L'être immense me gagne, et de mon cœur divin
L'encens qui brûle expire une forme sans fin ...
Tous les corps radieux tremblent dans mon essence ! ...

. . . .

... Alors, n'ai-je formé, vains adieux si je vis,[40]
Que songes ? ... Si je viens, en vêtements ravis,
Sur ce bord, sans horreur, humeur la haute écume,
Boire des yeux l'immense et riante amertume,
L'être contre le vent, dans le plus vif de l'air,
Recevant au visage un appel de la mer ;

Si l'âme intense souffle, et renfle furibonde
L'onde abrupte sur l'onde abattue, et si l'onde
Au cap tonne, immolant un monstre de candeur,[41]
Et vient des hautes mers vomir la profondeur
Sur ce roc, d'où jaillit jusque vers mes pensées,
Un éblouissement d'étincelles glacées,
Et sur toute ma peau que morde l'âpre éveil,
Alors, malgré moi-même, il le faut, ô Soleil
Que j'adore mon cœur où tu te viens connaître,
Doux et puissant retour du délice de naître,

Feu vers qui se soulève une vierge de sang[42]
Sous les espèces d'or[43] d'un sein reconnaissant!

1. "La Jeune Parque" is the crucial poem in Valéry's career. When he went back to writing in 1912, this is the poem that he produced. Intended originally as an adieu to poetry, the work of his youth, it turned out to be, rather, the start of a new career in poetry. Valéry had in mind something about forty verses strictly obedient to the classical rules. But, once underway, the exercise in an art form became a vehicle for the drama of consciousness, ten times longer than planned and, as Valéry acknowledged, a hundred times more difficult.

Valéry explains why a poem may be difficult even though the author does not make it so intentionally. First, the subject itself may be a difficult one. He tells us that the subject of "La Jeune Parque" is "la peinture d'une suite de substitutions psychologiques, et en somme le changement d'une conscience pendant la durée d'une nuit" (*Œuvres*, vol. 1, p. 1621). Second, the problem of adapting the material to the form that poetry demands (harmony, rhythm, etc.) may oblige the poet to resort to ellipses and other devices that are taxing for many readers. Third (a combination of points one and two), the effort of the poet, which is the inverse of the prose writer's, moves from the clear to the obscure. Valéry recognizes that there are other causes and perhaps more profound ones, but these are his reasons for the problems that "La Jeune Parque" presents for the readers and presented for the poet as well. It took Valéry four years to write the poem. They were the war years, and its writing had the virtue of taking his mind off what was going on in the world. It would seem, therefore, that the pains that he took with it were not entirely due to artistic zeal or to the recalcitrant nature of the material, but voluntarily taken for their therapeutic value.

J'ai trouvé alors que le moyen de lutter contre l'imagination des événements et l'activité consumante de l'impuissance était de s'astreindre à un jeu difficile; se faire un labeur infini, chargé de conditions et de clauses, tout gêné de strictes observances. Je pris la poésie pour charte privée. Je pris les ceintures les plus classiques. Je m'imposai en outre la continuité de l'harmonie, l'exactitude de la syntaxe, la détermination précise des mots, un à un triés, pesés, voulus, etc.

Twenty times, he says, he wanted to give it up, but he persisted. An additional incentive was patriotism. Since he was not at the front, he thought that perhaps he was still making a contribution in working for the French language, erecting in its honor "un petit monument peut-être funéraire, fait de mots les plus purs et de ses formes les plus nobles,—un petit tombeau sans date,—sur les bords menaçants de l'Océan du Charabia ..." (*Œuvres*, vol. 1, p. 1629)

The poem was ready in April 1917, and just before it appeared in print Léon-Paul Fargue was chosen to give it a public reading. The notorious success which the poem met with brought to Valéry many letters; his replies are the chief source of our knowledge concerning the circumstances of its writing and what Valéry was trying to say. Utterances such as the following have made him extremely popular among the advance-guard writers of the 1970s for whom language is something else than a vehicle to express thought:

> Oui, je me suis imposé pour *ce* poème des lois, observances constantes, *qui en constituent le véritable objet*. C'est bien un exercice, et voulu, et repris, et travaillé: œuvre seulement de volonté; et puis d'une seconde volonté, dont la tâche dure est de masquer la première. Qui saura me lire lira une autobiographie, dans la forme. Le *fond* importe peu. Lieux communs. La vraie pensée n'est pas adaptable au vers. (*Œuvres*, vol. 1, p. 1631)

Incidentally, to refer to the content as commonplace contradicts other statements to the effect that he put in "La Jeune Parque" all that he had learned in twenty years concerning the thought and feeling processes of manking. Undoubtedly, Valéry tailored his remarks to suit his audience. In accounting for the praise and respect that his poem received, we must not overlook this factor. By now treating it with profoundest seriousness, now dismissing it as a tedious futility, Valéry himself contributed to its success in the Parisian circles of the day. Unaffected by Valéry's words and in a time and place far removed from the Paris of Paul Valéry, it may be hard to see this poem, in spite of its beauties, as the summa of wisdom and the pious monument to the French language that its author represented it to be. The theme is indeed commonplace and the erotic evocation that fleshes it out is definitely dated. La jeune parque is a fake Greek maiden of 1900 manufacture. Moreover, the artificiality of praising her charms in a monologue spoken by the drowsy heroine herself prohibits credibility; the preciousness of her expression elicits amusement today probably as much as admiration. If Valéry appears in some respects as an ancestor of writing today, he belongs, by a work like "La Jeune Parque" to the past, to the Symbolist tradition. La jeune parque herself resembles all the heroines of the Hérodiade tradition and her to-be-or-not-to-be lucubrations represent a theme harking back to Jules Laforgue and beyond.

The argument of the poem is briefly this. La jeune parque, as depicted here, is an imprecise figure from Greek mythology, the youngest of the three Fates. She is a young woman, lovely and appealing, and a semi-goddess, therefore remote and noble enough to incarnate the problems of life and destiny (Fate) that Valéry wished to treat. The Fates preside over the stages of life, the youngest was doubtless chosen as the logical one to symbolize the awakening of self-consciousness, the crisis of adolescence which Valéry himself had experienced during the "nuit de Gênes" and which is recounted here in literary disguise. During the night, la jeune parque has had a bad dream and now, awake and filled with anxiety, she has left her bed to stand on a precipice over the Mediterranean. It is a chilly moment close to dawn, but the stars are still very bright. In her dream she had been bitten by a snake and was following it. She stops, declaring that now she needs nothing outside herself. Presumably as a result of the snake's poison, no longer is she one but two persons, the one watching, inhibiting, tormenting the other. Regretfully she recalls her former days lived spontaneously in the sun and feels that she can never again take innocent pleasure in life. Her mind now enables her to anticipate the future, thereby robbing it of all interest, and lets her know that death is ultimately in store. In thinking of her past, she blushes at her former immodesty. Death would be welcome, she decides, but spring is stirring in nature and, in spite of herself, she cannot resist its appeal. She calls upon Death and Life to vie for her being. May the first one take me, she cries. But she cannot die now, nor can she any longer fully live. In the early dawn she anticipates the familiar view of the sea and the islands that will soon spread before her, the same view as yesterday and any day. She returns to her bed and drowses off. The sun rises and the jeune parque, forgetting the conflicts of the night, awakes to greet the new day.

In its form as well as in its subject, "La Jeune Parque" has many ties with Symbolism. Valéry defined Symbolism as an attempt to bring poetry closer to music and pursued the dream entertained by Mallarmé and others of incorporating into the poem structures common to music. "La Jeune Parque," in its form, owes something to opera. In a letter to Aimé Lafont, Valéry confided:

> Vous observerez aussi que la coupe du poème peut rappeler celle d'une œuvre musicale. La notion de récitatifs de drame lyrique (à une seule voix) m'a hanté. Je vois, par exemple, un commencement d'*acte* à ce vers: "Mystérieuse *Moi*, pourtant tu vis encore!" J'avoue que Gluck et Wagner m'étaient des modèles secrets. (*Œuvres*, vol. 1, p. 1636)

If the metrical pattern betrays none of the innovations of the Symbolists, other elements of poetic diction suggest close kinship between Valéry and the elder poets. Inversions and syntactical transpositions and words used in an unusual sense are common devices to make of the language of communication the vehicle of suggestion and veiled beauty. The Symbolist concern for melody, particularly through repetitive devices such as alliteration, is clearly evident in Valéry. Likewise the precious epithet and the periphrase. Extreme density, many layered meanings based on allusion and wordplay are further insurance against the explicitness which for Symbolists was anathema.

2. The time and place of the poem are established gradually and indirectly. Wind is mentioned here, later waves, rocks, islands, etc. The first indication of the hour is given in line 2. Note the sensatory appeals. Wind sounds and wave sounds are alluded to through personification. Movement of the wind, fluttering and shivering of leaves and hands evoke tactile and thermic sensations which reinforce the coldness and the shimmer of the stars. Such harmonic and contrapuntal weaving create the remarkable dense pattern of the poem.

3. *diamants extrêmes* = distant stars. Use of words in a rare sense, frequently justified only by their Latin root, is one of Valéry's favorite devices. The combination here creates a very precious epithet.

4. *destins* = stars (destiny in stars)

5. *pur* = extrême (the purest star?)

6. *Gorges* is a pivot word, probably what suggests *bue* in the next line. Valéry is quite sensitive to the various meanings of a word which he exploits for suggestive ambiguity or humor.

7. Is there a second antecedent for *bue amèrement* in the tear of line 6?

8. *Plainte* coupled with *resserrement* creates a zeugma.

9. *Hérissée* refers to the young fate herself, standing. *Glacée* echoes the coldness of the stars (diamonds) and reinforces the impression of cold night at the edge of the sea and a shivering young fate, shivering, bristling (?), shimmering in the wind.

10. The fluttering of her heart? of her hand? (Cf. line 4.) Note the alliteration.

11. *Iles* is a feature of the setting for the poem (cf. p. 261, line 30) used metaphorically to describe breasts or possibly areas reserved for thought. (Cf. Hartmut Köhler, *Poésie et Profondeur sémantique dans "la Jeune Parque" de Paul Valéry*, Université de Nancy, 1965, p. 19.) *Ile* is used elsewhere by Valéry in the latter sense. Whether it is a hand or a heart or a thought which is fluttering, Valéry's figure links physical phenomena and establishes correspondences between the physical and the affective or intellectual.

12. Redundancy of *grappe* (meaning cluster of stars) and *désastres* (word containing *astre* = star). The word *grappe* calls forth *soif*. Thirst to know even though knowledge is unpleasant. The theme of the whole poem is knowledge.

13. The similarity between this line and the eighth line of the poem (see note 5) make this second section a sort of repetition and elucidation of the first.

14. Word play in *merveille* = la mer.

15. Within the parenthesis a pastiche of Mallarmé.

16. Note the tense change. It is not always easy to follow Valéry shifts in time throughout the poem. Here, of course, it indicates the dream that she has just had.

17. *Mordre* was anticipated by *mordu* of line bearing note 14.

18. *Soif de limpidité* repeats *soif de désastres* of line bearing note 12.

19. The serpent figure is ambiguous, although consistently an agent of temptation. Here the serpent tempts with knowledge. The young fate has been bitten by the serpent and, like Eve, henceforth bereft of innocence. Her knowledge is self-knowledge, self-awareness. The rest of the stanza alludes to the splitting of the personality into the two aspects described by Hegel as the "für sich" and the "an sich." Sartre will translate the terms as *pour soi* and *en soi*, the conscious side and the nescient side of personality.

20. Consciousness of self and conscience are serpents enough. There is no need for the old theater prop of a real snake. Leisure, lassitude, daydreaming are all conducive to self-torment. Possibly snake should be equated here with carnal problems, temptations, and la jeune parque realizes that they are nothing compared to the torments of the intellect.

21. The farewell is farewell to innocence, to youth whose only problem was one of the senses. La jeune parque regrets this former self, the *égale et épouse* of day. Daylight or sunlight is personified in this section.

22. This section goes on describing a jeune parque avid for sensual fulfillment.

23. Armed by my nothingness—by my awareness of my mortality?

24. She is no longer the equal of day.

25. Awareness of self increases mystery of self and deepens her (the poet's?) art.

26. The rest of the stanza deals with the parque's unhappiness, her temptation of suicide. The reference to a statue may mean just her motionless stance on the promontory

overlooking the sea at dawn as the sun rays touch her.

27. La jeune parque calls upon death to deliver her, for tomorrow spring will arrive and she fears that she will give in to life and to the senses.

28. Her wish for death had been a combination of shame for the past and of depression caused by the look into the future that imagination and introspection permit. This line echoes that depression.

29. The sun is meant.

30. *signes* = stars (Latin *signa*).

31. pink dawn = *pink* flesh?

32. *Vermeille* may pick up from preceding *aube*. See note 31.

33. tomb = sea, where she was about to throw herself.

34. Cf. Eschylus "Le sourire innombrable des flots" (*Prometheus* 89–90).

35. *Divinités* anticipates apposition to *îles* (two lines later) just as *ruche* (line 3) antici-pates *bourdonnerez* (four lines later).

36. Example of syllepsis: *bêtes/idées*. Continued on next line with *hymnes*.

37. The salutation to the islands as divinities is reinforced and made more specific throughout the strophe. Note the following build up; *féconde* of line 6 has prepared for *mères*. The *ceintures de mer* just previous (foam of waves around each island?) pivots by paranomasia into *mère*, whereas the adjective *vierges* leads into *Parques* of the following line.

38. *à genoux:* islands thought of as "crouching" female figures?

39. This stanza has prompted the remark, witty albeit of questionable taste, that the subject of "La Jeune Parque" is the drama of a girl's first menstruation! It might be better to link the bleeding with the suicide upon which la jeune parque has been reflecting. Valéry's esteem for this stanza is indicated in a letter to Albert Mockel: "De ces morceaux, il en est un qui, seul, représente pour moi le poème que j'aurais voulu faire. Ce sont les quelques vers qui commencent ainsi: *O n'aurait-il fallu, folle*" (*Œuvres*, vol. 1, p. 1630).

The rest of the stanza seems to imply that la jeune parque has been saved from suicide and is now prey to sensual thoughts.

40. The final lines of the poem describe dawn and the parque's arising. Night and sleep with its torments are over.

41. *candeur* = white foam

42. *sang* = reddened by the wind

43. *espèces d'or* = sun; Valéry said that these last three verses·came to him "tout rôtis, de la Muse, sans attente ni provocation, et dans la rue" (*Œuvres*, vol. 1, p. 1624).